Using Chinese

This is a guide to Chinese usage for students who have already acquired the basics of the language and wish to extend their knowledge. Unlike conventional grammars, it addresses many aspects of Chinese language usage, such as letter writing, idioms, proverbs, and riddles. It also provides new and recent words, including internet vocabulary, which enables students to understand and properly use the most up-to-date expressions alongside everyday language. Useful sections on common social interactions are included, along with an invaluable guide to the finer nuances of body language. Clear, readable, and easy to consult, this is an essential reference for learners seeking access to one of the world's most important languages.

YVONNE LI WALLS taught Chinese for over thirty years in North American universities, including Indiana University, the University of Washington, University of British Columbia, University of Victoria, and Simon Fraser University. She is now an editor and translator for the North America Fine Arts Publishing House in Vancouver, Canada.

JAN W. WALLS taught Chinese for over thirty years in North American universities, including Indiana University, the University of British Columbia, University of Victoria, and Simon Fraser University. He is now Professor Emeritus in Humanities, Simon Fraser University, Vancouver, Canada.

Companion titles to *Using Chinese*

Other titles in this series

Using French (third edition)
A guide to contemporary usage
R. E. BATCHELOR and M. H. OFFORD
(ISBN 9780521 64177 7 hardback)
(ISBN 9780521 64593 5 paperback)

Using Spanish (second edition)
A guide to contemporary usage
R. E. BATCHELOR and C. J. POUNTAIN
(ISBN 9780521 00481 7 paperback)

Using German (second edition)
A guide to contemporary usage
MARTIN DURRELL
(ISBN 9780521 53000 2 paperback)

Using Russian (second edition)
A guide to contemporary usage
DEREK OFFORD and NATALIA
GOGLITSYNA
(ISBN 9780521 54761 1 paperback)

Using Italian
A guide to contemporary usage
J. J. KINDER and V. M. SAVINI
(ISBN 9780521 48556 2 paperback)

Using Japanese
A guide to contemporary usage
WILLIAM MCLURE
(ISBN 9780521 64155 5 hardback)
(ISBN 9780521 64614 7 paperback)

Using Portuguese
A guide to contemporary usage
ANA SOFIA GANHO
and TIMOTHY MCGOVERN
(ISBN 9780521 79663 7 paperback)

Using Arabic
A guide to contemporary usage
MAHDI ALOSH
(ISBN 9780521 64832 5 paperback)

Using Korean
A guide to contemporary usage
MIHOO CHOO
(ISBN 9780521 66788 3 paperback)

Using Spanish Synonyms
R. E. BATCHELOR
(ISBN 9780521 44160 5 hardback)
(ISBN 9780521 44694 5 paperback)

Using German Synonyms
MARTIN DURRELL
(ISBN 9780521 46552 6 hardback)
(ISBN 9780521 46954 8 paperback)

Using Italian Synonyms
HOWARD MOSS
and VANNA MOTTA
(ISBN 9780521 47506 8 hardback)
(ISBN 9780521 47573 0 paperback)

Using French Synonyms
R. E. BATCHELOR
and M. H. OFFORD
(ISBN 9780521 37277 0 hardback)
(ISBN 9780521 37878 9 paperback)

Using Russian Synonyms
TERENCE WADE
and NIJOLE WHITE
(ISBN 9780521 79405 3 paperback)

Using French Vocabulary
JEAN H. DUFFY
(ISBN 9780521 57040 4 hardback)
(ISBN 9780521 57851 6 paperback)

Using German Vocabulary
SARAH FAGAN
(ISBN 9780521 79700 9 paperback)

Using Italian Vocabulary
MARCEL DANESI
(ISBN 9780521 52425 4 paperback)

Using Spanish Vocabulary
R. E. BATCHELOR
and MIGUEL A. SAN JOSÉ
(ISBN 9780521 00862 4 paperback)

Using Arabic Synonyms
DILWORTH PARKINSON
(ISBN 9780521 00176 2 paperback)

Using Russian Vocabulary
TERENCE WADE
(ISBN 9780521 61236 4 paperback)

Using Chinese

A guide to contemporary usage

YVONNE LI WALLS
and JAN W. WALLS

CAMBRIDGE
UNIVERSITY PRESS

CAMBRIDGE UNIVERSITY PRESS
Cambridge, New York, Melbourne, Madrid, Cape Town, Singapore, São Paulo, Delhi

Cambridge University Press
The Edinburgh Building, Cambridge CB2 8RU, UK

Published in the United States of America by Cambridge University Press, New York

www.cambridge.org
Information on this title: www.cambridge.org/9780521785655

First published 2009

Printed in the United Kingdom at the University Press, Cambridge

A catalogue record for this publication is available from the British Library

Library of Congress Cataloguing in Publication data

Walls, Jan.
Using Chinese : a guide to contemporary usage / Jan W. Walls and
Yvonne Li Walls.
    p.   cm.
Includes bibliographical references and index.
ISBN 978-0-521-78565-5
1. Chinese language – Textbooks for foreign speakers – English.
2. Chinese language – Grammar.   3. Chinese language – Usage.
I. Walls, Yvonne.   II. Title.
PL1129.E5W35   2009
495.1'82421 – dc22   2009000338

ISBN 978-0-521-78565-5 paperback

Contents

Contents

1 Varieties of language and register

1.1 Introduction

It has been several centuries since non-native speakers around the
world first began systematically learning the Chinese language.
In imperial China, the Jesuit order published Chinese language
textbooks for use by their missionaries. Chinese has been widely
taught in universities and colleges in the West for many decades now,
and the demand for Chinese language instruction has been increasing
steadily, to the point where it is now taught in many secondary and
even primary schools in Europe and North America. If grammar
is considered in the narrower sense of rules for the expression of
differences in case, number, person, tense, and voice, then Chinese
is said by some to have little or very simplistic grammar. As a result,
learning Chinese often has been believed to be a tedious exercise
in rote memorization of words and expressions. However, as a
human language, Chinese definitely has a well-ordered structure and
organization, and therefore has a grammar.

From the learner–user's point of view, Chinese grammar also
needs systematic treatment, so that learning can become a more
logical and orderly process. Once basic grammar has been mastered
in a number of conventional contexts, one must proceed to develop
command of a more extensive vocabulary in a variety of different
situations and contexts in order to truly master it. It is the intention
of *Using Chinese* to address these and a variety of other issues, with
a view towards making the learning of Chinese a more sensible and
pleasant experience. In this book, the target language is modern
standard Chinese, 现代汉语 xiàndài Hànyǔ, also called Mandarin,
the standard spoken form: 普通话 pǔtōnghuà; the standardized
(generally known as the simplified) character form, 简体字 jiǎntǐzì,
is used for the written script; and the Romanization adopted is
the 拼音 pīnyīn system, or more officially: the Scheme for the
Chinese Phonetic Alphabet, which has been officially used in
China since 1958 and has now become the most widely used

Romanization system in textbooks and dictionaries around the world. On January 1, 2001, "The Law of the People's Republic of China on the Standard Spoken and Written Language" went into effect. In this law the above-mentioned spoken, written, and Romanization forms are proclaimed as the standard.

The Chinese language, 中文 Zhōngwén, has a written history that can be traced back to about the middle of the second millennium BCE. It is one of two branches of the Sino-Tibetan family of languages and is used by the Han Chinese, 汉族 Hànzú, who make up 91.59% of China's 1.3 billion people, and by many Chinese who live elsewhere on every inhabited continent and on major islands around the world, estimated at around 30 million. The other 8.41% of the population in China speak one of many minority nationality languages, such as Mongolian, Tibetan, Uyghur, Dai, Naxi, Korean. The Chinese language in its many dialect forms is the native tongue of more people than any other language in the world, English being the second most widely spoken native tongue. Chinese is also one of the six official languages of the United Nations, the others being English, Arabic, French, Russian, and Spanish. Mandarin, 普通话 pǔtōnghuà, the standard language of China, is the native dialect of about 71% of its population, and is also spoken by educated speakers of other dialects. Mandarin is also the official language in Taiwan, and is one of the official languages in Singapore. In its broadest sense the Chinese language refers to all of the Chinese "dialects," so called because although they all read and write the same characters for the same meaning, their pronunciation of the same characters may differ as greatly as the Romance languages of Europe differ in their pronunciation of the same Latin root words, or their pronunciation of the Arabic numerals. The Chinese language, in both its written and spoken aspects, has been evolving for several millennia, but most historical linguistics scholars would say that the "modern Chinese" (Mandarin) era began around the time of the early Qing Dynasty (1644–1911).

There are a number of Chinese terms for the Chinese language: "汉语 Hànyǔ" meaning "Han language" and "中文 Zhōngwén," a more general term meaning "Chinese language" and "中国话 Zhōngguó huà" meaning "Chinese speech." There are also different terms used for what we call "Mandarin": "北方话 běifānghuà" meaning "northern speech"; "普通话 pǔtōnghuà" meaning "common speech" in mainland China; "华语 Huáyǔ" meaning "Chinese language," mostly used by overseas Chinese in Southeast Asia, and "国语 guóyǔ" meaning "national language" used mostly in Taiwan.

1.2 The Chinese language and its distribution

1.2.1 Modern Chinese

When we speak of the "modern Chinese language," 现代汉语 xiàndài Hànyǔ, or Mandarin 普通话 pǔtōnghuà, we refer to the language that is based on the northern dialect, taking Beijing pronunciation as its standard and taking well-known vernacular writings as the standard for its grammar. The origin of the term that we translate as "Mandarin" Chinese appears to be the older term "官话 guānhuà" which literally means "official speech." The English word "mandarin" is traceable to a Sanskrit term "mantrin," meaning "minister." The distinction between "Chinese language" and "Mandarin" is not just an academic one, for you may hear a Cantonese speaker say "Ngóh sik góng Jùngmàhn, ngh-sik góng gwok-yúeh," meaning "I speak Chinese, but not Mandarin." This makes sense when we consider that Mandarin is one of several dialects, all of which are "Chinese." While most urban Chinese today will be able to speak, or at least understand, Mandarin, it is spoken as the native tongue of Chinese in the area north of the Changjiang (Yangtze) River, and west of Hunan and Guangdong provinces.

Apart from Mandarin, other important dialect groups include: Wú (including Shanghainese), spoken in Jiangsu Province and Zhejiang Province; Mǐn (Fukienese), spoken in Fujian Province, Taiwan, and Southeast Asia; Yuè (Cantonese), spoken in Guangdong, Guangxi, Hong Kong, North America, and elsewhere by the Chinese diaspora; and Kèjiā (Hakka), spoken mostly in Guangdong and Jiangxi provinces. Following the growth of more universal education and mass media over the past century, Mandarin is now spoken by most educated Chinese in most cities throughout China.

1.2.2 Regional differences in spoken Chinese – the dialects

Most people living in northern, northeastern, and southwestern China, amounting to about three-quarters of all Chinese, are native speakers of a Mandarin sub-dialect: Beijing Mandarin, Shandong Mandarin, Sichuan Mandarin, etc. As mentioned above, the remaining quarter of the Chinese-speaking population is composed of about seven other major dialects, which mostly are mutually unintelligible. Their differences in pronunciation might be compared to the differences between French, Italian, Spanish, and Portuguese among the Romance languages.

1.2.3 Regional differences – within Mandarin

Regional differences in pronunciation of Mandarin within China are as great or greater than the varieties of English as spoken in England, Scotland, Ireland, Australia, the United States, and Canada. The difference between a Mandarin sub-dialect and a dialect is that sub-dialect speakers can mostly understand each other's speech, while the different dialects are often mutually unintelligible.

Major Chinese dialect distribution:

Dialect	Pop. (%)	Representative place where dialect is spoken	Region where dialect is spoken
普通话 pǔtōnghuà	71	北京 Běijīng	N of the Chángjiāng River 长江 & SW China
吴 Wú	9	上海 Shànghǎi	上海，苏州，杭州 Shànghǎi, Sūzhōu, Hángzhōu
湘 Xiāng	5	长沙 Chángshā	湖南 Húnán
粤 Yuè (Cantonese)	5	广州 Guǎngzhōu	广西，广东 Guǎngxī, Guǎngdōng
闽 Mǐn (Fukienese)	4	North: 福州 Fúzhōu South: 厦门 Xiàmén	福建，台湾，海南 Fújiàn, Táiwān, Hǎinán
客家 Kèjiā (Hakka)	4	梅县 Méixiàn	Mostly in Guǎngdōng, Jiāngxī, and Hakka communities in SE China
赣 Gàn	2	南昌 Nánchāng	江西 Jiāngxī

1.2.4 The spoken language

Spoken Chinese is an analytic, or isolating, language meaning that the vast majority of all morphemes, or syllables, are meaningful units of speech, which may in turn be combined with other meaningful syllables to form new words. There are only around 400 syllables in Modern Standard Chinese. Below are a few examples to illustrate the difference in the "feel" of a language whose words are mostly made up of meaningful syllables.

English	Chinese
crane	起重机 qǐ-zhòng-jī (raise-heavy-machine)
department store	百货公司 bǎi-huò-gōng-sī (100-goods-public-managed)
elevator	电梯 diàn-tī (electric-stairs)
encyclopedia	百科全书 bǎi-kē-quán-shū (100-category-total-book)

English	Chinese
escalator	滚梯 gǔn-tī (rolling-stairs)
library	图书馆 tú-shū-guǎn (chart-book-building)
microscope	显微镜 xiǎn-wēi-jìng (reveal-tiny-lens)
ophthalmology	眼科 yǎn-kē (eye department)
pedometer	计步器 jì-bù-qì (count-step-tool)
radio	收音机 shōu-yīn-jī (receive-sound-machine)
surgery	外科 wài-kē (external-department)
university	大学 dà-xué (major-learning)
telescope	望远镜 wàng-yuǎn-jìng (gaze-far-lens)
zebra	斑马 bān-mǎ (striped-horse)

All varieties (i.e. dialects or sub-dialects) of the Chinese language are tonal. Each Mandarin syllable has four tones, although not all toned syllables are meaningful syllables in modern Chinese.

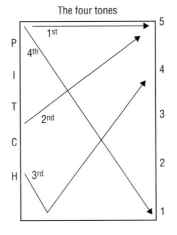

The four tones

There is also a "neutral" tone, which could be considered as a fifth tone.

First tone (high-level): mā, "妈, mother"
Second tone (high-rising): má, "麻, hemp"
Third tone (dip-low-rising): mǎ, "马, horse"
Fourth tone (falling): mà, "骂, scold"
Neutral tone ("toneless"): ma, 吗, verbalized question mark

These tonal distinctions are "built into" each spoken syllable, with or without reference to the Chinese character that would be used to write each different syllable. For example, the difference between "买菜 mǎi cài" and "卖菜 mài cài" is significant: the former means "buy groceries," while the latter means "sell groceries." "妈妈骂马 Māma mà mǎ" means "Mom scolds the horse," while "马骂妈妈 Mǎ mà Māma" means "The horse scolds Mom." Actually the meaning of the sample sentence "Māma mà mǎ," depending upon the context of the utterance, may be more general or more specific, and either singular or plural:

"(The) Mom(s) scold(s) (the) horse(s)."

In the context of speaking about things that happened yesterday, the utterance "Māma mà mǎ" would mean:

"(The) Mom(s) scolded (the) horse(s)."

Verbs are not conjugated in Chinese. If it is not clear whether we are talking about something in the past, present, or future, we may add a time expression before the verb or at the beginning of the utterance: for example, "妈妈昨天骂马 Māma zuótian mà mǎ," or "昨天妈妈骂马 Zuótian māma mà mǎ" where "昨天 zuótian, yesterday" shows it is a past action. Thus there is no need for verbalized declension to show past, present, and future tense of verbs in Chinese, since "yesterday" (or "today" or "tomorrow" or "last year"), which must always be expressed or implied before the verb, removes the need for the addition of tense markers in verbs.

Nor is there any need to verbalize distinctions between singular and plural forms of nouns. If it is necessary to refer specifically to more than one of a noun, it may be preceded by a specific number, or by "some," or "a few," or "many." Once you have uttered a number or a pluralizer like "several," then it is perfectly clear that the noun which follows has been pluralized, so there is no need to mark it any further: 书 shū, book or books; 一本书 yìběn shū, one book; 两本书 liǎngběn shū, "two book"; 很多书 hěnduō shū, "many book"; 几本书 jǐběn shū, "a few book," etc., is every bit as clear as "one book, two books, many books or a few books."

One way to turn an indicative sentence into an interrogative sentence is simply to add the interrogative particle (verbalized question marker) "吗 ma" at the end of the sentence. Thus, to ask the question "Does/Do Mom(s) scold(s) (the) horse(s)?" we may simply say: "妈妈骂马吗？Māma mà mǎ ma?"

1.2.5   The written language and writing system

When writing their language, Chinese speakers use a non-alphabetical script called "characters, 字 zì." 中华字海 Zhōnghuá zìhǎi, *Sea of Chinese Characters* (1994), contains 85,568 characters' entries, 3,500 of which are used the most frequently. In China, urban people are considered literate if they have mastered 2,000 of the most frequently used characters. In the countryside, the number is 1,500. However, a well-educated person should know 5,000 to 7,000 characters.

Most Chinese characters can be identified as belonging to one of the following categories:

1. Pictograms such as:

    木   mù, tree
    山   shān, mountain
    水   shuǐ, water
    人   rén, person
    日   rì, sun
    月   yuè, moon
    马   mǎ, horse

2. Ideograms such as:

    上   shàng, above
    下   xià, below
    凸   tū, protruding
    凹   āo, concave
    二   èr, two
    三   sān, three

3. Meaningful compounds such as:

    从   cóng, follow (person following a person)
    旦   dàn, dawn (sun above the horizon)
    林   lín, woods (two trees)
    森   sēn, forest (three trees)
    晶   jīng, bright (three suns), also means "crystal"
    众   zhòng, crowd (three people)

4. Ideophonetic compounds such as:

    沐   mù, bathe: has something to do with "water,氵," and
          sounds something like "木 mù, wood" = "mù," "bathe"

    栋   dòng, pillar: has something to do with "wood, 木," and
          sounds something like "东 dōng, east" = "dòng," "pillar"

    晴   qíng, fair: has something to do with "sun,日," and
          sounds something like "青 qīng, blue/green" = "qíng,"
          "fair" (weather)

    清   qīng, clear: has something to do with "water,氵," and
          sounds something like "青 qīng, blue/green" = "qīng,"
          "clear" or "pure"

    请   qǐng, request: has something to do with "words, 讠," and
          sounds something like "青 qīng, blue/green" = "qǐng,"
          "ask," or "invite"

About 94% of all characters used today are either meaningful
compounds or ideophonetic compounds, the latter being the
great majority. The remaining characters are either pictographs or
ideographs. Therefore we may say that most Chinese characters are
neither completely phonetic nor completely ideographic, but rather,
they contain a "semantic hint" and a "phonetic hint."

1.3 Overview of register in Chinese

When linguists speak of "register" in a language, they refer to a
subset of a language used for a particular purpose or in a particular

7

social setting. The famous linguistics scholar M. A. K. Halliday (1964) identified three broadly defined variables that help us understand different types of register in a language: field (the subject matter); tenor (the participants and their relationships); and mode (the channel of communication – spoken, written, chatroom, etc.). Martin Joos (1962) describes five styles: frozen (printed, unchanging phrases, such as canonical quotations); formal (one-way participation, no interruption, ritualistic); consultative (two-way participation, interruptions common); casual (in-group friends, ellipsis and slang common, interruptions common); and intimate (non-public, private vocabulary). Quirk *et al.* (1985) distinguish five different registers of formality in English, although they use the term "attitude" rather than register: very formal, formal, neutral, informal, and very informal. Such distinctions would seem to be quite helpful to understand how register works in Chinese.

Native speakers of North American English usually are not so conscious of the need to switch speech registers when talking with people of different social distance, different professions, different age groups, different degrees of closeness, or in different social contexts. Perhaps the implicit assumptions of equality and individuality among modern English speakers are not conducive to a focus on relationships, which is precisely what is required to trigger a switch in speech register.

1.3.1 Illustrations of register

You (normal)	你 nǐ
You (polite)	您 nín
My father (normal)	我父亲 wǒ fùqin
My father (normal, less formal)	我爸爸 wǒ bàba
Your father (more formal)	您父亲 nín fùqin
My mother (normal)	我母亲 wǒ mǔqin
My mother (normal, less formal)	我妈妈 wǒ māma
Your mother (more formal)	您母亲 nín mǔqin
To visit a friend (normal)	看朋友 kàn péngyou
To visit the teacher (more formal)	拜访老师 bàifǎng lǎoshī
To eat at a restaurant (informal)	吃馆子 chī guǎnzi
To eat at a restaurant (more formal)	在饭馆儿吃饭 zài fànguǎnr chīfàn
To go by taxi (informal)	打的去 dǎdī qù
To go by taxi (normal)	坐出租车去 zuò chūzūchē qù
To order drinks (informal)	要喝的 yào hēde
To order beverages (more formal)	点饮料 diǎn yǐnliào
What would you like to drink? (informal)	喝点儿什么？ Hē diǎnr shénme?
What would you like to drink? (more formal)	您喝点儿什么饮料？ Nín hē diǎnr shénme yǐnliào?

How old are you? (to children)	你几岁了？ Nǐ jǐsuì le?
How old are you? (to adults)	你多大了？ Nǐ duōdà le?
How old are you? (to older people)	您多大岁数了？ Nín duōdà suìshu le?
How old are you? (polite, to older people)	请问，您多大年纪？ Qǐngwèn, nín duōdà niánji?
How old are you? (extremely polite)	请问，您贵庚？ Qǐngwèn, nín guìgēng?
How are you? (informal)	怎么样啊？ Zěnmeyàng a?
How are you? (normal)	好吗？ Hǎo ma?
How are you? (normal)	你好！ Nǐ hǎo!
How are you? (more polite)	您好！ Nín hǎo!
My wife (to familiar people)	我那口子 wǒ nèikǒuzi
My wife (to familiar people)	我老爱 wǒ lǎo'ài
My wife (to familiar people)	我老伴儿 wǒ lǎobànr (also means "my husband")
My wife (to familiar people)	孩子他妈 háizi tā mā
My wife (common in PRC)	我爱人 wǒ àiren
My wife (normal)	我妻子 wǒ qīzi
My wife (normal now)	我太太 wǒ tàitai
My husband (to familiar people)	我那口子 wǒ nèikǒuzi
My husband (to familiar people)	我老爱 wǒ lǎo'ài
My husband (to familiar people)	我老伴儿 wǒ lǎobànr (also means "My wife")
My husband (to familiar people)	孩子他爸 háizi tā bà
My husband (common in PRC)	我爱人 wǒ àiren
My husband (normal)	我丈夫 wǒ zhàngfu
My husband (normal now)	我先生 wǒ xiānsheng
Your wife (normal)	你太太 nǐ tàitai
Your wife (a bit formal)	您太太 nín tàitai
Your wife (formal)	您夫人 nín fūren
Your husband (normal)	你丈夫 nǐ zhàngfu
Your husband (a bit formal)	您丈夫 nín zhàngfu
Your husband (formal)	您先生 nín xiānsheng
Teacher Liu (polite, to a teacher)	刘老师 Liú lǎoshī
Master Liu (polite, to skilled worker)	刘师傅 Liú shīfu
Section Chief Liu (formal)	刘科长 Liú kēzhǎng
Liu (older than speaker, familiar)	老刘 lǎo Liú (old Liu)
Liu (younger than speaker, familiar)	小刘 xiǎo Liú (young Liu)
Mr. Liu (normal, formal)	刘先生 Liú xiānsheng
Come in! (impolite, command)	进来！ Jìnlái!
Come in! (informal)	进来吧。 Jìnlai ba.
Please come in! (formal)	请进。 Qǐng jìn.

2 Vocabulary and usage

2.1 Parts of speech

Before they became aware of non-Chinese concepts of "parts
of speech" in the late nineteenth century, Chinese distinguished
primarily between "notional" words, 实词 shící, literally "substantive
words," and "function" words, 虚词 xūcí, literally "empty words."
The first Western-style grammar was that of Mǎ Jiànzhōng 马建忠
(1844–1900), the 1898 马氏文通 Mǎshì wéntōng, *Basic Principles for
Writing*. This very influential work introduced Chinese terminology
for parts of speech based on Latin, and cited classical Chinese
passages extensively to document short statements about syntax. The
book was revolutionary and remains a primary work. Over the last
century Chinese grammatical concepts such as nouns, 名词 míngcí,
literally "name words"; verbs, 动词 dòngcí, literally "motion words";
adjectives, 形容词 xíngróngcí, literally "description words"; adverbs,
副词 fùcí, literally "assisting words"; prepositions, 介词 jiècí, literally
"interface words"; conjunctions, 连词 liáncí, literally "connecting
words," etc., have become standard grammatical terms.

The most commonly used Chinese terms for what we consider to
be parts of speech are:

名词	míngcí	noun: 马 mǎ, horse
专有名词	zhuānyǒu míngcí	proper noun: 马玉婷 Mǎ Yùtíng
动词	dòngcí	verb: 骂 mà, to scold, to curse
代词	dàicí	pronoun: 她 tā, she
形容词	xíngróngcí	adjective: 美 měi, beautiful
副词	fùcí	adverb: 很 hěn, very
能愿动词	néngyuàn dòngcí	modal verb: 可以 kěyǐ, can; may
介词	jiècí	preposition: 替 tì, for
量词	liàngcí	measure word: 个 gè, as in 两个人, two people

数词	shùcí	numeral: 三 sān, 3
连词	liáncí	connecting word/conjunction: 和 hé, and
助词	zhùcí	particle: 了 le, perfective aspect particle
拟声词	nǐshēngcí	onomatopoeia: 嗡嗡 wēngwēng, buzzing sound
主语	zhǔyǔ	subject: 妈妈骂马 Māma mà mǎ (Māma = subject)
谓语	wèiyǔ	predicate: 妈妈骂马 (mà mǎ = predicate)
宾语	bīnyǔ	object: 妈妈骂马 (mǎ = object of verb 骂 mà)
补语	bǔyǔ	complement: 马跑得快 (得快 de kuài = complement)
陈述句	chénshùjù	declarative sentence, statement: 妈妈骂马 Māma mà mǎ, Mom scolds the horse.
疑问句	yíwènjù	interrogative sentence: 妈妈骂马吗? Māma mà mǎ ma?, Is Mom scolding the horse?
祈使句	qíshǐjù	imperative sentence: 别骂马! Bié mà mǎ!, Don't scold the horse!
感叹句	gǎntànjù	exclamatory sentence: 我的妈! Wǒde mā!, Oh my goodness!

2.2 Word formation

Chinese words are formed in a great variety of ways. There are simple words, which are monosyllabic and written with a single Chinese character such as "person, 人 rén," or polysyllabic and written with more than one character such as "command, 命令 mìnglìng"; and there are compound words such as "a switch, 开关 kāiguān," literally "open–close" or "happy, 开心 kāixīn," literally, "open-heart," or "pistachio nut, 开心果 kāixīn'guǒ," literally "[split-] open-heart-fruit."

2.2.1 Compounding

Listed below are some of the most characteristic ways of forming compound words:

Co-ordinate compounds	保卫 bǎowèi, protect, literally "protect–defend"
Attribute-head subordinate	电灯 diàndēng, electric light, literally "electric lamp"

Head-referent subordinate	吃力 chīlì, require strenuous effort, literally "eat-up strength"
Head-modifier subordinate	打倒 dǎdǎo, topple, literally "strike fall"
Referent-head subordinate	自豪 zìháo, pride oneself in, literally "self-proud"
Head-measure subordinate	车辆 chēliàng, vehicle, car; literally "vehicle + measure word used for vehicles"
Prefix-plus-root	老张 Lǎo Zhāng, Old Zhang (addressing or referring to a familiar person whose surname is Zhang)
Root-plus-suffix	桌子 zhuōzi, table; literally "table" + diminutive suffix "zi"
Reduplicated compounds	车车 chēche, little car or buggy (children's talk)
Abbreviated compounds	高教 gāojiào, higher education (from 高等教育 gāoděng jiàoyù)

2.2.2 Prefixes

Prefixes like 老 lǎo, old and 小 xiǎo, young, are often used before names of close friends and associates, such as 老张 Lǎo Zhāng, (Old) Zhang and 小王 Xiǎo Wáng, (Young) Wang, or before nouns, as in 老师 lǎoshī, teacher or 老乡 lǎoxiāng, fellow villager. Some compound verbs may consist of a verbal prefix plus an action, such as 打开 dǎkāi, to open; 打扫 dǎsǎo, to sweep; 打扮 dǎbàn, to apply makeup; 打听 dǎtīng, to make enquiry, and 打算 dǎsuàn, to plan. The English suffix "-able" is expressed by using the verbal prefix 可 kě, may, as with 可惜 kěxī, regretable; 可喜 kěxǐ, rejoiceable; 可悲 kěbēi, lamentable; 可怜 kělián, pitiable; 可恶 kěwù, detestable; 可能 kěnéng, possible; and 可笑 kěxiào, laughable.

2.2.3 Suffixes

The most common suffixes are:

儿 er	花儿, 刀儿, 棍儿, 瓶儿, 头儿, 画儿, 这儿, 那儿, 哪儿, etc.
子 zi	刀子, 叉子, 桌子, 面子, 法子, 帽子, 孩子, 儿子, 拍子, etc.
头 tou	里头, 外头, 上头, 下头, 后头, 前头, 斧头, 砖头, 木头, etc.
者 zhě	读者, 学者, 强者, 前者, 后者, 个人主义者, etc.
家 jiā	作家, 画家, 专家, 文学家, 书法家, 科学家, etc.

员 yuán	教员，研究员，演员，售货员，炊事员，运动员，etc.
士 shì	学士，硕士，博士，男士，女士，护士，etc.
们 men	我们，你们，他们，她们，朋友们，先生们，etc.
性 xìng	积极性，永久性，政治性，娱乐性，独特性，etc.
化 huà	绿化，深化，石化，机械化，老化，电脑化，正常化，etc.

Verbal aspect particles such as "了 le, perfective aspect," "着 zhe, progressive aspect" and "过 guò, experiential aspect" may also be regarded as suffixes, but will be treated in this book as aspect particles.

2.2.4　New words

Words imported from non-Chinese languages are created using one of four primary strategies:

1. Creating a new Chinese character using a semantic component related to the meaning of the new word, plus a phonetic component whose pronunciation is similar to that of the word being translated. Examples would be the word for the chemical element "erbium" – 铒 ěr, which has to do with "metal," and sounds like the "er" of "erbium"; another example is "magnesium" – 镁 měi, which has to do with "metal," and sounds like the "ma" of "magnesium."

2. Transliterating the sound of the polysyllabic foreign word into a series of Chinese characters used for their phonetic value only. One example from the early twentieth century would be the first term used for the Western concept of "democracy" – 德谟克拉西 démókèlāxī, whose components "virtue-plan-overcome-tug-west" representing no Chinese concept, are recognized as a transliteration of a foreign concept. Another early twentieth-century example would be the transliteration of "inspiration" – 烟士批里纯 yānshìpīlǐchún, literally: "mist-scholar-approve-hamlet-pure." Both of the above examples later were "domesticated" using the next translation technique below.

3. Translating the meaning of the foreign word into a meaningful Chinese compound of two or more characters. Examples would be the term now used for "democracy," 民主 mínzhǔ, whose components mean "people-sovereign," and "inspiration," 灵感 línggǎn, whose components mean "spirit-feeling."

4. Combining translation with transliteration. An example is the Chinese word for "ice cream" – 冰激凌 bīngjilíng or 冰淇淋 bīngqilín, in which "bīng" means "ice," and "jilíng" ("surge" + "encroach") or "qilín" ("Qí River" + "drench") represent the sound of "cream" in English. Other examples would be: "beer" – 啤酒 píjiǔ, in which "pí" represents the sound of "beer," and "jiǔ" means "alcoholic drink"; and "internet" – 因特网 yīntèwǎng, in

which "yīntè" represents the sound of "inter," and "wǎng" means "net."

2.3 Homonyms

In English, a homonym is a word which has the same spelling and pronunciation as another word but a different meaning. A few examples are: "ball: a sphere; a dance"; "band: something wrapped around the arm; musical group"; "box: a crate; engage in fisticuffs"; "bank: a financial institution; the edge of a river," etc. In Chinese, then, we might say that a homonym is one character which has only one pronunciation, but more than one meaning.

Because there are relatively fewer syllables in Chinese, even with their tonal distinctions, we would expect to see more different meanings attached to a typical Chinese word than we might expect to a typical English word. A good example would be "放 fàng" whose most basic meaning is "to let go of something, to release something." To "put" or to "place" is a logical extension of "release," as in: 把书放在桌子上 bǎ shū fàngzai zhuōzishang, Put the book on the table. Seen in this light, other extensions become quite reasonable, as shown in the following illustrations, each requiring different English words to express the same meaning:

放 fàng
set free, release
佛教提倡放生。
Fójiào tíchàng fàngshēng.
Buddhism advocates freeing captive animals.

put, place
她把衣服放在洗衣机里。
Tā bǎ yīfu fàngzai xǐyījī lǐ.
She put the clothes in the washer.

let off, give out
酒发酵时会放出气泡。
Jiǔ fājiàoshí huì fàngchū qìpāo.
When wine is fermented it gives off bubbles of gas.

put out to pasture
放牛；放羊
fàng niú; fàng yáng
put cows out to pasture; put sheep out to pasture

expand; make longer/larger
这条裤子能不能给我放长一寸？
Zhètiáo kùzi néngbuneng gěi wǒ fàngcháng yícùn?
Can you lengthen these pants by an inch for me?

blossom, bloom
百花齐放
Bǎihuā qífàng.
"Let a hundred flowers blossom" (Let different views be aired)

lend money, make loans
放款是银行生利的方式之一。
Fàngkuǎn shi yínháng shēnglì de fāngshì zhīyī.
Loans are one of the ways a bank earns a profit.

add something to something else
你喝咖啡放不放糖？
Nǐ hē kāfēi fàngbufàng táng?
Do you add sugar to your coffee?

Another good illustration of the same point would be "毛 máo," which originally means "body hair," which is short and fine, as opposed to "发 fà, hair on the head," which grows longer. In light of the principle of metaphorical extension, it becomes easy to understand the connection between "tiny hair," "down," "wool," "feather," "mildew," "small," "careless," "unfinished," and even "alarmed" (hair standing on end), as illustrated in the following utterances, each requiring different English words to translate:

毛 máo

hair, wool, down, feather
一般的洋人身上长的毛比中国人多。
Yìbānde yángrén shēnshang zhǎngde máo bǐ Zhōngguórén
    duō.
Westerners generally have more body hair than Chinese.

mildew, mold
这干酪已经长毛了！
Zhè gānlào yǐjīng zhǎngmáo le!
This cheese is already moldy!

little, small
他才不是大人，是个毛孩子！
Tā cái bushì dàrén, shige máoháizi!
He's no adult. He's just a little kid!

semifinished (product)
毛铁就是生铁的另外一个说法。
Máotiě jiùshi shēngtiě de lìngwài yige shuōfa.
"Rough iron" is another way of saying "pig iron."

gross (profit or income)
毛收入当然比净收入多啦。
Máoshōurù dāngrán bǐ jìngshōurù duō la.
Gross income is greater than net income, of course.

careless, crude, rash

喂！做事要小心点儿，别那么毛糙了！

Wei! Zuòshì yào xiǎoxīn diǎnr, bié nàme máocao le!

Hey! Be more careful with your work, don't be so careless!

alarmed, scared

她一看见厂长就发毛了。

Tā yíkànjian chǎngzhǎng jiù fāmáo le.

She became frightened (got goose flesh) at the sight of the factory
manager.

dime (1/10th of a yuan)

两毛五而已？真便宜！

Liǎngmáowǔ éryǐ? Zhēn piányi!

Only twenty-five cents? That's really cheap!

This phenomenon of extended metaphorical usage should be
quite familiar to English speakers when we think of words like "run,"
whose core meaning is "to move at a speed faster than a walk, never
having both or all the feet on the ground at the same time." Put
"run" in different contexts, and it will require entirely different words
to translate it into Chinese. For example, "the Yankees lead by one
run: 洋基棒球队领先一分 Yángjī bàngqiúduì lǐngxiān yìfēn," "to
run a business: 经营企业 jīngyíng qǐyè," "to run out of money: 钱
用光了 qián yòngguāng le," "to run up a huge bill: 开支的累积很
大 kāizhīde lěijī hěn dà," and "a run of bad luck: 一连串的坏运气
yìliánchuànde huàiyùnqi." All the previous examples require different
translations in Chinese and none of them involve "跑 pǎo," which is
the core meaning of "run" in Chinese. Following is a small sample
of common Chinese words with several different meanings, requiring
different English words in translation:

走	zǒu	to flee, to walk, to leave, to run
上	shàng	above, over, on, upper; previous; to ascend, to mount; to present to one's superiors; to go (to class or to work)
下	xià	below, under, lower; next; to descend, to dismount to send down (to one's subordinates); to finish (a class or a working day)
白	bái	white; clear, pure, plain; colloquial; free of charge; vainly; wrongly written; surname

2.4 Homophones

English homophones are words which have the same sound but
different meanings and different spelling, such as "air (atmosphere)"
and "heir (one who inherits wealth)"; or "to," "too," and "two."
Chinese homophones, 同音字 tóngyīnzì, by analogy, are syllables
which have the same pronunciation, but are written with different

Chinese characters and have different meanings. With a total inventory of just over 400 syllables (without considering tones) to pronounce the 2,000 or so characters needed to be basically literate in Chinese, it is statistically impossible to avoid a huge number of homophones, far more than we could ever expect to find through the vagaries of spelling words in English. In fact, any attempt to list the pǔtōnghuà homophones would amount to a pronunciation dictionary of pǔtōnghuà, so rather than list all the homophones, we shall simply take a few syllables, and list all the characters represented by each.

ān

安 ān still, quiet
庵 ān hut, nunnery
氨 ān ammonia
鞍 ān saddle
谙 ān learn by heart, be well versed in
桉 ān eucalyptus
鹌 ān quail

jiā

家 jiā home, house, family
加 jiā add
佳 jiā good, beautiful
夹 jiā press, squeeze; clip
嘉 jiā good, fine; praise
袈 jiā used in "袈裟 jiāshā," a Buddhist monk's outerwear
茄 jiā used in transliterated words, like "雪茄 xuějiā," cigar
枷 jiā cangue
伽 jiā a Galileo unit; used in transliterated words like "瑜伽 yújiā," yoga
珈 jiā woman's headdress in ancient China
痂 jiā scab, crust
跏 jiā used in "跏趺 jiāfū," a sitting posture of a Buddhist
迦 jiā used in transliterating names, such as "释迦牟尼 Shìjiāmóuní," Sakyamuni
浃 jiā wet through
葭 jiā tender shoot of a reed
镓 jiā gallium

yī

一 yī one
壹 yī one
医 yī medicine; medical profession; doctor
衣 yī clothing
依 yī approach; depend on; comply with; according to
伊 yī surname; he or she

呹 yī a character used for its sound in "呹呀 yīyā," babble, prattle
铱 yī iridium
噫 yī alas
猗 yī a character used to show exclamation in classical Chinese
漪 yī ripples
揖 yī bow with hands clasped together
黟 yī a character used in a place name "Yī xiàn," Yi County

zuò

作 zuò do, make
做 zuò do, make, be
坐 zuò sit, ride
座 zuò seat; a measure word for mountains, tall buildings
唑 zuò a character used in "噻唑 sāizuò," thiazole
怍 zuò shame
祚 zuò fortune
胙 zuò sacrifical meat in the ancient times
酢 zuò a character used in classical Chinese, "酬酢 chóuzuò," a
   return toast made by a guest
阼 zuò the stairs on the east side of the hall of a Chinese building
柞 zuò oak
凿 zuò certain (classic meaning); mortise

While it may be unrealistic to present a list of all the homophones
in the language, we should say a few words about the prevalence and
importance of the playful use of homophones by Chinese speakers.
This happens in the form of punning, both verbal and graphic.

Examples of verbal punning would be:

"逃之夭夭, táo zhī yāoyāo" is an idiom meaning "to flee," but the
first character is a punning allusion to the first line of a famous folk
ballad in the *Classic of Songs*, 诗经 Shījīng, "桃之夭夭," meaning
"peach tree, young and fresh." The cleverness of this pun is in
its simultaneously calling forth images of classical dignity and an
undignified departure.

Domino's Pizza, which currently dominates around 60% of the
market in Taiwan, is famous for its use of puns in Chinese marketing.
First, its registered Chinese corporate name is "达美乐 Dáměilè"
which means "Achieving Beautiful Joy" while sounding like
"Domino." Three of the puns associated with Domino's are:

达美乐
dáměilè,
打了没
dǎle méi?
Translation: Answering the phone: "Domino's, you called?"

饿爸爸饿, 我饿我饿
è bàba è, wǒ è wǒ è

2882-5252
èr-bā-bā-èr wǔ-èr-wǔ-èr (Domino's phone number)
Hungry Papa hungry; I'm hungry I'm hungry

快乐颂
kuàilèsòng
Ode to Joy

快热送
kuàirèsòng
Delivered fast and hot

2.5 Homographs

Chinese homographs, 多音字 duōyīnzì, are characters that have more than one pronunciation, depending upon different meanings or their use in different character compounds. Here are some examples:

阿	ā	阿飞, 阿米巴, 阿姨
	ē	阿弥陀佛, 阿谀
背	bèi	背书, 背后, 背景, 背面, 背叛, 背心
	bēi	背包, 背带
别	bié	别名, 别墅, 别针, 别致, 辨别, 差别, 辞别, 个别, 永别
	biè	别扭
卜	bǔ	占卜, 生死未卜
	bo	萝卜, 胡萝卜
参	cān	参考, 参赞, 参政, 参观, 参加, 参谋, 参与
	cēn	参差, 参差不齐
	shēn	党参, 海参, 人参
藏	cáng	藏书, 躲藏, 收藏, 蕴藏, 珍藏, 贮藏, 捉迷藏
	zàng	藏族, 藏红花, 宝藏
曾	céng	曾经, 不曾, 未曾
	zēng	曾姓, 曾孙, 曾祖
差	chā	差额, 差距, 差别, 差错, 差异
	chà	差劲, 差不多, 差不离
	chāi	差遣, 差事, 出差, 公差
	cī	参差
场	cháng	场院, 一场雨
	chǎng	操场, 登场, 广场, 冷场, 牧场, 怯场, 现场

朝	cháo	朝阳, 朝政, 朝代, 朝鲜族, 王朝
	zhāo	朝气, 朝露, 朝日, 朝夕, 朝霞
称	chēng	称呼, 称谓, 称谢, 称赞, 号称, 简称, 名称, 人称, 职称, 自称, 尊称
	chèn	称心, 称愿, 称职, 相称
重	chóng	重婚, 重孙, 重演, 重阳, 重奏, 重叠, 重复, 重新, 双重
	zhòng	重创, 重负, 重任, 重托, 重担, 重地, 重活, 重用
臭	chòu	臭虫, 臭骂, 臭豆腐, 臭烘烘, 臭乎乎, 狐臭, 口臭, 腥臭, 乳臭未干
	xiù	无色无臭, 臭味相投
处	chǔ	处女, 处世, 处暑, 处死, 处方, 处分, 处境, 处刑, 处罚, 处理品, 相处
	chù	处所, 长处, 害处, 益处
畜	chù	家畜, 牲畜, 种畜, 畜肥, 畜生
	xù	畜牧, 畜产品
传	chuán	传播, 传单, 传递, 传授, 传统, 传真, 传布, 传教, 传神, 传染病, 失传, 谣传, 祖传
	zhuàn	传略, 传记, 评传, 自传
创	chuàng	创刊, 创办, 创业, 创举, 创作, 创立, 创新, 创造, 创始, 首创
	chuāng	创痕, 创伤, 重创
答	dā	答应, 答腔
	dá	答案, 答辩, 答复, 答卷, 答话, 答谢, 回答, 解答, 问答
打	dá	一打鸡蛋
	dǎ	打岔, 打工, 打官司, 打行李, 打抱不平
大	dà	大地, 大脑, 大雪, 大城市, 大白菜, 大慈大悲
	dài	大夫, 大黄
倒	dǎo	倒塌, 打倒, 颠倒
	dào	倒立, 倒流, 倒影, 倒转, 倒栽葱
的	de	似的, 是的, 有的是
	dí	的确, 的确良
	dì	目的

得	dé	得当, 得胜, 得失, 得手, 懂得, 心得, 值得
	de	靠得住,了不得, 晓得, 认得
	děi	你得当心
调	diào	调查, 调子, 强调, 曲调
	tiáo	调理, 调料, 调情, 调停, 调味, 烹调, 失调, 协调
恶	è	恶毒, 恶化, 恶劣, 恶习, 恶意, 恶作剧, 丑恶, 险恶, 凶恶, 罪恶
	ě	恶心
	wù	可恶
分	fēn	分辨, 分泌, 分期, 分布, 分寸, 分工, 分红, 分解, 分裂, 分明, 分配, 分批, 分散, 分数, 分析, 分钟, 分担, 分店, 分居, 分开, 分娩, 分秒, 分身, 分手, 分头, 瓜分, 平分, 区分
	fèn	分量, 分外, 安分, 处分, 过分, 情分, 缘分
	fen	成分, 身分
干	gān	干杯, 干瘪, 干扰, 干涉, 干燥, 风干, 若干, 相干
	gàn	干部, 干劲, 干吗, 干事, 干线, 才干, 骨干, 能干, 主干
更	gēng	更动, 更改, 更换, 更生, 更新, 更衣, 更正
	gèng	更加
行	háng	行当, 行家, 行列, 行情, 行业, 发行, 同行, 外行, 银行, 行话
	xíng	行程, 行军, 行李, 行动, 行径, 行人, 行驶, 行星, 行好, 行善, 行事, 行医, 行走, 行装, 行人, 行为, 行政, 行踪, 暴行, 德行, 发行, 横行, 盛行, 运行
好	hǎo	好歹, 好汉, 好受, 好意, 友好, 好听, 好人, 好像, 好似, 好笑, 好心, 好些, 好比, 好处, 好在, 好坏, 好久, 好看, 好说, 美好, 恰好
	hào	好强, 好客, 好奇, 好胜, 好事, 爱好, 嗜好
和	hé	和蔼, 和睦, 和平, 和尚, 和谐, 和风, 和好, 和缓, 和善, 和解, 和谈, 温和
	he	说和
	huo	搅和, 暖和, 热和, 软和, 温和
	hè	一唱百和
	hú	和牌了
	huó	和面, 和泥

	huò	和稀泥, 藕粉里和点糖
还	hái	还是
	huán	还本, 还手, 还债, 还价, 还礼, 还原, 还嘴, 偿还, 退还
假	jiǎ	假扮, 假冒, 假设, 假释, 假定, 假如, 假若, 假使, 假山, 假意, 假装, 虚假, 作假
	jià	假期, 假条, 假日, 病假, 请假
间	jiān	车间, 房间, 民间, 期间, 时间
	jiàn	间谍, 间断, 间接, 间隙, 间歇
强	jiàng	强嘴, 倔强
	qiáng	强度, 加强, 强奸, 强健, 强壮, 强盗, 强权, 强盛, 强烈, 强化, 强调, 强大
	qiǎng	强迫, 强词夺理, 强人所难, 强颜欢笑
教	jiāo	教书
	jiào	教导, 教会, 教练, 教师, 教训, 教育, 教材, 教室, 教堂, 教条, 教学, 教员
角	jiǎo	角度, 角落
	jué	角色, 角逐
将	jiāng	将近, 将军, 将来
	jiàng	将官, 将领
校	jiào	校订, 校对, 校勘, 校样, 校阅, 校正
	xiào	校风, 校规, 校刊, 校徽, 校园, 校长
结	jié	结构, 结果, 结婚, 结晶, 结局, 结论, 结业, 结帐, 结识, 结束, 结业, 团结, 总结
	jiē	结实
	jie	巴结
尽	jǐn	尽先, 尽管
	jìn	尽力, 尽量, 尽兴, 尽职
禁	jīn	禁得起, 禁不住, 禁得住
	jìn	禁忌, 禁区, 禁止, 禁令, 监禁, 拘禁, 违禁
看	kàn	看望, 看相, 看待, 看法, 看见, 看重, 看齐, 看轻, 看台, 看不起, 难看, 小看, 看病
	kān	看管, 看护, 看家, 看守, 看孩子

空	kōng	空腹, 空论, 空头, 空洞, 空旷, 空话, 空谈, 空投, 空袭, 空运, 空间, 空军, 气, 空调, 空想, 空虚, 空中, 天空
	kòng	空白, 空儿, 空隙, 空缺, 空暇, 空闲, 填空, 偷空
乐	lè	乐观, 乐趣, 乐意, 乐园, 乐呵呵, 康乐, 快乐, 欢乐, 娱乐
	yuè	乐理, 乐谱, 乐曲, 乐器, 乐团, 乐章, 声乐, 音乐, 奏乐
了	le	除了, 算了, 为了
	liǎo	了得, 了解, 了结, 了不起, 了不得, 终了, 不得了
累	léi	累赘, 果实累累
	lěi	累积, 连累, 罪行累累
	lèi	劳累, 受累
量	liáng	量杯, 量度, 测量, 估量
	liàng	量词, 量力, 产量, 度量, 气量
	liang	商量
蒙	méng	蒙蔽, 蒙昧, 蒙受
	mēng	蒙骗
	měng	蒙古族
难	nán	难产, 难处, 难说, 难道, 难得, 难度, 难怪, 难堪, 难免, 难受, 难题, 艰难, 为难
	nàn	难胞, 难友, 避难, 难兄难弟
	nan	困难
漂	piāo	漂泊, 漂浮, 漂流
	piǎo	漂白, 漂染, 漂白粉
	piào	漂亮, 漂亮话
切	qiē	切除, 切磋, 切割, 切片, 切面
	qiè	切合, 切记, 切忌, 切身, 切题, 切实, 关切, 恳切, 密切, 亲切, 确切, 一切
曲	qū	曲尺, 曲解, 曲直, 曲折, 曲线, 曲棍球, 蜷曲
	qǔ	曲艺, 插曲, 歌曲, 戏曲, 组曲, 奏鸣曲
散	sǎn	散光, 散漫, 散文, 散装, 懒散, 松散, 闲散
	sàn	散播, 散场, 散心, 散步, 散发, 散会, 散戏
扫	sǎo	扫盲, 扫地, 扫墓, 扫描, 扫兴, 打扫

	sào	扫帚, 扫帚星
舍	shě	舍得, 舍命, 舍弃, 舍身, 舍不得
	shè	舍下, 宿舍
省	shěng	省城, 俭省, 省事, 省心, 省份, 省略号, 俭省, 节省
	xǐng	省亲, 省悟, 反省
似	sì	似乎, 相似
	shì	似的
挑	tiāo	挑选, 挑剔, 挑眼
	tiǎo	挑拨, 挑战, 挑逗
吐	tǔ	吐蕃, 吐露, 谈吐, 吞吐
	tù	吐沫, 吐血, 吐泻, 呕吐
为	wéi	为人, 为难, 为期, 为首, 为止, 成为, 行为, 以为, 作为
	wèi	为何, 为了, 为什么, 因为
	wei	难为
相	xiāng	相称, 相处, 相传, 相比, 相差, 相当, 相等, 相对, 相反, 相关, 相互, 相似, 相识, 相同, 相逢, 相干, 相思, 相象, 相依, 相互
	xiàng	相机, 相貌, 相面, 相声, 相片, 扮相, 看相, 亮相, 识相, 照相, 真相
血	xiě	血晕, 血淋淋
	xuè	血管, 血压, 血液, 血癌, 血案, 血崩, 血迹, 血浆, 血库, 血泪, 血脉, 血气, 血清, 血球, 血肉, 血色, 血书, 血水, 血糖, 血统, 血腥, 血型, 血缘, 血债, 血战, 血渍
兴	xīng	兴办, 兴奋, 兴建, 兴旺, 兴隆, 兴盛, 兴衰, 兴亡, 兴修, 兴许, 振兴, 中兴, 复兴
	xìng	兴趣, 高兴, 即兴, 扫兴, 雅兴, 助兴
要	yāo	要求, 要挟
	yào	要不, 要道, 要地, 要犯, 要害, 要价, 要件, 要强, 要人, 要闻, 要职, 要点, 要领, 要命, 要是, 要素, 要面子, 要不然, 要不是, 扼要, 需要, 摘要, 重要
应	yīng	应当, 应该, 应声, 应许, 应允

	yìng	应变, 应酬, 应答, 应对, 应付, 应急, 应景, 应考, 应试, 应验, 应用, 应诊, 应征, 报应, 答应, 反应, 响应, 照应
载	zài	载重, 超载, 运载, 装载, 载歌载舞
	zǎi	记载, 刊载, 连载, 转载
折	zhē	折腾
	zhé	折合, 折磨, 折叠, 折扣, 折中, 波折, 存折, 骨折, 曲折
	shé	打折了腿, 折本
挣	zhēng	挣扎
	zhèng	挣命, 挣钱
中	zhōng	中餐, 中断, 中坚, 中间儿, 中介, 中看, 中立, 中东, 中古, 中华, 中级, 中流, 中外, 中西, 中止, 中年, 中文, 中式, 中枢, 中听, 中心, 中学, 中药, 中庸, 中用, 中游
	zhòng	中毒, 中风, 中奖, 中伤, 中暑, 中选, 中意, 看中
种	zhòng	种痘, 种地, 种花, 种田, 种植, 栽种, 耕种
	zhǒng	种畜, 种类, 种子, 种族, 播种, 剧种, 育种
作	zuō	作弄, 作死, 作揖
	zuó	作料
	zuò	作保, 作恶, 作怪, 作假, 作乐, 作孽, 作祟, 作废, 作风, 作家, 作品, 作为, 作文, 作业, 作用, 作者, 作主, 作弊, 作对
	zuo	做作

2.6 New and recent words

With the changes in society and technologies, some words (vocabulary) fall into disuse and many more new words are added. In addition, some existing words take on new meanings. In recent years, many new Chinese words have appeared. The following is a selection from the reservoir of new words that accumulated in the 1990s and shortly beyond.

A	爱疗	àiliáo	healing with love
	爱绿	àilǜ	love and protect green space
	爱之角	àizhījiǎo	love corner, match-making corner
	艾滋病	àizībìng	AIDS

	安乐死	ānlèsǐ	euthanasia, mercy-killing
B	白色消费	báisè xiāofèi	funeral expenses (funerals are referred to as "white event"); also, spend money according to income
	白噪音	báizàoyīn	white noise, a sound that promotes sleep
	帮忙公司	bāngmáng gōngsī	home service company
	保险菜	bǎoxiǎn cài	safe vegetables, vegetables not sprayed with insecticides
	背黑锅	bēihēiguō	to be a scapegoat
	比基尼挂历	bǐjīní guàlì	bikini calendar, calendar with pictures of bikini-clad women
	病区	bìngqū	geographic areas with serious problems
C	财经小说	cáijīng xiǎoshuō	novels whose main theme is finances and economy
	厕所广告	cèsuǒ guǎnggào	advertisments inside and outside public bathrooms
	炒股	chǎogǔ	speculate in stocks
	炒鱿鱼	chǎoyóuyú	to fire, to dismiss; to be fired, to be dismissed
	吃饭农业	chīfàn nóngyè	traditional agricultural activities which only produce grains
	吃旧	chījiù	one whose profession is buying and selling used goods
	持卡族	chíkǎzú	those who possess credit cards
	赤脚新闻	chìjiǎo xīnwén	"barefoot" news, news that comes from real life

持续农业	chíxù nóngyè	sustainable agriculture
充电	chōngdiàn	charge batteries; recharge oneself by going back to school
聪明卡	cōngmingkǎ	"clever electronic" card, debit card
促销小姐	cùxiāo xiǎojie	young women who promote sales

D

打的	dǎdī	to take a taxi
大锅债	dàguōzhài	debts incurred from guaranteed lifelong work and the equal distribution system
打工文学	dǎgōng wénxúe	literature on the subject of short-term laborers
大耳朵	dà ěrduo	satellite dish
大哥大	dàgēdà	cellular phone; also called "手机 shǒujī" which is a more popular term now
大脚男人	dàjiǎo nánren	men who can take risks
大款	dàkuǎn	a very wealthy person
大款商品	dàkuǎn shāngpǐn	expensive goods which only the very rich can afford
大腕儿	dàwànr	big shot, celebrity, expert
大腕企业	dàwàn qǐyè	solid and reputable enterprises
单身用品	dānshēn yòngpǐn	items suitable for singles to use; small packages of frozen foods, small utensils, small furniture, etc.
的	dī	taxi, short for "的士 dīshi, taxi"
的士快餐	dīshi kuàicān	fast food originally designed for taxi drivers
的爷	dīyé	taxi driver
地铁广告	dìtiě guǎnggào	advertisements on subway trains and at subway stations

27

第五产业	dìwǔ chǎnyè	the fifth industry: psychology and career development consulting services
第一厨房	dìyī chúfáng	first kitchen: the processing plant for partial or fully prepared foods
第一者	dìyīzhě	a married person who has a lover
电红娘	diànhóngniáng	computer, television and telephone matchmakers
电话拜年	diànhuà bàinián	wishing someone Happy New Year by telephone (traditionally done only in person)
电话恋爱	diànhuà liànài	"love" by telephone
电话律师	diànhuà lǜshī	"telephone lawyers," a service provided by some telephone companies
电话商场	diànhuà shāngchǎng	"telephone markets," shopping services via telephone
电话营销	diànhuà yíngxiāo	telemarketing
电话推销	diànhuà tuīxiāo	telemarketing
电话银行	diànhuà yínháng	telebanking
电脑茶馆	diànnǎo cháguǎn	tea houses with computers, offering shopping and consulting services
电脑盲	diànnǎománg	computer illiterate
电脑族	diànnǎozú	people who own and use personal computers at home
电视大锅	diànshì dàguō	television satellite receiver
电视商场	diànshì shāngchǎng	info-mercial
电邮	diànyóu	e-mail, short for 电子邮件 diànzǐ yóujiàn
电子钱包	diànzǐ qiánbāo	"electronic wallet": credit card
点子公司	diǎnzi gōngsī	services which give people ideas, provide information, design

	点子人	diǎnzirén	advertisements, marketing, etc. consultants who plan for industries
	点子投资	diǎnzi tóuzī	investing in valuable ideas in industries
	电影茶座	diànyǐng cházuò	places where people can drink tea and watch movies at the same time
	电影人	diànyǐngrén	people who work in the movie industry
	丁克夫妇	dīngkè fūfù	DINK couple: double income no kids
	多余会议	duōyú huìyì	superfluous meetings
E	二老外	èrlǎowài	Chinese employees who are hired by foreign companies in China and receive higher salaries and better benefits
	二一家庭	èryī jiātíng	families consisting of two parents and one child
	二职	èrzhí	second job which people take on in order to earn more money
F	方便菜	fāngbiancài	instant dishes in pouches which can be cooked very quickly
	方便面	fāngbianmiàn	instant noodles
	房龄	fánglíng	age of a house
	仿生树	fǎngshēngshù	artificial trees for decoration
	飞天计划	fēitiān jìhuà	flying plan: a plan that involves inviting overseas Chinese scholars to China to develop projects
G	工厂旅游	gōngchǎng lǚyóu	factory tourism, touring factories as part of tourist industry

29

	股票情绪	gǔpiào qíngxù	stock emotions, stress created by the changes in stocks
	鬼价	guǐjià	extremely high prices
	贵族商店	guìzú shāngdiàn	nobility shops: shops with very expensive goods
	贵族商品	guìzú shāngpǐn	merchandise of excellent quality and high price
	国有私营	guóyǒu sīyíng	industries owned by the state but managed by the private sector
	国资	guózī	state-owned capital
H	海撒	hǎisǎ	funeral services which spread the dead person's ashes into the ocean
	汉语明星	Hànyǔ míngxīng	non-Chinese who become famous because they speak very good Chinese
	含知量	hánzhīliàng	"knowledge content," referring to how learned a person is
	黑面	hēimian	the dark and ugly side of society
	黑五类	hēiwǔlèi	a processed health food made of five kinds of "black" ingredients: 黑豆 hēidòu, black soy beans; 黑米 hēimǐ, black rice; 黑芝麻 hēizhīma, black sesame seeds; 黑松子 hēisōngzǐ, black pine seeds; and 黑加仑 hēijiālún, black currants. Note: "hēiwǔlèi" used to refer to landlords, rich

		farmers, counter-revolutionaries, rightists, and criminals, during the Cultural Revolution.
红色消费	hóngsè xiāofèi	expenses using public funds. For example: dining, dancing, gift-giving.
呼机	hūjī	a pager, a beeper
候鸟型人才	hòuniǎoxíng réncái	high-tech specialists who come and go wherever projects need their skills
环保	huánbǎo	environmental protection
环保名片	huánbǎo míngpiàn	environmental business cards; business cards with colored earth, ocean, seaweed, butterflies, etc. printed on them to call attention to environmental protection
胡同游	hútòngryóu	special tours for tourists who ride in pedicabs and are driven through designated traditional alleys in Beijing
环发	huánfā	environment and development
环境音乐	huánjìng yīnyuè	"background music": music broadcast in factories, shops, restaurants, etc.
黄金档	huángjīndǎng	prime time on television
黄金教育	huángjīn jiàoyù	valuable training for entrepreneurs and education for the staff
灰化	huīhuà	greying or blurring of distinctions, as between good and bad, moral and immoral, in society

混血车	hùnxuèchē	"mixed blood cars": cars made with parts from different countries
火招	huǒzhāo	most popular and most welcome ways of doing things

<table>
<tr><td>J</td><td>吉利号</td><td>jílìhàor</td><td>auspicious numbers, such as 8888 which sounds like "fā fā fā fā" which means "having great prosperity"</td></tr>
<tr><td></td><td>机译</td><td>jīyì</td><td>machine translation</td></tr>
<tr><td></td><td>技援</td><td>jìyuán</td><td>technical assistance</td></tr>
<tr><td></td><td>假唱</td><td>jiǎchàng</td><td>lip-sync (singing)</td></tr>
<tr><td></td><td>家庭出租</td><td>jiātíng chūzū</td><td>a service which earns money by providing a family or family-like atmosphere to lonely elders who have no family of their own</td></tr>
<tr><td></td><td>假日集市</td><td>jiàrì jíshì</td><td>markets held during holidays for shoppers' convenience</td></tr>
<tr><td></td><td>讲价公司</td><td>jiǎngjià gōngsī</td><td>companies who bargain on behalf of their clients</td></tr>
<tr><td></td><td>轿的</td><td>jiàodī</td><td>sedan car type of taxi, as opposed to "面的 miàndī" which is a van type of taxi</td></tr>
<tr><td></td><td>接送族</td><td>jiēsòngzú</td><td>parents who deliver and pick up children from schools in cities</td></tr>
<tr><td></td><td>借脑</td><td>jiènǎo</td><td>"borrowing brains": hiring, with very high pay, highly intelligent people from other regions</td></tr>
<tr><td></td><td>金本位</td><td>jīnběnwèi</td><td>the concept that money is the most important thing of all</td></tr>
</table>

金点子	jīndiǎnzi	especially good ideas
金耳朵	jīn'ěrduo	sharp ears
经济餐	jīngjìcān	affordable, good meals
经盲	jīngmáng	people who have no knowledge of market economy
精神快餐	jīngshen kuàicān	spiritual fast-food: short reading
精神粮店	jīngshen liángdiàn	"spiritual food store": bookstores in rural areas
酒经济	jiǔjīngji	economy based on marketing liquor
巨无霸	jùwúbà	superlative things, the best

K

卡拉ok病	kǎlā ok bìng	sore throat from singing too many karaoke songs
卡爷	kǎyé	those who have the authority to stop someone from doing anything whenever they want to
侃价市场	kǎnjià shìchǎng	markets where the buyers can bargain
侃文化	kǎn wénhuà	the common phenomenon of the Chinese chatting and talking about anything and everthing when they get together
康居住宅	kāngjūzhùzhǎi	affordable housing in Beijing for low and mid-income earners
科企	kēqǐ	technology industry
啃老	kěnlǎo	young people who should have been independent but still depend on their parents
空巢阶段	kōngcháo jiēduàn	empty-nest period in one's life when all children have left home

空哥	kōnggē	male cabin personnel on airplanes	
空姐	kōngjiě	stewardess, short for "空中小姐 kōngzhōng xiǎojie"	
空嫂	kōngsǎo	stewardesses who range from 30 to 35 years of age, and are married and have children	
空白婚姻	kòngbái hūnyīn	a marriage on paper only. The purpose is for a foreigner to get permanent resident status.	
恐龙症	kǒnglóng zhèng	dinosaur-like organizations where there are too many employees and efficiency is substandard	
空中礼物	kōngzhōng lǐwù	"cyber-space gifts": greetings or good wishes given to people with songs over radio or television	
酷	kù	"cool" (transliteration)	
款娘	kuǎnniáng	super-rich women	
款族	kuǎnzú	very rich people	
困难公司	kùnnán gōngsī	consulting companies who help enterprises to solve problems in such things as capital, management, policy, and development	

L	蓝天计划	lántiān jìhuà	blue sky plan: environmental plans to keep the sky blue
	老板市场	lǎobǎn shìchǎng	employment market, job market
	老大	lǎodà	mid-sized and large-sized state enterprises
	老欧	lǎo'ōu	a person from Europe

老外	lǎowài	one who does not understand a particular profession; used to refer to a foreigner since the 1970s.
礼品市场	lǐpǐn shìchǎng	markets specializing in selling gift items
丽人职业	lìrén zhíyè	"beauty" profession: models, promotion ladies, etc.
礼仪广告	lǐyí guǎnggào	newspaper advertisements announcing weddings, birthdays, etc.
礼仪消费	lǐyí xiāofèi	expenses for social and protocol activities
廉价房	liánjiàfáng	affordable housing
廉商	liánshāng	ethical business practice, ethical business person
两岸三地	liǎng'àn sāndì	three places on two shores: mainland China, Hong Kong, and Taiwan
两岸四地	liǎng'àn sìdì	four places on two shores: mainland China, Hong Kong, Macau, and Taiwan
两乐	liǎnglè	"two joys" or "two colas," referring to Coca Cola 可口可乐 kěkǒukělè and Pepsi Cola 百事可乐 bǎishìkělè
两条腿凳子	liǎngtiáotuǐ dèngzi	two-legged chairs: unstable careers, jobs, and wages
两制家庭	liǎngzhì jiātíng	two-system family: either husband or wife is from mainland China and the other one from Taiwan
猎才	liècái	head-hunting, also known as 猎头 liètóu

35

留守男士	liúshǒu nánshì	husbands who stay home and take care of everything when their wives go abroad
留守女士	liúshǒu nǚshì	wives who stay home and take care of everything when their husbands go abroad
留守子女	liúshǒu zǐnǚ	children whose parents went abroad and are taken care of by relatives
绿地公司	lǜdì gōngsī	"green companies": companies who create green space in urban environments
绿色电脑	lǜsè diànnǎo	environmentally sound computers, energy saving and easily recycleable
绿色顾客	lǜsè gùkè	customers with strong environmental consciousness
绿色管理	lǜsè guǎnlǐ	green management: management that takes environmental protection into consideration
绿色科技	lǜsè kējì	science and technology which promote environmental protection and sustainable ecological balance
绿色汽车	lǜsè qìchē	"green cars": environmentally sound, low-emission cars
绿色食品	lǜsè shípǐn	"green food": unpolluted food, organic food
旅游学习	lǚyóu xuéxí	tourism that involves some learning

M	买单	mǎidān	asking for the check (at a restaurant)

买全国，	mǎi quánguó	management policies and directions that promote buying
卖全国	mài quánguó	selling and distributing to the whole country, not just locally
美食	měishí	good food, delicious food
迷你市场	mínǐ shìchǎng	mini-markets: markets with stalls by the streets and in residential lanes
面的	miàndī	inexpensive, yellow mini-van type of taxis
明星广告	míngxīng guǎnggào	commercials or advertisements with famous movie stars, singers, dancers, and sports figures promoting goods
明星衫	míngxīngshān	T-shirts with pictures of movie stars, singers, etc. on them
模拟警察	móní jǐngchá	virtual police: police statues placed at intersections
母城	mǔchéng	mother cities: cities around which satellite cities and development zones have developed
N 脑矿	nǎokuàng	brain mine: resource base for talents and intelligence
脑民	nǎomín	people whose work depends on using their brains (intelligence). This type of work is called "脑业 nǎoyè."
农大款	nóngdàkuǎn	extremely rich farmers
弄股	nònggǔ	buy and sell stocks, play with stocks
农事秘书	nóngshì mìshū	technical people hired by farmers to

37

		improve the products by employing new technology

P	泡沫经济	pàomò jīngjì	bubble economy
	泡沫合同	pàomò hétong	bubble contract: a contract which promises to supply more than one can produce in order to control the market
	泡沫图书	pàomò túshū	bubble books: books which do not have substantial content or value but are published in great quantities
	泡沫文化	pàomò wénhuà	bubble culture: a false, pretentious culture, such as the mass creation of low-quality cultural goods
	泡沫新闻	pàomò xīnwén	false news
	跑腿公司	pǎotuǐ gōngsī	service companies who will do chores of any kind for clients
	陪产	péichǎn	accompanying childbirth: husband stands by his wife when she is giving birth
	捧爷	pěngyé	flatterer, brown-nose, apple polisher, bootlicker
	贫法	pínfǎ	poor legal knowledge, lacking legal concepts
	贫老	pínlǎo	poor old-aged people, particularly those without a spouse, old-age pension, or ability to work
	破铁捧金	pòtiě pěngjīn	break the "3 irons" and hold "gold"; 3 irons: iron office

			chair, iron wage, iron rice bowl; gold: gold rice bowl, particularly more work for more pay and a rich and comfortable life
	普九	pǔjiǔ	nine years of compulsory public education
	铺路费	pūlùfèi	money, "fee," given to someone who will help to get things done
Q	7-11 商店	qīyīyī shāngdiàn	7-11 stores
	钱盲	qiánmáng	people who are blinded by, and blindly worship, money
	巧克力式	qiǎokèlì shì	the pampering way of bringing up children
	轻轨交通	qīngguǐ jiāotōng	light rail transit
	企业人	qǐyèrén	enterprise members who have a solemn and proud air
	青春合同	qīngchūn hétong	"youth contract": contracts between enterprises and their employees, where they agree that the employees only work for them when they are young
	清咖	qīngkā	black coffee, with no cream or sugar
	情感促销	qínggǎn cùxiāo	promotions which appeal to buyers' emotions for sales
R	热点	rèdiǎn	"hot spots": popular spots or places
	热点话题	rèdiǎn huàtí	hot conversation topics
	人才潮	réncáicháo	"brain tide": qualified people relocating for better jobs

人才夜市	réncái yèshì	night job market
儒商	rúshāng	Confucian merchant: a scholarly merchant
软广告	ruǎn guǎnggào	soft advertisement: for example, through the props or words in movies
软资源	ruǎn zīyuán	soft resource: science, technology, information, etc.
软管理	ruǎn guǎnlǐ	"soft management": a management method where people are left alone to be proactive and creative

S

三币	sānbì	three kinds of currency: Renminbi, Hong Kong dollar, and Taiwan dollar
三懂律师	sāndǒng lùshī	lawyers who know law, foreign language, and economics
三替公司	sāntì gōngsī	"three 4 U company": a service company who will do almost anything for the client for a fee
色盲镜	sèmángjìng	corrective lenses for color blindness
商海	shānghǎi	commodity market which is as vast and changeable as an ocean
商广	shāngguǎng	commercial advertising or commercials
商书	shāngshū	books on economics or commerce
商友	shāngyǒu	friends who do business together
上花班	shànghuābān	"spotty work": some state government workers only go to their own workplace when they are not

		working on the side elsewhere
少犯	shàofàn	juvenile delinquent
涉外厕所	shèwài cèsuǒ	good, clean washrooms for people from overseas
涉外红娘	shèwài hóngniáng	matchmakers who try to find foreign partners for Chinese
生态道德	shēngtài dàodé	ecological ethics: regulations and norms which keep harmony between humans and the natural ecological environment
生态旅游	shēngtài lǚyóu	eco-tourism
世贸	shìmào	WTO, World Trade Organization, short for 世界贸易组织 shìjiè màoyì zǔzhī
世银	shìyín	World Bank, short for 世界银行 shìjiè yínháng
手机	shǒujī	cellular phone; the older term is "dàgēdà"
手语市场	shǒuyǔ shìchǎng	"sign language market," where only hand signs are used for trade
寿险	shòuxiǎn	life insurance, short for 人寿保险 rénshòu bǎoxiǎn
书民	shūmín	people who truly love books
双休日	shuāngxiūrì	both Saturday and Sunday off work
双赢	shuāngyíng	win–win situation or strategy
水货	shuǐhuò	low quality, fake goods, as opposed to 行货 hánghuò, genuine goods
水泥森林	shuǐní sēnlín	concrete jungle: tall buildings in cities
四合院	sìhéyuànr	conservative and closed way of

			thinking, like the traditional enclosed courtyard homes
死亡婚姻		sǐwáng hūnyīn	a marriage in which husband and wife still maintain the relationship although the marriage has broken down and they have no more feelings towards each other
四小龙		sìxiǎolóng	Four Little Dragons: Singapore, South Korea, Taiwan, and Hong Kong
	T	跳板婚姻	tiàobǎn hūnyīn	a marriage without love, based purely on achieving a certain goal
头脑公司		tóunǎo gōngsī	"talent company" which gathers engineering and technical talents and provides them to organizations
	W	娃娃教授	wáwa jiàoshòu	"baby professors": very young professors
网吧		wǎngbā	internet cafe
网虫		wǎngchóng	nethead, webaholic
网民		wǎngmín	internet surfers
围裙丈夫		wéiqún zhàngfu	husbands who take care of household work
危机管理		wēijī guǎnlǐ	crisis management
文化餐		wénhuà cān	foods which have historical, folk, or other kinds of cultural meaning
问题家庭		wèntí jiātíng	dysfunctional family, where husband and wife do not get along or are divorced
无店铺销售		wúdiànpù xiāoshòu	sales without shops: direct sales
无孩族		wúháizú	childless people

	舞疗	wǔliáo	dancing as a way of healing, dance therapy
	无烟校	wúyānxiào	non-smoking schools
X	夕阳市场	xīyáng shìchǎng	sunset market: markets catering to older people
	下海	xiàhǎi	to quit one's official job and go into private business
	心疗	xīnliáo	psychological healing, psychotherapy
	信息贩子	xìnxī fànzi	one who sells information
	信息污染	xìnxī wūrǎn	disturbance caused by inaccurate or mistaken information
	形象推销	xíngxiàng tuīxiāo	marketing of a corporate, product, or personal image
Y	洋打工	yángdǎgōng	foreigners who work and earn wages in China
	一国两制	yìguó liǎngzhì	one country, two systems, such as China and Hong Kong, or China and Macau
	硬广告	yìng guǎnggào	hard advertisements: commercials shown on television
	有病	yǒubìng	sick, wacky, abnormal
Z	宰家	zǎijiā	people who demand high prices and try to make money without mercy
	宰外	zǎiwài	cheating foreigners out of their money, or getting more money out of foreigners
	阵热	zhènrè	short temporary social trend or fashion
	知本家	zhīběnjiā	intellectual capitalist: one who has keen

43

		business skills and a creative mind, a term coined from 资本家 zīběnjiā, capitalist
智力回流	zhìlì huíliú	Chinese science and technology intellectuals who studied, stayed abroad, and then returned to work in China
钟点工	zhōngdiǎngōng	people who are paid by the hour, doing odd jobs such as shopping, laundry, window cleaning, taking care of a sick person
筑巢引凤	zhùcháo yǐnfèng	"building a nest to attract the phoenix": a term meaning creating a favorable environment in order to attract investments
追潮族	zhuīcháozú	those who follow the trends
追车族	zhuīchēzú	those who love to own or enjoy the use of cars
追款族	zhuīkuǎnzú	people who chase after money
准顾客	zhǔngùkè	potential customers
自助银行	zìzhù yínháng	automatic banking, ATM, automatic teller machine
自助照	zìzhùzhào	camera booth where one puts in coins, and photos are automatically dispensed

2.7   Computer and internet-related words

2.7.1   Terms for things

address book	地址簿 dìzhǐbù	
attachment	附件 fùjiàn	

Big 5	the traditional (or complex) Chinese standard fonts
blog/blogger	博客 bókè
chatroom	聊天室 liáotiānshì
domain	域名 yùmíng
e-mail	电子邮件 diànzǐ yóujiàn/电邮 diànyóu/伊媚尔 yīmèi'ěr
file	文件 wénjiàn
forum	论坛 lùntán
GB	abbreviation for 国标 guóbiāo, the simplified Chinese standard fonts
Google	谷歌 gǔgē
hacker	黑客 hēikè
hardware	硬件 yìngjiàn
home page	主页 zhǔyè
host (computer)	主机 zhǔjī
internet	互联网 hùliánwǎng, the older name is 因特网 yīntèwǎng
internet cafe	网吧 wǎngbā
keyword	关键字 guānjiànzì/ 关键词 guānjiàncí
message	消息 xiāoxi
netizen/nettizen	网民 wǎngmín
online	在线 zàixiàn
password	密码 mìmǎ
platform	平台 píngtái
site	站点 zhàndiǎn
software	软件 ruǎnjiàn
user name	用户 yònghù/用户名 yònghù míng
virus	病毒 bìngdú
webaholic/nethead	网虫 wǎngchóng
webpage	网页 wǎngyè
website	网站 wǎngzhàn
Wikipedia	维基百科 wéijībǎikē
Yahoo	雅虎 yǎhǔ

2.7.2   Terms for actions

back, return	返回 fǎnhuí
browse	浏览 liúlǎn
chat	聊天 liáotiān
check one's mail	查邮件 chá yóujiàn
check one's mailbox	查邮箱 chá yóuxiāng
click on a link	点击 diǎnjī
decode	解码 jiěmǎ
download	下载 xiàzǎi
go online	上网 shàngwǎng
log in	登录 dēnglù
log out	登出 dēngchū

register	注册 zhùcè
search	搜索 sōusuǒ
send e-mail	发邮件 fā yóujiàn
surf/go online	上网 shàngwǎng
upload	上载 shàngzǎi

2.7.3   Text messaging, blogging, and online chatting abbreviations

::>_<::	weeping eyes
3Q	Junglish pun: pronounced "sān Q," thank you
3x	bilingual pun: "sān x" sounds like "thanks"
"42"	yes (sounds like "shì")
"88"	"bābā," similar to "bye bye," goodbye
"94"	"jiǔ sì," short for 就是 jiù shì, that is
"520"	I love you (sounds like "wǒ ài nǐ")
"5555"	short for "wū wū wū wū," the sound of sobbing
bt	变态 biàntài, abnormal
fb	腐败 fǔbài, corruption, dining out on public funds
ft	分特 fēntè, short for "faint"
GG	short for "哥哥 gēge," "elder brother," boy
JJ	short for "姐姐 jiějie," older sister
konglong	恐龙 kǒnglóng, dinosaur, ugly girl
MM	short for "妹妹 mèimei," "younger sister," a girl
mm	美眉 měiméi, beautiful eyebrows, a girl
偶稀饭	ǒuxīfàn = 我喜欢 wǒ xǐhuān, I like (+ an object)
PF	short for "佩服 pèifu," admire
PLMM	acronym for "漂亮妹妹 piàoliang mèimei," beautiful girl
PMP	short for "拍马屁 pāimǎpì," to bootlick, to brown-nose
qingwa	青蛙 qīngwā, frog, ugly boy
史弟弟	shǐdìdi = 傻瓜 shǎguā, short for "史努比的弟弟 shǐnúbǐde dìdì, Snoopy's younger brother," meaning "stupid"
TMD	acronym for "他妈的 tāmāde," expletive "his mother's"

2.8   Quotable quotes from the classics

One of the most favored ways to display wisdom and/or erudition when using Chinese to discuss matters is to be able to quote a well-known line from one of the great classics, such as *The Analects of Confucius, The Writings of Mencius, The Middle Way, The Great Learning, The Writings of Zhuangzi, The Classic of the Way and Its Virtue, The Writings of Master Han Fei,* and the like, which will suggest a perspective that not only makes sense, but also imposes a proper moral or ethical interpretation on the matter at hand. For example, after discussing at length the pros and cons of undertaking a project that clearly cannot be completed in the foreseeable future, but should be started regardless of the challenge, one might quote a line from the Daoist classic, *The Classic of the Way and Its Virtue*: "A thousand-league journey begins with a first step, 千里之行始于足下 qiānlǐzhīxíng shǐyú zúxià." There are countless others, but we may cite a few of the best-known quotations here:

From *The Analects of Confucius*, 论语 Lúnyǔ:

不患人之不己知，患不知人也。

búhuàn rénzhī bùjǐzhī, huàn bùzhīrén yě

I am not bothered by others not understanding me; I am bothered that I do not understand others.

富而不骄易，贫而无怨难。

fù ér bùjiāo yì, pín ér wúyuàn nán

It is easier to resist being arrogant when wealthy than to avoid being resentful when poor.

君子欲讷於言，而敏於行。

jūnzi yù nàyúyán, ér mǐnyúxíng

The superior person should be slow in speech and earnest in conduct.

君子喻於义，小人喻於利。

jūnzi yùyúyì, xiǎorén yùyúlì

The mind of the superior person is conversant with righteousness; the mind of the petty person is conversant with gain.

其身正，不令而行，其身不正，虽令不从。

qíshēn zhèng, búlìng érxíng; qíshēn búzhèng, suīlìng bùcóng

An upright person will be obeyed without issuing orders; a deviant person will not be followed even after issuing orders.

三人行，必有我师焉，择其善者而从之。

sānrénxíng, bìyǒu wǒshī yān, zé qí shànzhě ér cóngzhī

Among any three people, one will be worthy of being my teacher. I can choose the best to follow.

温故而知新，可以为师矣。

wēngù érzhīxīn, kěyǐ wéishīyǐ

One who learns something new from reviewing something old may be a teacher of others.

学而时习之，不亦悦乎？

xué ér shíxízhī, búyì yuèhū?

Isn't it pleasant to learn with constant application?

有朋自远方来，不亦乐乎？

yǒupéng zìyuǎnfāng lái, búyì lè hū?

Isn't it delightful to have friends coming from far away?

知者不惑，仁者不忧，勇者不惧。

zhīzhě búhuò, rénzhě bùyōu, yǒngzhě bújù

The wise are free from perplexity, the kind free from anxiety,
and the bold free from fear.

知之者不如好之者，好之者不如乐之者。

zhīzhīzhě bùrú hàozhīzhě, hàozhīzhě bùrú lèzhīzhě

They who know the truth are not as great as those who love
it, and they who love it are not as great
as those who delight in it.

From *The Great Learning*, 大学 Dàxué

君子无所不用其极。

jūnzi wúsuǒ búyòngqíjí

The superior person puts everything into every endeavor.

物格而后知至。

wù gé érhòu zhīzhì

Knowledge is achieved only after things have been
investigated.

物有本末，事有终始。

wù yǒuběnmò; shì yǒuzhōngshǐ

Things have fundamentals and incidentals. Matters have
beginnings and endings.

心不在焉，视而不见，听而不闻，食而不知其味。

xīnbúzàiyān, shì ér bújiàn, tīng ér bùwén, shí ér bùzhīqíwèi

When the mind is not focused, we look without seeing,
listen without hearing, and eat without tasting.

欲治其国者，先齐其家，欲齐其家者，先修其身。

yù zhìqíguózhě, xiān qíqíjiā, yù qíqíjiāzhě, xiān xiūqíshēn

Whoever would rule a nation should first put their house
in order; whoever would put their house in order should
first perfect self-cultivation.

自天子以至於庶人，壹事皆以修身为本。

zì tiānzǐ yǐzhìyú shùrén, yīshì jiēyǐ xiūshēn wéiběn

From the emperor down to the common people, all must
consider self-cultivation to be the fundamental issue.

From *The Middle Way*, 中庸 Zhōngyōng

诚者, 天之道也。诚之者, 人之道也。

chéngzhě, tiānzhīdàoyě. chéngzhīzhě, rénzhīdàoyě

Sincerity is the Way of Heaven. Making oneself sincere is
the Way of humanity.

诚者，物之终始。不诚无物。

chéngzhě, wùzhī zhōngshǐ. bùchéng wúwù

Sincerity is the beginning and end of all things. Without
sincerity there is nothing.

诚者自成也，而道自道也。

chéngzhě zìchéngyě, ér dào zìdàoyě

Sincerity is perfected in people as the Way is followed in Nature.

道不远人。人之为道而远人，不可以为道。

dào bùyuǎn rén. rén zhī wéidào ér yuǎnrén, bùkěyi wéidào

The Way is not something separate from humankind. If you practice a Way that is apart from humankind, this cannot be the Way.

和也者，天下之达道也。

héyězhě, tiānxià zhī dádàoyě

Harmony is the most advanced Way in the world.

或生而知之，或学而知之，或困而知之，及其知之，一也。

huò shēng ér zhīzhī, huò xué ér zhīzhī, huò kùn ér zhīzhī, jíqí zhīzhī, yī yě

Some are born understanding; some understand by learning and some have to struggle to understand. Nevertheless, their understanding has the same value.

君子之道，费而隐。

jūnzi zhī dào, fèi ér yǐn

The Way of superior people is to go into seclusion when their talents are unused.

君子之道，辟如行远必自迩。

jūnzǐ zhī dào, pìrú xíngyuǎn bìzì'ěr

The Way of superior people can be compared to traveling: to go far, you must start from close by.

人莫不饮食也。鲜能知味也。

rén mòbùyǐnshíyě. xiǎnnéng zhīwèiyě

Everyone eats and drinks, but few are they who really appreciate flavor.

如此者，不见而章，不动而变，无为而成。

rúcǐzhě, búxiàn érzhāng, búdòng érbiàn, wúwéi érchéng

In this way, it manifests without show, it changes without moving, and achieves without effort.

From *The Classic of Filial Piety*, 孝经 Xiàojīng

夫孝，德之本也，教之所由生也。

fū xiào, dézhīběnyě, jiào zhī suǒyóushēngyě.

Filial piety is the root of all virtue, and the stem out of which grows all moral teaching.

夫孝，天之经也，地之义也，民之行也。

fū xiào, tiānzhījīngyě, dìzhīyìyě, mínzhīxíngyě.

Filial piety is the constant way of Heaven, the righteous way of Earth, and the practical duty of the populace.

身体发肤，受之父母，不敢毁伤，孝之始也。

shēntǐ fàfū, shòuzhī fùmǔ, bùgǎn huǐshāng, xiàozhìshǐyě.

Our bodies, even every hair and bit of skin, are received by
us from our parents, and not daring to injure or wound
them is the beginning of filial piety.

事亲者，居上不骄，为下不乱，在丑不争。

shìqīnzhě, jūshàng bùjiāo, wéixià búluàn, zàichǒu bùzhēng.

They who serve their parents well, when in a high position
will be free from pride, in a low position will avoid
insubordination, and among equals will not be quarrelsome.

From *The Ritual Records*, 礼记 Lǐjì

大道之行也，天下为公。

dà dào zhī xíng yě, tiān xià wéi gōng

The Greatest Truth proceeds this way: the world is for the
public.

苛政猛于虎。

kēzhèng měngyú hǔ

Tyrannical government is more fierce than a tiger.

礼尚往来。

lǐ shàng wǎnglái

Courtesy demands reciprocity.

学然后知不足，教然后知困。

xué ránhòu zhībùzú, jiāo ránhòu zhīkùn

Through studying we understand deficiency; through
teaching we understand difficulty.

玉不琢不成器，人不学不知道。

yù bùzhuó bùchéngqì, rén bùxué bùzhīdào

Unpolished jade is useless; uneducated people are ignorant.

知耻近乎勇。

zhīchǐ jìnhū yǒng

Having a sense of shame is close to being courageous.

From *The Writings of Mencius*, 孟子 Mèngzǐ

得道多助，失道寡助。

dédào duōzhù, shīdào guǎzhù

Just causes find much support; unjust causes enjoy little
support.

老吾老，以及人之老，幼吾幼，以及人之幼，天下可运
于掌。

lǎo wúlǎo, yǐjí rénzhīlǎo, yòu wúyòu, yǐjí rénzhīyòu, tiānxià
kěyùnyúzhǎng

If we treat our own elders with respect and extend that
treatment to the elders of other families, and treat our
own young with great care and extend that treatment to
the young of other families, we will have a peaceful world
in our hands.

人皆可以为尧舜。

rén jiēkěyǐ wéi Yáo Shùn

Anyone may become a Sage King.

王顾左右而言他。

wáng gù zuǒyòu ér yántā

The King looks left and right, then changes the subject.

(Used to describe someone who changes the subject when he/she can't answer a difficult or embarrassing question.)

以五十步笑百步。

yǐ wǔshíbù xiào bǎibù

Those who retreat fifty feet scoff at those who retreat a hundred feet.

From *The Classic of the Way and Its Virtue* 道德经 Dàodéjīng

大道废，有仁义。。。国家昏乱，有忠臣。

dàdào fèi, yǒu rényì....guójiā hūnluàn, yǒu zhōngchén

When the Great Truth has been abandoned, benevolence and righteousness appear... When the country is in chaos, loyal ministers appear.

道常无为而无不为。

dào cháng wúwéi ér wú bùwéi

The Way always does without ado, leaving nothing left undone.

道可道，非常道。名可名，非常名。

dào kě dào, fēi cháng dào. Míng kě míng, fēi cháng míng

Truths may be told, but not eternal Truth. Names may be named, but not eternal names.

九层之台起于累土，千里之行始于足下。

jiǔcéngzhītái qǐyúlěitǔ, qiānlǐzhīxíng shǐyúzúxià

A nine-story tower starts with a pile of dirt; a thousand-league journey starts with a first step.

人法地，地法天，天法道，道法自然。

rén fǎ dì, dì fǎ tiān, tiān fǎ dào, dào fǎ zìrán

Humanity is patterned after Earth; Earth is patterned after Heaven; Heaven is patterned after the Way. The Way simply is.

上善若水。水善利万物而不争。

shàngshàn ruò shuǐ. shuǐ shàn lì wànwù ér bùzhēng

The greatest good is like water. Water benefits all things and struggles against none.

胜人者有力，自胜者强。

shèngrénzhě yǒulì, zìshèngzhě qiáng

He who overcomes others has power; he who overcomes himself has strength.

知人者智，自知者明。

zhīrénzhě zhì, zìzhīzhě míng

One who understands others is wise; one who understands
oneself is brilliant.

From *The Writings of Zhuangzi*, 庄子 Zhuāngzǐ

哀莫大于心死，而身死次之。

āi mòdàyú xīnsǐ, ér shēnsǐ cìzhī

Nothing is sadder than the death of a heart, and the death of
a body is the next saddest.

君子之交淡如水，小人之交甘若醴

jūnzi zhījiāo dànrúshuǐ, xiǎorén zhījiāo gānruòlǐ

Superior people's friendship is pure as water; petty people's
friendship is too sweet, like a liqueur.

小巫见大巫

xiǎowū jiàn dàwū

A lesser shaman meets a greater shaman (a novice meets a
master).

From *The Writings of Master Han Fei*, 韩非子 Hánfēizǐ

千里之堤，溃于蚁穴

qiānlǐ zhī dī, kuì yú yǐxuè

A thousand-league dike may collapse because of an ant hole
(minor causes may lead to major disasters).

2.9   Idioms

The four-character idioms, 四言成语 sìyánchéngyǔ, are expressions
derived from classical writings. They are concise summaries of well-
known anecdotes or parables from classical Chinese texts, crystallizing
the main point or lesson of the stories. They are analogous to English
expressions like "slow but steady wins the race," which finds its
source in "The Tortoise and the Hare" from *Aesop's Fables*. A typical
Chinese idiom is a string of four characters that may constitute a
complete sentence, such as "老马识途 lǎomǎshítú, the old horse
knows the route," or may simply constitute a comment on a
previously stated topic, such as "井底之蛙 jǐngdǐzhīwā, a frog at the
bottom of the well." Educated Chinese, like learned English speakers,
derive pleasure from using classical allusions to crystallize the essence
of a current situation both in speech and in writing. The difference
is that Chinese speakers have such a huge collection of classical
works from which to draw their allusions when a comparable parallel
is noticed in contemporary situations. Not only is it not deemed
pretentious, it is widely admired and appreciated when one idiom,
drawn from a rich reservoir of classical citations, is recollected and
aptly applied to a contemporary scenario.

The following are examples of idioms, along with their classical
sources:

百发百中	bǎifābǎizhòng	To hit the bull's eye every time.	(*Strategies of the Warring States*, 战国策 Zhànguócè)
半途而废	bàntú'érfèi	To give up halfway through the task.	(The *Writings of Lie Yukou*, 列子 Lièzǐ)
不耻下问	bùchǐxiàwèn	Not ashamed to learn from one's subordinates.	(*The Analects of Confucius*, 论语 Lúnyǔ)
出尔反尔	chū'ěrfǎn'ěr	You reap what you sow./What goes around, comes around.	(*The Writings of Mencius*, 孟子 Mèngzǐ)
唇亡齿寒	chúnwángchǐhán	Share a common lot; when one is lost, dependents will suffer.	(*The Zuo Commentary on the Spring and Autumn Annals*, 左传 Zuǒzhuàn)
东施效颦	Dōng Shī xiàopín	Ugly people's affectations make them appear even uglier, referring to Xi Shi's ugly neighbor Dong Shi, who tried to imitate Xi Shi's cute frown.	(*The Writings of Zhuangzi*, 庄子 Zhuāngzǐ)
对牛弹琴	duìniútánqín	Cast pearls before swine.	(庄子 Zhuāngzǐ)
多言何益	duōyánhéyì	There is no use talking too much.	(*The Writings of Mozi*, 墨子 Mòzǐ)
狐假虎威	hújiǎhǔwēi	To feign powerful airs by positioning oneself near one who wields real power.	(战国策 Zhànguócè)
画蛇添足	huàshétiānzú	Ruin the project by adding something superfluous.	(战国策 Zhànguócè)
井底之蛙	jǐngdǐzhīwā	A person with a very limited outlook, who has seen no more of the world outside than a frog who lives at the bottom of a well.	(庄子 Zhuāngzǐ)
刻舟求剑	kēzhōuqiújiàn	To base one's actions on irrelevant history, like the man who carved a notch on the side of the boat where his sword dropped in the river during	(*The Lü Historical Annals.*, 吕氏春秋 Lǚshì Chūnqiū)

		the crossing, with the intention of searching under the notch once they reached the other side.	
滥竽充数	lànyúchōngshù	One's incompetence may go unnoticed in a large group.	(*The Writings of Master Han Fei*, 韩非子 Hánfēizǐ)
老马识途	lǎomǎshítú	An old hand; a veteran who knows how to perform the task.	(韩非子 Hánfēizǐ)
乐极生悲	lèjíshēngbēi	Extremes generate opposite extremes.	(*Records of the Grand Historian*, 史记 Shǐjì)
梁上君子	liángshàngjūnzǐ	A euphemistic reference to a cat-burglar.	(*History of the Later Han Dynasty*, 后汉书 Hòuhànshū)
毛遂自荐	Máo Suí zìjiàn	Used apologetically when recommending oneself for a job or a task.	(史记 Shǐjì)
骑虎难下	qíhǔnánxià	To find it impossible to back down once a challenge has been taken up.	(*History of the Jin Dynasty*, 晋书 Jìn Shū)
杞人忧天	qǐrényōutiān	To worry about misfortunes that will never happen.	(列子 Lièzǐ)
起死回生	qǐsǐhuíshēng	To snatch life from the jaws of death; to have a very close call.	(史记 Shǐjì)
如鱼得水	rúyúdéshuǐ	Happy as a fish in water.	(*Annals of the Three Kingdoms*, 三国志 Sānguózhì)
孺子可教	rúzǐkějiāo	A young person who is capable of learning great things.	(史记 Shǐjì)
塞翁失马	sàiwēngshīmǎ	A potential blessing in disguise.	(*The Writings of Huáinánzǐ*, 淮南子 Huáinánzǐ)
食言而肥	shíyán'érféi	Habitually making idle promises.	(左传 Zuǒzhuàn)
守株待兔	shǒuzhūdàitù	Foolishly wait for an unrepeatable windfall.	(韩非子 Hánfēizǐ)
徒劳无功	túláowúgōng	Work to no avail; to work hard and achieve nothing.	(庄子 Zhuāngzǐ)
望洋兴叹	wàngyángxīngtàn	Feeling utterly helpless and powerless.	(庄子 Zhuāngzǐ)

先发制人	xiānfāzhìrén	The one who makes the first move has the advantage.	(史记 Shǐjì)
掩耳盗铃	yān'ěrdàolíng	To use "ostrich head" tactics. To bury one's head in the sand.	(淮南子 Huáinánzǐ)
言过其实	yánguòqíshí	An overstatement.	(三国志 Sānguózhì)
揠苗助长 / 拔苗助长	yàmiáozhùzhǎng bámiáozhùzhǎng	Engage in counterproductive measures to hasten or increase production.	(孟子 Mèngzǐ)
一败涂地	yíbàitúdì	Suffer a crushing defeat; to be wiped out by the enemy.	(史记 Shǐjì)
一字千金	yízìqiānjīn	Worth its weight in gold (said of great calligraphy or poetry).	(史记 Shǐjì)
因小失大 / 贪小失大	yīnxiǎoshīdà tānxiǎoshīdà	Penny wise and pound foolish.	(吕氏春秋 Lǚshì Chūnqiū)
有备无患	yǒubèiwúhuàn	Preparedness averts peril; be prepared and have no worries.	(左传 Zuǒzhuàn)
愚公移山	yúgōngyíshān	Where there's a will, there's a way.	(列子 Lièzǐ)
朝三暮四	zhāosānmùsì	To deceive by juggling the figures.	(列子 Lièzǐ)
纸上谈兵	zhǐshàngtánbīng	Be an armchair quarterback.	(史记 Shǐjì)
自相矛盾	zìxiāngmáodùn	Make self-contradictory statements.	(列子 Lièzǐ)
自知之明	zìzhīzhīmíng	To know one's own strengths and weaknesses.	(战国策 Zhànguócè)

2.10   Four-character set phrases

Four-character set phrases are structurally the same as idioms, since they also consist of four characters. Chinese usually put these two into the same category and call them "四言成语 sìyán chéngyǔ, four-character idioms." However, unlike the idioms, these are not usually crystallizations of stories from classical writings and their usage is more common and their occurrence is more frequent in modern Chinese.

A	爱不释手	àibùshìshǒu	like something so much one would not let go of it
	爱财如命	àicáirúmìng	money-grabbing, miserly
	爱莫能助	àimònéngzhù	willing but unable to help
	安步当车	ānbùdāngchē	walking, go on foot
	安分守己	ānfènshǒujǐ	well behaved and law abiding, mind one's own business
	安居乐业	ānjūlèyè	live and work in peace and contentment
	安贫乐道	ānpínlèdào	live contentedly even though poor, and enjoying what one does
	安然无恙	ānránwúyàng	safe and sound
	按部就班	ànbùjiùbān	doing things according to rules
	暗箭伤人	ànjiànshāngrén	stab people in the back
	昂首阔步	ángshǒukuòbù	march forward with head high, strut about
B	八面玲珑	bāmiànlínglóng	pleasing everyone, an artful person
	白发苍苍	báifàcāngcāng	with white/grey hair
	白日做梦	báirìzuòmèng	day-dreaming
	白手起家	báishǒuqǐjiā	build up a fortune from scratch
	白头偕老	báitóuxiélǎo	husband and wife live together through old age
	百读不厌	bǎidúbúyàn	something one never gets tired of reading
	百发百中	bǎifābǎizhòng	always on target
	百感交集	bǎigǎnjiāojí	moved by many different emotions
	百花齐放	bǎihuāqífàng	let a hundred flowers blossom, let all talents be revealed

百思不解	bǎisībùjiě	absolutely cannot understand
百依百顺	bǎiyībǎishùn	totally obedient
百战百胜	bǎizhànbǎishèng	ever victorious
百折不挠	bǎizhébùnǎo	unyielding and persistent, unrelenting, never frustrated
半途而废	bàntú'érfèi	give up half way
半信半疑	bànxìnbànyí	not quite convinced, half believing, half doubting
半夜三更	bànyèsāngēng	in the middle of the night
暴跳如雷	bàotiàorúléi	fly into a rage, stomp around with rage
杯盘狼籍	bēipánlángjí	cups and dishes in disarray after a dinner or party
本来面目	běnláimiànmù	one's true colors
本末倒置	běnmòdàozhì	confuse cause and effect, put the cart before the horse
笨手笨脚	bènshǒubènjiǎo	clumsy
笨头笨脑	bèntóubènnǎo	block-headed, stupid
比手画脚	bǐshǒuhuàjiǎo	to gesticulate (while talking)
必恭必敬	bìgōngbìjìng	extremely respectful
闭门造车	bìménzàochē	work on a project without knowing what everyone else is doing on the same project
鞭长莫及	biānchángmòjí	beyond one's reach (of authority)
彬彬有礼	bīnbīnyǒulǐ	very well mannered
冰天雪地	bīngtiānxuědì	the whole landscape covered with ice and snow
病入膏肓	bìngrùgāohuāng	sick to the core, incurable
博古通今	bógǔtōngjīn	well versed in knowledge old and new, very learned
博学多才	bóxuéduōcái	learned and talented
不耻下问	bùchǐxiàwèn	feel at ease asking and learning from people below oneself

不打自招	bùdǎzìzhāo	confess without being pressed, confess on one's own
不动声色	búdòngshēngsè	not showing any feelings, poker-faced, not batting an eyelid
不好意思	bùhǎoyìsi	embarrassed, shy
不欢而散	bùhuān'érsàn	end in discord
不慌不忙	bùhuāngbùmáng	calmly, not in any hurry
不计其数	bújìqíshù	countless, uncountable
不拘小节	bùjūxiǎojié	not constrained by formalities, unconventional
不堪回首	bùkānhuíshǒu	cannot bear to look back to the past
不堪设想	bùkānshèxiǎng	unimaginable, inconceivable
不可救药	bùkějiùyào	incurable, beyond remedy
不可胜数	bùkěshèngshǔ	countless, numerous
不可收拾	bùkěshōushi	beyond help, unretractable
不可思议	bùkěsīyì	unthinkable, incomprehensible
不劳而获	bùláo'érhuò	reap without sowing
不了了之	bùliǎoliǎozhī	settle something by leaving it unsettled
不露声色	búlùshēngsè	not revealing one's feelings, intentions, etc.
不伦不类	bùlúnbúlèi	neither fish nor fowl
不明不白	bùmíngbùbái	pointless, with no clear reason
不三不四	bùsānbúsì	neither one nor the other; neither fish, flesh, nor fowl
不声不响	bùshēngbùxiǎng	quiet, silent
不胜枚举	búshèngméijǔ	too numerous to mention, too numerous to count
不疼不痒	bùténgbùyǎng	effortless, perfunctory
不闻不问	bùwénbúwèn	turn a blind eye to, turn a deaf ear to, be indifferent to

	不相上下	bùxiāngshàngxià	comparable, well matched, on a par
	不学无术	bùxuéwúshù	ignorant, not learned
	不厌其烦	búyànqífán	taking great pains, very patient
	不翼而飞	búyì'érfēi	vanish into the thin air, disappear suddenly
	不约而同	bùyuē'értóng	coincide, think alike, in concert
	不择手段	bùzéshǒuduàn	by hook or by crook
	不知不觉	bùzhībùjué	unaware, unconsciously
	不知所措	bùzhīsuǒcuò	at a loss, not knowing what to do
	不足挂齿	bùzúguàchǐ	not worth mentioning, not important
	步人后尘	bùrénhòuchén	follow in someone's footsteps
C	才貌双全	cáimàoshuāngquán	beautiful/handsome and talented
	惨无人道	cǎnwúréndào	inhumane, brutal
	藏龙卧虎	cánglóngwòhǔ	hidden talents
	参差不齐	cēncībùqí	uneven, not uniform
	层出不穷	céngchūbùqióng	emerging endlessly, one coming after another
	插翅难飞	chāchìnánfēi	difficult to escape
	长篇大论	chángpiāndàlùn	very lengthy, long-winded
	车水马龙	chēshuǐmǎlóng	heavy traffic
	沉默寡言	chénmòguǎyán	keeping quiet, habitually silent
	趁火打劫	chènhuǒdǎjié	take advantage of others' misfortune to benefit oneself
	称心如意	chēngxīnrúyì	just as one wishes, to one's own liking
	成千上万	chéngqiānshàngwàn	thousands upon thousands
	成群结队	chéngqúnjiéduì	in large groups
	成人之美	chéngrénzhīměi	helping others to achieve their goals
	乘虚而入	chéngxū'érrù	take advantage of a chance

驰名中外	chímíngzhōngwài	famous in China and abroad
赤手空拳	chìshǒukōngquán	empty-handed
愁眉苦脸	chóuméikǔliǎn	distressed looks
丑态百出	chǒutàibǎichū	acting like a buffoon
出口成章	chūkǒuchéngzhāng	articulate, be able to speak well extemporaneously
出人头地	chūréntóudì	stand a cut above others
出生入死	chūshēngrùsǐ	risk one's life, go through thick and thin
初出茅庐	chūchūmáolú	totally inexperienced in society
处之泰然	chǔzhītàirán	take things calmly
处处碰壁	chùchùpèngbì	run against obstacles everywhere
吹毛求疵	chuīmáoqiúcī	fault-finding, hair-splitting
垂涎三尺	chuíxiánsānchǐ	greedily hankering after something
春风满面	chūnfēngmǎnmiàn	beaming with smiles and happiness
词不达意	cíbùdáyì	words fail to express the real meaning
粗心大意	cūxīndàyì	careless, negligent
寸步不离	cùnbùbùlí	follow someone closely
措手不及	cuòshǒubùjí	caught unprepared

D	打抱不平	dǎbàobùpíng	lend a helping hand to right a wrong
	大材小用	dàcáixiǎoyòng	underuse of great talents and material
	大吃一惊	dàchīyìjīng	astounded, greatly shocked
	大发雷霆	dàfāléitíng	fly into a rage, flare up
	大功告成	dàgōnggàochéng	a great task is successfully accomplished
	大公无私	dàgōngwúsī	totally selfless
	大海捞针	dàhǎilāozhēn	look for a needle in a haystack
	大惊小怪	dàjīngxiǎoguài	fuss over something small, a storm in a teacup

大名鼎鼎	dàmíngdǐngdǐng	very well known, celebrated
大器晚成	dàqìwǎnchéng	great talents mature late, Rome was not built in a day
大失所望	dàshīsuǒwàng	greatly disappointed
大同小异	dàtóngxiǎoyì	nearly the same, differing only in details
大显身手	dàxiǎnshēnshǒu	show off one's skill, distinguish oneself
大摇大摆	dàyáodàbǎi	strut; walk with big, swinging steps
呆头呆脑	dāitóudāinǎo	idiotic, tactless
呆若木鸡	dāiruòmùjī	dumb as a wooden chicken, dumbstruck, rendered speechless
单枪匹马	dānqiāngpīmǎ	single-handed
胆大包天	dǎndàbāotiān	fearless, extremely brave
胆小如鼠	dǎnxiǎorúshǔ	timid as a mouse, cowardly
胆战心惊	dǎnzhànxīnjīng	tremble with fear
当之无愧	dāngzhīwúkuì	worthy of great reputation, worthy of merit
倒行逆施	dàoxíngnìshī	do things backward, retrogressive attempt
道听途说	dàotīngtúshuō	hearsay, gossip
得不偿失	débùchángshī	more loss than gain, waste effort on pointless things
得寸进尺	décùnjìnchǐ	give him an inch and he'll take a mile
得过且过	déguòqiěguò	muddle through, get by
得天独厚	détiāndúhòu	particularly blessed
得意忘形	déyìwàngxíng	beside oneself with joy
得意洋洋	déyìyángyáng	very pleased with oneself
地大物博	dìdàwùbó	vast terrritory and rich resources
颠三倒四	diānsāndǎosì	upside-down, in utter confusion, incoherent
顶天立地	dǐngtiānlìdì	towering (said of a person), heroic and great

丢三落四	diūsānlàsì	missing this and that, losing this and that
东奔西走	dōngbēnxīzǒu	running to and fro busily, going in all directions
东拉西扯	dōnglāxīchě	do things in a disorderly way; ramble in speech
东山再起	dōngshānzàiqǐ	stage a comeback
东张西望	dōngzhāngxīwàng	look this way and that
独一无二	dúyīwú'èr	one of a kind, unique, unmatched
度日如年	dùrìrúnián	a day seems as long as a year, time passes slowly
断章取义	duànzhāngqǔyì	take things out of context
对答如流	duìdárúliú	give quick and fluent answers
对牛弹琴	duìniútánqín	cast pearls before swine
对症下药	duìzhèngxiàyào	prescribe specific cures for specific problems
多才多艺	duōcáiduōyì	talented in many things, versatile
多愁善感	duōchóushàngǎn	overly sentimental
多多益善	duōduōyìshàn	the more the merrier
多管闲事	duōguǎnxiánshì	stick one's nose in other's business, finger in many pies

E	恩将仇报	ēnjiāngchóubào	repay kindness with hatred
	耳目一新	ěrmùyìxīn	find everything new and fresh
	耳提面命	ěrtímiànmìng	give earnest advice
	耳闻目睹	ěrwénmùdǔ	what one witnesses directly, what one hears and sees

F	发奋忘食	fāfènwàngshí	work so hard as to forget to eat
	发号施令	fāhàoshīlìng	give orders
	翻来覆去	fānláifùqù	toss and turn; say things repeatedly

翻天覆地	fāntiānfùdì	earth-shaking; make a shambles of
反复无常	fǎnfùwúcháng	change one's mind frequently, blow hot and cold
废寝忘食	fèiqǐnwàngshí	forget to eat or sleep
分道扬镳	fēndàoyángbiāo	to go separate ways
分门别类	fēnménbiélèi	sort into different categories
丰衣足食	fēngyīzúshí	have plenty of food and clothes
风靡一时	fēngmíyìshí	become fashionable for a time
风平浪静	fēngpínglàngjìng	no wind or waves, all is calm
风调雨顺	fēngtiáoyǔshùn	everything goes smoothly
风烛残年	fēngzhúcánnián	old age, like a candle in the wind
夫唱妇随	fūchàngfùsuí	husband and wife are in sync
敷衍了事	fūyánliǎoshì	do things in a perfunctory way
赴汤蹈火	fùtāngdǎohuǒ	undaunted by danger, through thick and thin

G

改过自新	gǎiguòzìxīn	mend one's ways and start over, turn over a new leaf
改头换面	gǎitóuhuànmiàn	make superficial changes
改邪归正	gǎixiéguīzhèng	mend one's ways
甘拜下风	gānbàixiàfēng	willing to admit defeat or inferiority
高枕无忧	gāozhěnwúyōu	rest without worry, rest easy
格格不入	gégébúrù	incompatible, misfit
隔墙有耳	géqiángyǒu'ěr	walls have ears
隔靴搔痒	géxuēsāoyǎng	a vain effort, useless attempt
各持己见	gèchíjǐjiàn	each holds on to his/her own opinion, uncompromising
各尽所能	gèjìnsuǒnéng	each according to his/her ability
各式各样	gèshìgèyàng	all kinds

各有所长	gèyǒusuǒcháng	each has his/her/its own merits
各有所好	gèyǒusuǒhào	each has his/her own taste, each to his/her own liking
根深蒂固	gēnshēndìgù	deep-rooted, deep-seated, ingrained
功成名就	gōngchéngmíngjiù	to have achieved success and recognition
勾心斗角	gōuxīndòujiǎo	plot against each other, mutual rivalry
狗急跳墙	gǒujítiàoqiáng	take desperate measures if pushed to the limit
狗仗人势	gǒuzhàngrénshì	a bully who relies on powerful backing
古今中外	gǔjīnzhōngwài	at all times and in all countries
孤陋寡闻	gūlòuguǎwén	ill-informed
骨肉相连	gǔròuxiānglián	flesh and blood
骨瘦如柴	gǔshòurúchái	thin as a bag of bones
拐弯抹角	guǎiwānmòjiǎo	beat about the bush, to be roundabout
鬼鬼祟祟	guǐguǐsuìsuì	secretive, stealthy
过河拆桥	guòhéchāiqiáo	burn the bridge after crossing it, be ungrateful
过目不忘	guòmùbúwàng	will not forget after reading, great retentive memory

H

海底捞月	hǎidǐlāoyuè	make a futile attempt, attempt something illusory
含含胡胡	hánhanhūhū	ambiguous, evasive, muttering
毫不含糊	háobùhánhu	unambiguous, clear-cut
好吃懒做	hàochīlǎnzuò	gluttonous and lazy, good for nothing
和蔼可亲	hé'ǎikěqīn	kind and gentle
和平共处	hépínggòngchǔ	live at peace with, peaceful coexistence
鹤立鸡群	hèlìjīqún	stand out, outstanding

横七竖八	héngqīshùbā	spread out in disorder
哄堂大笑	hōngtángdàxiào	all burst out into laughter
后会有期	hòuhuìyǒuqī	will meet again
糊里糊涂	húlihūtū	muddle-headed
囫囵吞枣	húluntūnzǎo	swallow without chewing, accepting without thinking
胡说八道	húshuōbādào	talk nonsense, stuff and nonsense
胡思乱想	húsīluànxiǎng	let one's imagination run wild
虎头蛇尾	hǔtóushéwěi	good beginning with a weak ending, peter out
花言巧语	huāyánqiǎoyǔ	artful talk, lip service
欢天喜地	huāntiānxǐdì	overjoyed, extremely delighted
恍然大悟	huǎngrándàwù	suddenly realize, a great revelation
挥金如土	huījīnrútǔ	spend money like dirt, squander
诲人不倦	huǐrénbújuàn	tireless in teaching
浑水摸鱼	húnshuǐmōyú	to fish in troubled waters
昏头昏脑	hūntóuhūnnǎo	muddle-headed, become muddled
火上加油	huǒshàngjiāyóu	add fuel to flames, stir things up

J

饥不择食	jībùzéshí	beggars can't be choosers
饥寒交迫	jīhánjiāopò	suffer from both hunger and cold
积少成多	jīshǎochéngduō	many a little makes a mickle, many a little makes a lot
既往不咎	jìwǎngbújiù	let bygones be bygones
家常便饭	jiāchángbiànfàn	ordinary meal, home cooking
家喻户晓	jiāyùhùxiǎo	known to every household
假公济私	jiǎgōngjìsī	exploit public offices for private gains
假心假意	jiǎxīnjiǎyì	insincere, feigned sincerity

见死不救	jiànsǐbújiù	doing nothing to save someone in grave danger
见义勇为	jiànyìyǒngwéi	gallantly rise to the occasion
交头接耳	jiāotóujiē'ěr	whisper into each other's ears, talk confidentially
脚踏实地	jiǎotàshídì	feet solidly on the ground
叫苦连天	jiàokǔliántiān	complain bitterly
教学相长	jiàoxuéxiāngzhǎng	teaching and learning stimulate each other
皆大欢喜	jiēdàhuānxǐ	everyone concerned is greatly pleased
接二连三	jiē'èrliánsān	one after another, successively
捷足先登	jiézúxiāndēng	fastest person gets there first
借花献佛	jièhuāxiànfó	make a gift of something given by others
斤斤计较	jīnjīnjìjiào	caculate everything, haggle over everything
锦上添花	jǐnshàngtiānhuā	make what is good better, icing on the cake
近在眼前	jìnzàiyǎnqián	right under one's nose
进退两难	jìntuìliǎngnán	in a dilemma
惊天动地	jīngtiāndòngdì	earth-shaking, incredible
精疲力尽	jīngpílìjìn	completely exhausted
井井有条	jǐngjǐngyǒutiáo	in good order, tidy
敬而远之	jìng'éryuǎnzhī	keep at a respectful distance
九死一生	jiǔsǐyìshēng	a narrow escape, close shave
就事论事	jiùshìlùnshì	deal with a matter on its own merits
举世闻名	jǔshìwénmíng	world famous
举一反三	jǔyīfǎnsān	make inference by analogy

K	开门见山	kāiménjiànshān	no beating about the bush

侃侃而谈	kǎnkǎn'értán	talk at ease and fluently
可想而知	kěxiǎng'érzhī	as can be imagined
空空洞洞	kōngkōngdòngdòng	completely empty, no content
空前绝后	kōngqiánjuéhòu	unprecedented and unrepeatable
空中楼阁	kōngzhōnglóugé	castles in the air, daydreams
口若悬河	kǒuruòxuánhé	eloquent, nimble of speech
口是心非	kǒushìxīnfēi	say one thing and mean another
脍炙人口	kuàizhìrénkǒu	widely quoted, on everyone's lips
狂风暴雨	kuángfēngbàoyǔ	storms and hurricanes

L

邋里邋遢	lālilātā	sloppy, slovenly
拉线搭桥	lāxiàndāqiáo	pull strings and make contacts
来来往往	láiláiwǎngwǎng	coming and going, to and fro
来龙去脉	láilóngqùmài	sequence of actions, the complete process, the ins and outs
来者不拒	láizhěbújù	refuse no one, refuse nothing
狼狈为奸	lángbèiwéijiān	in cahoots
狼吞虎咽	lángtūnhǔyàn	wolf down, gobble up
老当益壮	lǎodāngyìzhuàng	the older the more energetic, old and vigorous
老奸巨滑	lǎojiānjùhuá	old and cunning, old and crafty
老生常谈	lǎoshēngchángtán	cliché expression
乐极生悲	lèjíshēngbēi	extreme joy gives rise to sorrow
泪如雨下	lèirúyǔxià	tears fall like rain
冷若冰霜	lěngruòbīngshuāng	(manner) cold as ice
冷眼旁观	lěngyǎnpángguān	look on with indifference
愣头愣脑	lèngtóulèngnǎo	rash, reckless
恋恋不舍	liànliànbùshě	reluctant to part
两全其美	liǎngquánqíměi	satisfy both parties, have it both ways

两袖清风	liǎngxiùqīngfēng	penniless, having nothing but bare hands
零七八碎	língqībāsuì	odds and ends, odd pieces
六神无主	liùshénwúzhǔ	out of sorts, at sixes and sevens
乱七八糟	luànqībāzāo	messy, chaotic, topsy-turvy
罗里罗嗦	luōliluōsuō	fussy, nagging
M 埋头苦干	máitóukǔgàn	work very hard, industrious
满面春风	mǎnmiànchūnfēng	face beaming with smiles
满载而归	mǎnzài'érguī	come home with a full load
毛手毛脚	máoshǒumáojiǎo	careless, rough-handed
慢条斯理	màntiáosīlǐ	slowly and unperturbed
毛遂自荐	Máo Suí zìjiàn	recommend oneself for something
眉飞色舞	méifēisèwǔ	enraptured, delighted
美中不足	měizhōngbùzú	slight imperfection
面红耳赤	miànhóng'ěrchì	blushing
面黄肌瘦	miànhuángjīshòu	thin and colorless (person), emaciated
面目一新	miànmùyìxīn	take on a new look
妙手回春	miàoshǒuhuíchūn	wonderful skill in curing illnesses
名不虚传	míngbùxūchuán	well-deserved reputation
名副其实	míngfùqíshí	the name matches the reality, worthy of the name
明知故犯	míngzhīgùfàn	violate knowingly, do something wrong knowingly
莫名其妙	mòmíngqímiào	inexplicable, without reason or rhyme
漠不关心	mòbùguānxīn	indifferent, totally unconcerned
目不识丁	mùbùshídīng	completely illiterate
目瞪口呆	mùdèngkǒudāi	dumbfounded, stunned

N	拿手好戏	náshǒuhǎoxì	one's specialty, what one is best at
	南腔北调	nánqiāngběidiào	a mixed accent
	难舍难分	nánshěnánfēn	difficult to part from each other
	难言之隐	nányánzhīyǐn	something difficult to disclose
	恼羞成怒	nǎoxiūchéngnù	embarrassment turned into anger
	能者多劳	néngzhěduōláo	capable people do more work
	念念不忘	niànniànbúwàng	unable to forget, unforgettable
	弄假成真	nòngjiǎchéngzhēn	something playful becomes serious, false becomes true
	怒发冲冠	nùfàchōngguān	so angry that one's hair stands on end
	怒目而视	nùmù'érshì	stare with angry eyes, to glare at
O	藕断丝连	ǒuduànsīlián	relationships that cannot be entirely severed
	呕心沥血	ǒuxīnlìxuè	work one's heart out, work one's fingers to the bone
	偶一为之	ǒuyīwéizhī	do something once in a while
P	拍案叫绝	pāi'ànjiàojué	praise the excellence of something
	排难解纷	páinànjiěfēn	settle disputes, clear up misunderstandings
	庞然大物	pángrándàwù	something formidable, colossus
	旁观者清	pángguānzhěqīng	the by-stander always sees more clearly
	旁若无人	pángruòwúrén	act as if no one is nearby, supercilious
	披头散发	pītóusǎnfà	with hair disheveled
	捧腹大笑	pěngfùdàxiào	split one's sides with laughter, roar with laughter
	否极泰来	pǐjítàilái	something good follows something very bad

	皮毛之见	pímáozhījiàn	superficial views
	平心静气	píngxīnjìngqì	calm, dispassionate
	平易近人	píngyìjìnrén	amicable and easy to get along with
	萍水相逢	píngshuǐxiāngféng	casual and brief encounter, meet by chance
	披星戴月	pīxīngdàiyuè	work or travel night and day
	破镜重圆	pòjìngchóngyuán	reunion of a couple after separation or divorce
	破口大骂	pòkǒudàmà	shout abuse at someone
	普天同庆	pǔtiāntóngqìng	the whole country/ world joins in celebration
Q	七拼八凑	qīpīnbācòu	piece together from various sources
	七上八下	qīshàngbāxià	in a mental flurry of indecision, at sixes and sevens
	七手八脚	qīshǒubājiǎo	everyone lending a hand; too many cooks may spoil the broth
	七嘴八舌	qīzuǐbāshé	all talking at once, tongues wagging
	奇形怪状	qíxíngguàizhuàng	odd shape or appearance
	奇装异服	qízhuāngyìfú	exotic or bizarre clothes
	骑虎难下	qíhǔnánxià	no way of backing out of something already started
	骑马找马	qímǎzhǎomǎ	keeping what one has while looking for something better
	起死回生	qǐsǐhuíshēng	bring the dying back to life
	岂有此理	qíyǒucǐlǐ	sheer nonsense
	恰到好处	qiàdàohǎochù	just right
	恰恰相反	qiàqiàxiāngfǎn	just the opposite, on the contrary
	千变万化	qiānbiànwànhuà	unending changes, myriad changes

千方百计	qiānfāngbǎijì	by one means or another, by hook or by crook
千里迢迢	qiānlǐtiáotiáo	from afar
千篇一律	qiānpiānyílǜ	all alike, a set formula, following the same pattern
千奇百怪	qiānqíbǎiguài	all kinds of strange things
千辛万苦	qiānxīnwànkǔ	spare no pains
千真万确	qiānzhēnwànquè	as sure as can be
千头万绪	qiāntóuwànxù	(of things) extremely complicated and difficult to unravel
千言万语	qiānyánwànyǔ	innumerable words, a host of words
千载难逢	qiānzǎinánféng	once in a blue moon
前车之鉴	qiánchēzhījiàn	past examples to take warnings from
前程似锦	qiánchéngsìjǐn	a bright future
前程万里	qiánchéngwànlǐ	a great future, bright prospects
前功尽弃	qiángōngjìnqì	all previous work is wasted, all labor lost
前因后果	qiányīnhòuguǒ	cause and effect, antecedents and consequences
亲如手足	qīnrúshǒuzú	as close as siblings
亲自出马	qīnzìchūmǎ	come out in person, make a personal appearance
青黄不接	qīnghuángbùjiē	a gap in succession
青梅竹马	qīngméizhúmǎ	the period of time when boy and girl grow up together
轻而易举	qīng'éryìjǔ	easy to undertake
倾盆大雨	qīngpéndàyǔ	torrential downpour
青天霹雳	qīngtiānpīlì	a bolt from the blue, a terrible blow
穷途末路	qióngtúmòlù	at the end of one's rope, at the end of one's tether
秋高气爽	qiūgāoqìshuǎng	dry, crisp air of autumn
求之不得	qiúzhībùdé	just what one has wanted
屈指可数	qūzhǐkěshǔ	can be counted on one hand, not many

取长补短	qǔchángbǔduǎn	draw on others' strong points to offset one's weaknesses
取而代之	qǔ'érdàizhī	replace, take over, step into someone else's shoes
全力以赴	quánlìyǐfù	totally devote oneself to, do one's utmost
全神贯注	quánshénguànzhù	absorbed in, utterly concentrate on
全心全意	quánxīnquányì	whole-hearted, complete devotion
裙带关系	qúndàiguānxi	nepotism
群龙无首	qúnlóngwúshǒu	a group without a leader

R	燃眉之急	ránméizhījí	as urgent as eyebrows on fire
	惹是生非	rěshìshēngfēi	be meddlesome
	人才济济	réncáijìjǐ	many talented people, full of talented people
	人定胜天	réndìngshèngtiān	human determination can overcome destiny
	人间地狱	rénjiāndìyù	hell on earth
	人间天堂	rénjiāntiāntáng	heaven on earth, paradise on earth
	人力不足	rénlìbùzú	insufficient manpower
	人面兽心	rénmiànshòuxīn	a person with a cruel heart
	人山人海	rénshānrénhǎi	huge crowds
	人所共知	rénsuǒgòngzhī	well known, known to everyone
	人烟稠密	rényānchóumì	densely populated
	人之常情	rénzhīchángqíng	human nature
	忍气吞声	rěnqìtūnshēng	endure without any protest
	忍无可忍	rěnwúkěrěn	beyond endurance, beyond tolerance
	任劳任怨	rènláorènyuàn	work hard without complaint
	任重道远	rènzhòngdàoyuǎn	able to carry heavy responsibilities through thick and thin
	日积月累	rìjīyuèlěi	gradual accumulation

日久天长	rìjiǔtiāncháng	for a long, long time; after a considerable period of time
日日夜夜	rìrìyèyè	day and night
日新月异	rìxīnyuèyì	new changes day after day
容光焕发	róngguānghuànfā	glowing with health
如法炮制	rúfǎpàozhì	follow suit, model after
如获至宝	rúhuòzhìbǎo	as if hitting the jackpot, rejoice over a windfall
如饥似渴	rújīsìkě	thirst for, seek eagerly
如雷贯耳	rúléiguàn'ěr	(your reputation) is resounding
如梦初醒	rúmèngchūxǐng	just like waking from a dream
如释重负	rúshìzhòngfù	as if relieved of a heavy burden, heave a sigh of relief
如数家珍	rúshǔjiāzhēn	speak on a subject with great familiarity
如所周知	rúsuǒzhōuzhī	as is generally known
如意算盘	rúyìsuànpán	wishful thinking
如鱼得水	rúyúdéshuǐ	like a fish in water, in one's natural element
如愿以偿	rúyuànyǐcháng	a wish come true, fulfill a wish
如坐针毡	rúzuòzhēnzhān	on pins and needles, feeling extremely uneasy
乳臭未干	rǔchòuwèigān	still wet behind the ears
入木三分	rùmùsānfēn	(said of views, ideas) penetrating, sharp
入情入理	rùqíngrùlǐ	perfectly reasonable and logical
若无其事	ruòwúqíshì	as if nothing has happened
若有所失	ruòyǒusuǒshī	look distracted
S 三长两短	sānchángliǎngduǎn	unexpected disaster or misfortune
三番五次	sānfānwǔcì	time and again, over and over again

三更半夜	sāngēngbànyè	in the dead of night, middle of the night, about midnight
三生有幸	sānshēngyǒuxìng	extremely lucky, a stroke of luck
三心二意	sānxīn'èryì	indecisive, whimsical, have two minds
三言两语	sānyánliǎngyǔ	in a few words
杀一儆百	shāyījǐngbǎi	punish one to warn others
山盟海誓	shānménghǎishì	pledge of eternal love
山明水秀	shānmíngshuǐxiù	beautiful scenery, beautiful mountains and rivers
山南海北	shānnánhǎiběi	the four corners of the land
姗姗来迟	shānshānláichí	arriving slowly and late
山珍海味	shānzhēnhǎiwèi	delicacies from mountains and seas
善有善报	shànyǒushànbào	good is always rewarded
少见多怪	shǎojiànduōguài	one who has seen little finds more things strange, ignorant
少年老成	shàoniánlǎochéng	young but experienced
舍己为人	shějǐwèirén	sacrifice oneself for others
设身处地	shèshēnchǔdì	place oneself in other's position, put oneself in another's shoes
身败名裂	shēnbàimíngliè	lose all standing and reputation, be utterly discredited
深更半夜	shēngēngbànyè	in the dead of night
深入浅出	shēnrùqiǎnchū	to treat a difficult matter in a simple and understandable way
深思熟虑	shēnsīshúlǜ	weigh and consider, ponder over
深信无疑	shēnxìnwúyí	thoroughly convinced

神通广大	shéntōngguǎngdà	infinitely powerful, very capable
生死存亡	shēngsǐcúnwáng	a matter of life and death
省吃俭用	shěngchījiǎnyòng	try to save money on food and other expenses
声东击西	shēngdōngjīxī	feign attack on the east and strike on the west
升官发财	shēngguānfācái	win promotion and get rich
生气勃勃	shēngqìbóbó	lively and full of vigor
胜任愉快	shèngrènyúkuài	equal to the task
盛行一时	shèngxíngyìshí	in vogue, become current
事半功倍	shìbàngōngbèi	get twice the result with half the effort
失而复得	shī'érfùdé	lost and found again
十冬腊月	shídōnglàyuè	winter months, the cold months of the year
十拿九稳	shínájiǔwěn	almost certain
十全十美	shíquánshíměi	perfect, flawless
视财如命	shìcáirúmìng	worship money
视而不见	shì'érbújiàn	turn a blind eye to
世外桃源	shìwàitáoyuán	Shangri-la, Utopia, paradise on earth
史无前例	shǐwúqiánlì	unprecedented, unparalleled in history
事与愿违	shìyǔyuànwéi	things do not turn out the way one wishes
始终不渝	shǐzhōngbùyú	unswerving, steady
手疾眼快	shǒujíyǎnkuài	quick of eye and deft of hand, dexterous
手忙脚乱	shǒumángjiǎoluàn	frantic, panic-stricken
手舞足蹈	shǒuwǔzúdǎo	waving and jumping up and down with joy, dance for joy
手足无措	shǒuzúwúcuò	perplexed, not knowing what to do
守口如瓶	shǒukǒurúpíng	tight-lipped, keeping a secret
首屈一指	shǒuqūyìzhǐ	the best, number one, second to none

受宠若惊	shòuchǒngruòjīng	overwhelmed by someone's favor or flattery
熟能生巧	shúnéngshēngqiǎo	practice makes perfect
殊途同归	shūtútóngguī	different paths to the same goal, there is more than one way of doing things
束手无策	shùshǒuwúcè	at a loss as to what to do, at one's wit's end
双管齐下	shuāngguǎnqíxià	using two different ways to deal with one matter
水落石出	shuǐluòshíchū	truth will emerge eventually
水涨船高	shuǐzhǎngchuángāo	ships rise with the tide
顺手牵羊	shùnshǒuqiānyáng	make off with something
顺水推舟	shùnshuǐtuīzhōu	go with the current, go with the flow
说来话长	shuōláihuàcháng	it's a long story
说一不二	shuōyībú'èr	one means what one says
说做就做	shuōzuòjiùzuò	suit the action to the word, act on one's word
死灰复燃	sǐhuīfùrán	like dying embers that flare up, resurging
死气沉沉	sǐqìchénchén	without vitality, lifeless
四分五裂	sìfēnwǔliè	falling apart, torn apart by disunity
四海为家	sìhǎiwéijiā	able to regard anywhere as home
四面八方	sìmiànbāfāng	all directions
四通八达	sìtōngbādá	can lead to all directions
似是而非	sìshì'érfēi	appearing right but really wrong, specious
随时随地	suíshísuídì	any time and anywhere, whenever and wherever

	随心所欲	suíxīnsuǒyù	as one pleases, as one sees fit
	随遇而安	suíyù'ér'ān	take what comes and be contented
	岁月无情	suìyuèwúqíng	time and tide wait for no one
T	太平无事	tàipíng wúshì	there is no trouble, peace and tranquility
	泰然处之	tàiránchǔzhī	take things calmly
	泰然自若	tàiránzìruò	unperturbed, with great composure
	贪得无厌	tāndéwúyàn	greedy, avaricious
	贪官污吏	tānguānwūlì	corrupt officials
	贪生怕死	tānshēngpàsǐ	afraid of death, cowardly
	贪小失大	tānxiǎoshīdà	penny wise and pound foolish
	昙花一现	tánhuāyíxiàn	rare and brief appearance
	谈天说地	tántiānshuōdì	talk about everthing under the sun
	谈笑风生	tánxiàofēngshēng	light-hearted and fascinating
	忐忑不安	tǎntèbù'ān	restless, fidgety, feeling uneasy
	叹为观止	tànwéiguānzhǐ	what perfection!, nothing could be better
	滔滔不绝	tāotāobùjué	spout words in a steady flow
	逃之夭夭	táozhīyāoyāo	run away, take to one's heels
	讨价还价	tǎojiàhuánjià	haggle, bargain
	提心吊胆	tíxīndiàodǎn	have one's heart in one's mouth, sick with worry or fear
	啼笑皆非	tíxiàojiēfēi	one can neither cry nor laugh
	天崩地裂	tiānbēngdìliè	earthshaking changes
	天长地久	tiānchángdìjiǔ	everlasting and unchanging
	天翻地覆	tiānfāndìfù	chaos, earthshaking changes
	天花乱坠	tiānhuāluànzhuì	an extravagant and colorful description, wonderful event or news

天昏地暗	tiānhūndì'àn	darkness all around, chaos and darkness
天伦之乐	tiānlúnzhīlè	family happiness
天南地北	tiānnándìběi	separated by great distance, from different places
甜言蜜语	tiányánmìyǔ	honey-tongued
天衣无缝	tiānyīwúfèng	flawless, faultless
天渊之别	tiānyuānzhībié	worlds apart, vastly different
天灾人祸	tiānzāirénhuò	natural and man-made disasters
天作之合	tiānzuòzhīhé	a match made in heaven
挑拨离间	tiǎobōlíjiàn	pit one against another, sow dissension
铁面无私	tiěmiànwúsī	(a person) of unbending principles
铁石心肠	tiěshíxīncháng	heart of steel, hard-hearted, resolute
听而不闻	tīng'érbùwén	listen without paying attention
听其自然	tīngqízìrán	let matters take their natural course
听天由命	tīngtiānyóumìng	be resigned to fate
挺身而出	tǐngshēn'érchū	step forward bravely
同病相怜	tóngbìngxiānglián	fellow sufferers sympathize with one another
同床异梦	tóngchuángyìmèng	strange bedfellows, partners with different agendas
同甘共苦	tónggāngòngkǔ	stick together through thick and thin
同归于尽	tóngguīyújìn	end in common ruin
同流合污	tóngliúhéwū	wallow in mire together
同心协力	tóngxīnxiélì	(work) united as one
同舟共济	tóngzhōugòngjì	in the same boat, stick together through thick and thin
童颜鹤发	tóngyánhèfà	(old man) with white hair and ruddy complexion

痛改前非	tònggǎiqiánfēi	thoroughly mend one's ways
痛哭流涕	tòngkūliútì	cry and shed bitter tears
痛骂一顿	tòngmàyídùn	give a sound scolding
头昏眼花	tóuhūnyǎnhuā	feel dizzy
头重脚轻	tóuzhòngjiǎoqīng	top-heavy
突飞猛进	tūfēiměngjìn	progress by leaps and bounds
突如其来	tūrúqílái	happens abruptly, arise suddenly
土生土长	tǔshēngtǔzhǎng	locally born and brought up, locally grown
团结一致	tuánjiéyízhì	in unity and solidarity
推陈出新	tuīchénchūxīn	put forth new ideas in place of old ones
推己及人	tuījǐjírén	treat others as you would yourself, be considerate
吞吞吐吐	tūntūntǔtǔ	mutter, hem and haw, be evasive
脱离苦海	tuōlíkǔhǎi	to get over hardship, to escape from difficulties of life
脱胎换骨	tuōtāihuàngǔ	create new things out of old, thoroughly remold oneself
拖泥带水	tuōnídàishuǐ	sloppy, slovenly, half-heartedly
W 歪曲事实	wāiqūshìshí	distort facts
歪歪扭扭	wāiwāiniǔniǔ	twisted, crooked
外强中干	wàiqiángzhōnggān	strong in appearance but weak inside
外为中用	wàiwéizhōngyòng	make things foreign serve China
万不得已	wànbùdéyǐ	when there is no alternative, as a last resort
万古流芳	wàngǔliúfāng	leave a good name to posterity
万念俱灰	wànniànjùhuī	all hopes dashed to pieces
万事如意	wànshìrúyì	have all one's wishes come true

万寿无疆	wànshòuwújiāng	to wish a long, long life to (someone)
万无一失	wànwúyìshī	absolutely certain, no chance of a mistake
万象更新	wànxiànggēngxīn	with the beginning of a new year, everything is renewed
万众一心	wànzhòngyìxīn	united as one, with one heart and one mind
万紫千红	wànzǐqiānhóng	a profusion of colors, a riot of colors
汪洋大海	wāngyángdàhǎi	vast sea, boundless ocean
枉费心机	wǎngfèixīnjī	rack one's brains in vain, all the attempts are futile
妄自菲薄	wàngzìfěibó	think lightly of oneself, feel inferior to others
妄自尊大	wàngzìzūndà	conceited, arrogant
忘恩负义	wàng'ēnfùyì	have no sense of gratitude
望尘莫及	wàngchénmòjí	fall far behind, unequal to
望风捕影	wàngfēngbǔyǐng	pursuing a phantom, on a wrong track
望梅止渴	wàngméizhǐkě	feed on fancies, castles in the air
望眼欲穿	wàngyǎnyùchuān	gaze anxiously till one's eyes are overstrained
望子成龙	wàngzǐchénglóng	long to see one's son succeed in life
危机重重	wēijīchóngchóng	riddled with crises
危机四伏	wēijīsìfú	be threatened by growing crises all around
威风凛凛	wēifēnglǐnlǐn	awe-inspiring
威风扫地	wēifēngsǎodì	be completely discredited
威武不屈	wēiwǔbùqū	not be subdued by force
微不足道	wēibùzúdào	insignificant, trivial
为非作歹	wéifēizuòdǎi	commit evil deeds
为人师表	wéirénshībiǎo	be a model for others

为所欲为	wéisuǒyùwéi	do whatever one pleases
惟利是图	wéilìshìtú	profit-grabbing, seek only profit
惟我独尊	wéiwǒdúzūn	assume airs of self-importance, autocratic, bossy
未卜先知	wèibǔxiānzhī	have foresight, be able to foretell
未老先衰	wèilǎoxiānshuāi	prematurely senile, older than one's years
未雨绸缪	wèiyǔchóumiù	save for a rainy day
温故知新	wēngùzhīxīn	learn something new by reviewing the old
文质彬彬	wénzhìbīnbīn	with elegant manners
闻所未闻	wénsuǒwèiwén	unprecedented, unheard of
问长问短	wènchángwènduǎn	make detailed enquiries, ask about this and that
问寒问暖	wènhánwènnuǎn	enquire with concern about someone's well-being
问心无愧	wènxīnwúkuì	have a clear conscience, not feel guilty about something
问心有愧	wènxīnyǒukuì	feel guilty about something
我行我素	wǒxíngwǒsù	stick to one's old ways
无边无际	wúbiānwújì	boundless, vast
无病呻吟	wúbìngshēnyín	moan and groan without being ill, make a fuss about nothing
无的放矢	wúdìfàngshǐ	aimless and fruitless, shoot without aiming
无地自容	wúdìzìróng	ashamed to show one's face
无动于衷	wúdòngyúzhōng	unmoved, aloof and indifferent
无独有偶	wúdúyǒu'ǒu	not unique; by coincidence
无法无天	wúfǎwútiān	violate all laws, run wild

无稽之谈	wújīzhītán	fabrication, fiddlesticks, nonsense
无计可施	wújìkěshī	at a loss as to what to do, at one's wit's end
无济于事	wújìyúshì	to no effect, irrelevant, of no help
无家可归	wújiākěguī	homeless
无价之宝	wújiàzhībǎo	priceless treasure, invaluable asset
无精打采	wújīngdǎcǎi	listless, in low spirits
无拘无束	wújūwúshù	free and easy, without any restraint
无可非议	wúkěfēiyì	blameless, beyond reproach
无可数计	wúkěshùjì	a countless amount of something
无可奈何	wúkěnàihé	having no alternative
无孔不入	wúkǒngbúrù	seize every opportunity, have a finger in every pie
无理取闹	wúlǐqǔnào	refuse to listen to reason, unprovoked quarrel
无路可走	wúlùkězǒu	no way out, helpless
无论如何	wúlùnrúhé	no matter what, in any event
无名小卒	wúmíngxiǎozú	a nobody
无名英雄	wúmíngyīngxióng	unknown hero
无能为力	wúnéngwéilì	powerless, incapable
无奇不有	wúqíbùyǒu	no lack of strange things, lots of bizarre things
无求于人	wúqiúyúrén	independent, be one's own master
无人问津	wúrénwènjīn	nobody is interested, unclaimed
无伤大雅	wúshāngdàyǎ	not matter much, not affecting things as a whole
无师自通	wúshīzìtōng	self-taught
无事生非	wúshìshēngfēi	much ado about nothing, make uncalled-for trouble
无所不为	wúsuǒbùwéi	stop at nothing, do all manner of evil
无所不知	wúsuǒbùzhī	know everything

无所不至	wúsuǒbúzhì	spare no pains, penetrate everywhere
无所事事	wúsuǒshìshì	idle, have nothing to do
无所适从	wúsuǒshìcóng	not knowing what to do
无微不至	wúwēibúzhì	meticulous, in every possible way
无隙可乘	wúxìkěchéng	no loophole to exploit
无依无靠	wúyīwúkào	be alone in the world, friendless and helpless
无以为生	wúyǐwéishēng	have no means of livelihood
无影无踪	wúyǐngwúzōng	without a trace, disappeared without a trace
无忧无虑	wúyōuwúlǜ	no worries whatsoever, carefree
无缘无故	wúyuánwúgù	without rhyme or reason
无中生有	wúzhōngshēngyǒu	sheer fabrication, groundless, out of thin air
无足轻重	wúzúqīngzhòng	insignificant, of little importance
五彩缤纷	wǔcǎibīnfēn	full of colors, very colorful
五福临门	wǔfúlínmén	the five blessings come to the house, the house is blessed
五光十色	wǔguāngshísè	resplendent with many colors
五湖四海	wǔhúsìhǎi	every corner of the country
五花八门	wǔhuābāmén	kaleidoscopic, a variety of
五体投地	wǔtǐtóudì	show someone profound admiration
五颜六色	wǔyánliùsè	very colorful
物极必反	wùjíbìfǎn	things always reverse themselves after reaching an extreme
物以类聚	wùyǐlèijù	birds of a feather flock together

误人子弟	wùrénzǐdì	mislead and cause harm to young people
误入歧途	wùrùqítú	take a wrong path (in doing things)

X

息事宁人	xīshìníngrén	compromise so that everyone can have peace
息息相关	xīxīxiāngguān	closely linked to each other
稀里糊涂	xīlihútū	muddle-headed
熙熙攘攘	xīxīrǎngrǎng	bustling with activity, hustle and bustle
习以为常	xíyǐwéicháng	become accustomed to
席地而坐	xídì'érzuò	sit on the floor
洗耳恭听	xǐ'ěrgōngtīng	listen with reverent attention, be all ears
洗手不干	xǐshǒubúgàn	wash one's hands of something
喜出望外	xǐchūwàngwài	overjoyed, happy beyond expectations
喜怒哀乐	xǐnù'āilè	delight, anger, joy and sorrow; full range of emotions
喜怒无常	xǐnùwúcháng	capricious, subject to changing moods
喜气洋洋	xǐqìyángyáng	jubilant, overwhelmed with joy
喜笑颜开	xǐxiàoyánkāi	beaming with smiles
喜新厌旧	xǐxīnyànjiù	fickle in one's affections
喜形于色	xǐxíngyúsè	radiant with joy
细水常流	xìshuǐchángliú	do something little by little in a constant way
下不了台	xiàbùliǎotái	caught in a dilemma, be in an embarrassing situation with no way out
下不为例	xiàbùwéilì	not to be taken as a precedent
下落不明	xiàluòbùmíng	not knowing the whereabouts of
显而易见	xiǎn'éryìjiàn	obvious, evident

先发制人	xiānfāzhìrén	gain mastery by striking first
先见之明	xiānjiànzhīmíng	able to predict, ability to discern what is coming
先决条件	xiānjuétiáojiàn	prerequisite
先钱后酒	xiānqiánhòujiǔ	pay first, deliver later
先入为主	xiānrùwéizhǔ	first impressions are most important; one who enters first is the master
先知先觉	xiānzhīxiānjué	having foresight, a person of foresight
鲜艳夺目	xiānyànduómù	brilliant colors, splendor blinding the eye
闲情逸致	xiánqíngyìzhì	carefree, leisurely and carefree mood
贤妻良母	xiánqīliángmǔ	a virtuous wife and loving mother
相得益彰	xiāngdéyìzhāng	bring out the best in each other, complement each other
相辅相成	xiāngfǔxiāngchéng	supplement and complement
相敬如宾	xiāngjìngrúbīn	(of married couples) treat each other with respect
相提并论	xiāngtíbìnglùn	mention in the same breath
想入非非	xiǎngrùfēifēi	indulge in wishful thinking, have fantasies
相依为命	xiāngyīwéimìng	depend on each other for survival
逍遥法外	xiāoyáofǎwài	(of criminals) be at large
逍遥自在	xiāoyáozìzài	be at peace with the world and oneself
消息灵通	xiāoxilíngtōng	well informed
霄壤之别	xiāorǎngzhībié	a great difference, as that between heaven and earth
小道消息	xiǎodàoxiāoxi	grapevine news
小心谨慎	xiǎoxīnjǐnshèn	careful, cautious
小心翼翼	xiǎoxīnyìyì	extremely careful

小题大做	xiǎotídàzuò	make much ado about nothing, make a mountain out of a molehill
笑里藏刀	xiàolǐcángdāo	murderous intent behind one's smiles
笑容可掬	xiàoróngkějū	beaming with smiles, with a charming smile
笑逐颜开	xiàozhúyánkāi	beaming with smiles
谢绝参观	xièjuécānguān	visitors not admitted
谢天谢地	xiètiānxièdì	thank goodness, thank heavens
心安理得	xīn'ānlǐdé	feel at ease, with mind at ease and conscience clear
心不在焉	xīnbúzàiyān	absent-minded
心烦意乱	xīnfányìluàn	confused and worried, with a heavy heart
心服口服	xīnfúkǒufú	utterly convinced
心腹之患	xīnfùzhīhuàn	danger from within, serious hidden trouble
心腹之交	xīnfùzhījiāo	bosom friends
心甘情愿	xīngānqíngyuàn	be most willing to
心花怒放	xīnhuānùfàng	wild with joy, elated
心怀鬼胎	xīnhuáiguǐtāi	have evil intentions
心慌意乱	xīnhuāngyìluàn	nervous and flustered, all in a fluster
心灰意冷	xīnhuīyìlěng	disheartened
心惊胆战	xīnjīngdǎnzhàn	tremble with fear
心惊肉跳	xīnjīngròutiào	jumpy, have the jitters
心口如一	xīnkǒurúyī	speak from the heart, frank and forthright
心旷神怡	xīnkuàngshényí	relaxed and happy
心里有数	xīnlǐyǒushù	know what's what, know what's going on
心乱如麻	xīnluànrúmá	very confused
心满意足	xīnmǎnyìzú	perfectly content
心平气和	xīnpíngqìhé	calm, even-tempered and good-humored
心如刀割	xīnrúdāogē	heart-rending, hurt to the quick

心如古井	xīnrúgǔjǐng	apathetic
心如火焚	xīnrúhuǒfén	torn by anxiety
心如死灰	xīnrúsǐhuī	hopelessly apathetic
心如针扎	xīnrúzhēnzhā	greatly distressed, as if pricked to the heart
心如止水	xīnrúzhǐshuǐ	mind as tranquil as still waters
心神不宁	xīnshénbùníng	out of sorts, the mind wanders
心心相连	xīnxīnxiānglián	closely attached to each other
心心相印	xīnxīnxiāngyìn	(normally said of lovers) share the same feelings, see eye to eye
心胸开阔	xīnxiōngkāikuò	broad-minded, light-hearted
心虚胆怯	xīnxūdǎnquè	have a guilty conscience
心血来潮	xīnxuèláicháo	seized by a whim, suddenly hit upon an idea
心猿意马	xīnyuányìmǎ	restless, fickle
心悦诚服	xīnyuèchéngfú	completely convinced
心照不宣	xīnzhàobùxuān	have a tacit understanding
心直口快	xīnzhíkǒukuài	outspoken
心中有鬼	xīnzhōngyǒuguǐ	have a guilty conscience
心中有数	xīnzhōngyǒushù	know the score, understand the situation
辛辛苦苦	xīnxīnkǔkǔ	take great pains, work laboriously
欣喜若狂	xīnxǐruòkuáng	wild with joy, beside oneself with joy
欣欣向荣	xīnxīnxiàngróng	thriving, prospering
行尸走肉	xíngshīzǒuròu	one who vegetates, utterly useless person
兴高采烈	xìnggāocǎiliè	elated, jubilant
幸灾乐祸	xìngzāilèhuò	gloat over other people's disasters
胸有成竹	xiōngyǒuchéngzhú	have a preconceived idea or vision before one does something
雄心勃勃	xióngxīnbóbó	very ambitious

熊熊烈火	xióngxiónglièhuǒ	raging fire, raging flames
羞羞答答	xiūxiūdādā	bashful, shy, timid
虚度光阴	xūdùguāngyīn	waste one's time, idle away time
虚情假意	xūqíngjiǎyì	a false display of affection, a hypocritical show of friendship
虚有其表	xūyǒuqíbiǎo	appear better than it is
虚张声势	xūzhāngshēngshì	make an empty show of strength, bluff
袖手旁观	xiùshǒupángguān	stand by with indifference
雪中送炭	xuězhōngsòngtàn	give timely assistance

Y

鸦雀无声	yāquèwúshēng	dead silent
哑口无言	yǎkǒuwúyán	tongue-tied, dumbfounded
言多必失	yánduōbìshī	one who talks too much is prone to error
言归正传	yánguīzhèngzhuàn	to return to the subject, return from the digression
言过其实	yánguòqíshí	exaggerate, overstate
言行一致	yánxíngyízhì	deeds match the words, action in accord with words
奄奄一息	yǎnyǎnyìxī	at one's last gasp, on the verge of death
掩人耳目	yǎnrén'ěrmù	hoodwink others, deceive the public
眼高手低	yǎngāoshǒudī	fastidious but incompetent, have high ambition but lack ability
眼花缭乱	yǎnhuāliáoluàn	dazzled
眼见为实	yǎnjiànwéishí	seeing is believing
扬眉吐气	yángméitǔqì	feel proud and elated, a feeling of exaltation upon fulfillment
养儿防老	yǎng'érfánglǎo	raise children as old-age security

咬文嚼字	yǎowénjuézì	pedantic, paying too much attention to wording
摇摇摆摆	yáoyáobǎibǎi	swagger, wobble, wobbly
咬牙切齿	yǎoyáqièchǐ	gnash the teeth in deep-seated hatred, clench the teeth
野心勃勃	yěxīnbóbó	extremely ambitious
叶落归根	yèluòguīgēn	what comes from the soil will return to the soil
夜长梦多	yèchángmèngduō	a long night is fraught with dreams, a long delay brings trouble
一本正经	yìběnzhèngjīng	in all seriousness, in deadly earnest
一笔勾销	yìbǐgōuxiāo	write off in one stroke, reject off-hand
一臂之力	yíbìzhīlì	a helping hand
一唱一和	yíchàngyìhé	chime in with, in perfect harmony
一尘不染	yìchénbùrǎn	spotless, not stained with even a speck of dust, pure
一筹莫展	yìchóumòzhǎn	at a loss, no way out, at one's wit's end
一刀两断	yìdāoliǎngduàn	make a clean break
一帆风顺	yìfānfēngshùn	smooth sailing
一概而论	yígài'érlùn	generalize, lump people or things under one heading
一干二净	yìgān'èrjìng	lock, stock, and barrel; altogether, completely
一呼百诺	yìhūbǎinuò	have hundreds at one's beck and call
一呼百应	yìhūbǎiyìng	hundreds respond to a single call
一技之长	yíjìzhīcháng	having one single skill, capable of one specific job
一见如故	yíjiànrúgù	hit it off right from the start
一见钟情	yíjiànzhōngqíng	love at first sight

一箭双雕	yíjiànshuāngdiāo	kill two birds with one stone, achieve two things at one stroke
一举两得	yìjǔliǎngdé	gain two ends at once, kill two birds with one stone
一劳永逸	yìláoyǒngyì	settle a matter once and for all
一了百了	yìliǎobǎiliǎo	all troubles end when the main trouble ends
一路平安	yílùpíng'ān	bon voyage, have a safe journey
一毛不拔	yìmáobùbá	miserly, parsimonious, stingy
一鸣惊人	yìmíngjīngrén	achieve overnight success, set the world on fire
一模一样	yìmóyíyàng	identical, exactly the same
一目了然	yímùliǎorán	be clear at a single glance
一贫如洗	yìpínrúxǐ	penniless, utterly destitute, as poor as a church mouse
一气呵成	yíqìhēchéng	complete something at a stretch
一钱不值	yìqiánbùzhí	utterly worthless, not worth a penny
一窍不通	yíqiàobùtōng	utterly ignorant of something, know nothing about
一清二楚	yìqīng'èrchǔ	perfectly clear, as clear as daylight
一视同仁	yíshìtóngrén	treat all alike without discrimination, treat equally
一事无成	yíshìwúchéng	nothing accomplished, get nowhere
一丝不苟	yìsībùgǒu	conscientious and meticulous
一死百了	yìsǐbǎiliǎo	death pays all scores, death squares all accounts

一塌糊涂	yìtāhútú	in a complete mess, in a great mess
一天到晚	yìtiāndàowǎn	all day long
一网打尽	yìwǎngdǎjìn	make a clean sweep
一无可取	yìwúkěqǔ	good for nothing, worthless
一无所长	yìwúsuǒcháng	having no special skill
一无所有	yìwúsuǒyǒu	not having a thing to one's name
一五一十	yìwǔyìshí	(narrate) systematically and in full detail
一笑置之	yíxiàozhìzhī	laugh it off, dismiss with a smile
一心一意	yìxīnyíyì	wholeheartedly, heart and soul
一言难尽	yìyánnánjìn	it's a long story, difficult to put in a nutshell
一言为定	yìyánwéidìng	it's settled then!
一叶知秋	yíyèzhīqiū	one falling leaf heralds the autumn, a small sign can indicate the whole trend, a straw shows which way the wind blows
一意孤行	yíyìgūxíng	insist on having one's own way, act willfully
一饮而尽	yìyín'érjìn	quaff in one gulp, drink up
一应俱全	yīyīngjùquán	complete in every line, complete with everything
一针见血	yìzhēnjiànxiě	hit the nail on the head
一知半解	yìzhībànjiě	half-baked knowledge, with a smattering of knowledge
衣锦荣归	yījǐnróngguī	glorious home-coming after having won high honors and wealth

衣食住行	yīshízhùxíng	clothing, food, shelter, and transportation – the basic necessities of life
依依不舍	yīyībùshě	reluctant to part (from someone or some place)
疑神疑鬼	yíshényíguǐ	extremely suspicious
以毒攻毒	yǐdúgōngdú	fight poison with poison
以防万一	yǐfángwànyī	provide for any contingencies
以己度人	yǐjǐdùrén	judge others by oneself, measure another's corn by one's own bushel
以假乱真	yǐjiǎluànzhēn	mix the false with the true, pass the fake for genuine
以身作则	yǐshēnzuòzé	set an example with one's own conduct
以十当百	yǐshídāngbǎi	pit ten against a hundred
义不容辞	yìbùróngcí	be duty-bound, act from a strong sense of duty
异口同声	yìkǒutóngshēng	with one voice, in unison
异曲同工	yìqǔtónggōng	same satisfactory results produced by different methods
异想天开	yìxiǎngtiānkāi	indulge in the wildest fantasy, wishful thinking, have a bee in one's bonnet
意想不到	yìxiǎngbúdào	unexpected, never thought of it
易如反掌	yìrúfǎnzhǎng	as easy as falling off a log, as easy as ABC
因祸得福	yīnhuòdéfú	derive gain from misfortune, luck grows out of adversity
因人而异	yīnrén'éryì	vary with each individual

因小失大	yīnxiǎoshīdà	penny wise, pound foolish; to save a little only to lose a lot
引狼入室	yǐnlángrùshì	open the door to an enemy, lead a wolf into the sheepfold
引人注目	yǐnrénzhùmù	attract attention, conspicuous
饮水思源	yǐnshuǐsīyuán	when drinking water, think of its source – bear in mind where one's happiness comes from, feel grateful
应有尽有	yīngyǒujìnyǒu	everything one could wish for is there
应对如流	yìngduìrúliú	reply readily and fluently
永垂不朽	yǒngchuíbùxiǔ	be immortal, live forever in the hearts of
游手好闲	yóushǒuhàoxián	idle, loaf about
有备无患	yǒubèiwúhuàn	preparedness prevents calamity
有教无类	yǒujiàowúlèi	in education, there should be no class distinction
有口皆碑	yǒukǒujiēbēi	universally acclaimed, universally praised
有利可图	yǒulìkětú	there is profit to be reaped
有名无实	yǒumíngwúshí	exist in name only, nominal
有目共睹	yǒumùgòngdǔ	obvious to all
有气无力	yǒuqìwúlì	lifeless, feeble, lackluster
有求必应	yǒuqiúbìyìng	grant whatever is asked, never refuse a request
有声有色	yǒushēngyǒusè	very vivid and dramatic
有失身份	yǒushīshēnfen	beneath one's dignity
有始有终	yǒushǐyǒuzhōng	do something well from beginning to end, from beginning to end

有说有笑	yǒushuōyǒuxiào	talking and laughing
有头有尾	yǒutóuyǒuwěi	do something from beginning to end, have a beginning and an end
有朝一日	yǒuzhāoyírì	one day, some day, if by chance
鱼米之乡	yúmǐzhīxiāng	land of fish and rice, bread basket
鱼目混珠	yúmùhùnzhū	pass off fish eyes for pearls, pass off something sham as genuine
愚昧无知	yǔmèiwúzhī	stupid and ignorant
雨后春笋	yǔhòuchūnsǔn	spring up like mushrooms
与虎谋皮	yǔhǔmóupí	ask a tiger for its hide – a useless petition or act
与日俱增	yǔrìjùzēng	increase daily
与世无争	yǔshìwúzhēng	stand aloof from worldly strife
与众不同	yǔzhòngbùtóng	different from the others, showing originality
雨过天晴	yǔguòtiānqíng	sunshine after the rain, difficult period gives way to bright future
语无伦次	yǔwúlúncì	rambling, incoherent, nonsensical
语重心长	yǔzhòngxīncháng	in all earnestness
欲速不达	yùsùbùdá	haste makes waste
冤家对头	yuānjiāduìtóu	opponent and foe
冤家路窄	yuānjiālùzhǎi	one cannot avoid running into an enemy
原封不动	yuánfēngbúdòng	intact, left untouched
原来如此	yuánláirúcǐ	so that's how it is, I see
原形毕露	yuánxíngbìlù	show one's true colors
缘木求鱼	yuánmùqiúyú	a fruitless approach, attempt the impossible
远走高飞	yuǎnzǒugāofēi	flee to distant places

Z	杂乱无章	záluànwúzhāng	without pattern or order, confused and disorderly
	杂七杂八	záqīzábā	a mix of bits of everything
	再接再厉	zàijiēzàilì	make persistent effort, with ever-renewed efforts
	载歌载舞	zàigēzàiwǔ	singing and dancing
	再三再四	zàisānzàisì	again and again, time and again
	在所难免	zàisuǒnánmiǎn	unavoidable
	赞不绝口	zànbùjuékǒu	full of praise, praise unceasingly
	早出晚归	zǎochūwǎnguī	leave home or go to work at the crack of dawn and return by starlight
	扎扎实实	zhāzhāshíshí	sturdy, in a down-to-earth manner
	债台高筑	zhàitáigāozhù	debt-ridden, up to the ears in debt
	沾沾自喜	zhānzhānzìxǐ	self-satisfied, self-complacent
	瞻前顾后	zhānqiángùhòu	overly cautious and indecisive
	斩草除根	zhǎncǎochúgēn	when cutting weeds, remove the roots – remove the source of trouble
	斩钉截铁	zhǎndīngjiétiě	resolute and decisive, adamant
	战战兢兢	zhànzhanjīngjīng	tremble with fear, very cautious
	张灯结彩	zhāngdēngjiécǎi	decorate with lanterns and festoons (for an auspicious event)
	张冠李戴	zhāngguānlǐdài	mistake one thing or person for another
	张口结舌	zhāngkǒujiéshé	aghast and tongue-tied, at a loss for words
	张三李四	zhāngsānlǐsì	this or that person; Tom, Dick or Harry
	张牙舞爪	zhāngyáwǔzhuǎ	make threatening gestures

掌上明珠	zhǎngshàngmíngzhū	a dearly beloved daughter, apple of one's eye
仗势欺人	zhàngshìqīrén	abuse one's power and bully people
朝不保夕	zhāobùbǎoxī	live from hand to mouth, in a precarious state
朝气蓬勃	zhāoqìpéngbó	full of youthful vigor, fresh and vigorous
朝三暮四	zhāosānmùsì	play fast and loose, be fickle; hoodwink the gullible
针锋相对	zhēnfēngxiāngduì	diametrically opposed to, give tit for tat
真凭实据	zhēnpíngshíjù	indisputable evidence
真相大白	zhēnxiàngdàbái	the truth has come out, the case is entirely cleared up
真知灼见	zhēnzhīzhuójiàn	real knowledge and deep insight
争风吃醋	zhēngfēngchīcù	vie for a man's or woman's favor
争名夺利	zhēngmíngduólì	struggle for fame and wealth
争先恐后	zhēngxiānkǒnghòu	strive to be the first, in a mad rush to be first
正人君子	zhèngrénjūnzǐ	respectable gentleman
蒸蒸日上	zhēngzhēngrìshàng	ever flourishing
直接了当	zhíjiēliǎodàng	straightforward
执迷不悟	zhímíbúwù	refuse to come to one's senses
直言不讳	zhíyánbúhuì	speak without reservation, mince no words
指不胜屈	zhǐbúshèngqū	more than can be counted on the fingers, countless
只管吩咐	zhǐguǎnfēnfù	your wish is my command
指桑骂槐	zhǐsāngmàhuái	indirect, veiled accusation; make oblique accusations

指手画脚	zhǐshǒuhuàjiǎo	gesticulate
趾高气扬	zhǐgāoqìyáng	put on airs and swagger about, behave arrogantly
志同道合	zhìtóngdàohé	having same interests or goals, in the same camp
置若罔闻	zhìruòwǎngwén	turn a deaf ear to, take no notice
置之不理	zhìzhībùlǐ	pay no attention to, ignore
忠言逆耳	zhōngyánnì'ěr	good advice grates on the ear, the truth hurts
众口铄金	zhòngkǒushuòjīn	public clamor can confound right and wrong
众目睽睽	zhòngmùkuíkuí	under the watchful eyes of the public
众说纷纭	zhòngshuōfēnyún	opinions are widely divided
众所周知	zhòngsuǒzhōuzhī	as everyone knows
众志成城	zhòngzhìchéngchéng	unity is strength
周而复始	zhōu'érfùshǐ	move in cycles, go round and begin
周转不灵	zhōuzhuǎnbùlíng	not enough to meet the needs, problem with cashflow
转败为胜	zhuǎnbàiwéishèng	turn defeat into victory
转弯抹角	zhuǎnwānmòjiǎo	beat about the bush, in a devious way, in a roundabout way
装摸作样	zhuāngmózuòyàng	behave in an affected way, assume airs
装腔作势	zhuāngqiāngzuòshì	make pretence of dignity, put on airs
谆谆善诱	zhūnzhūnshànyòu	teach and guide untiringly
捉襟见肘	zhuōjīnjiànzhǒu	cannot make ends meet, too many (financial) problems to deal with
自吹自擂	zìchuīzìlěi	blow one's own horn, brag and boast
自告奋勇	zìgàofènyǒng	volunteer for (difficult or dangerous) tasks

自高自大	zìgāozìdà	self-important, self-aggrandizing, conceited
自顾不暇	zìgùbùxiá	unable even to fend for oneself
自给自足	zìjǐzìzú	self-sufficient
自力更生	zìlìgēngshēng	self-reliance, self-reliant, rely on oneself
自卖自夸	zìmàizìkuā	indulge in self-glorification, praise one's own goods
自鸣得意	zìmíngdéyì	sing one's own praises, be puffed up with pride
自命不凡	zìmìngbùfán	have an unduly high opinion of oneself, consider oneself above the crowd
自欺欺人	zìqīqīrén	deceive oneself as well as others, self-deceit
自然而然	zìrán'érrán	very naturally, automatically
自食其力	zìshíqílì	live by one's own labor, live on one's own toil, paddle one's own canoe
自始至终	zìshǐzhìzhōng	from start to finish, from beginning to end
自私自利	zìsīzìlì	selfish
自讨苦吃	zìtǎokǔchī	ask for trouble and get it
自投罗网	zìtóuluówǎng	walk into a trap, put one's head in a noose
自我陶醉	zìwǒtáozuì	self-intoxicated
自相残杀	zìxiāngcánshā	mutual annihilation, fratricide
自相矛盾	zìxiāngmáodùn	self-contradictory
自言自语	zìyánzìyǔ	mutter to oneself
自以为是	zìyǐwéishì	consider oneself in the right, be opinionated
自由竞争	zìyóujìngzhēng	free competition
自由自在	zìyóuzìzài	leisurely and carefree
自圆其说	zìyuánqíshuō	justify oneself

自作聪明	zìzuòcōngmíng	fancy oneself to be clever, try to be smart
自做主张	zìzuòzhǔzhāng	decide for oneself, have one's own way of doing things
自作自受	zìzuòzìshòu	suffer the consequences of one's own actions, as you make your own bed so you must lie on it
总而言之	zǒng'éryánzhī	in summary, in a few words, in short, in a nutshell
走投无路	zǒutóuwúlù	have no way out, be in an impasse, be in a hopeless situation
醉生梦死	zuìshēngmèngsǐ	lead a happy-go-lucky life
尊师重道	zūnshīzhòngdào	honor the teacher and respect his/her teachings
左顾右盼	zuǒgùyòupàn	glance left and right, feel uneasy
左邻右舍	zuǒlínyòushè	next-door neighbors
左思右想	zuǒsīyòuxiǎng	think over and over again, turn over in one's mind
左右逢源	zuǒyòuféngyuán	everything going one's way, win advantage from both sides
左右为难	zuǒyòuwéinán	in a dilemma, in an awkward predicament
作茧自缚	zuòjiǎnzìfù	caught in one's own trap, enmeshed in one's own web
作威作福	zuòwēizuòfú	act like a tyrant, assume great airs of authority
做贼心虚	zuòzéixīnxū	have a guilty conscience
坐吃山空	zuòchīshānkōng	fritter away a great fortune

坐立不安	zuòlìbù'ān	be fidgety, be on tenterhooks, on pins and needles
坐失良机	zuòshīliángjī	let a golden opportunity slip by
坐享其成	zuòxiǎngqíchéng	reap what one has not sown
座无虚席	zuòwúxūxí	all seats are occupied, a full house

2.11   Proverbs and common sayings

Proverbs and common sayings, 谚语 yànyǔ or 俗语 súyǔ, are a very important part of Chinese language usage. They are crystallizations of historical experience and popular wisdom. They are used so often because so much meaning is compressed and expressed in a single phrase.

* indicates English equivalents of sayings.
( ) indicates similar meanings in English.

| B | 八字衙门朝南开，有理无钱莫进来 | bāzìyámen cháonánkāi, yǒulǐ wúqián mòjìnlái | The court faces south, but do not enter if you have only reasons but no money. *Possession is nine-tenths of the law. *Rich men have no faults. *The reasons of the poor weigh not. |
| | 白猫黑猫，抓到老鼠就是好猫 | báimāo hēimāo, zhuādaolǎoshǔ jiùshi hǎomāo | It doesn't matter if it is a white cat or a black cat; as long as it catches mice, it is a good cat. (Whatever the method, as long as it works.) |

	百闻不如一见，百见不如一干	bǎiwén bùrú yíjiàn, bǎijiàn bùrú yígàn	Hearing it a hundred times is not as good as seeing it once, and seeing it a hundred times is not as good as doing it once. *Seeing is believing.
	病从口入，祸从口出	bìng cóngkǒurù, huò cóngkǒuchū	Illness enters from the mouth and calamity comes out of the mouth. *A closed mouth catches no flies. *Let not your tongue cut your throat.
	不当家不知柴米贵，不养儿不知父母恩	bùdāngjiā bùzhī cháimǐguì, bùyǎng'ér bùzhī fùmǔ'ēn	If you don't manage the household, you don't know the cost of fuel and food, and if you do not have children, you do not know how much gratitude you owe to your parents.
	不经一事，不长一智	bùjīng yíshì, bùzhǎng yízhì	Without experiencing things, you cannot grow wiser. *A stumble may prevent a fall. *Wisdom comes from experience.

	不听老人言，吃亏在眼前	bùtīng lǎorényán, chīkuī zàiyǎnqián	If you do not listen to an old person's advice, you will suffer soon. (One should listen to an old person's advice because he/she is wiser.)
	不入虎穴，焉得虎子	búrù hǔxuè, yāndé hǔzǐ	One cannot get the tiger's cub without entering the tiger's lair. *Nothing ventured, nothing gained. *Nothing venture, nothing win.
C	差之毫厘，失之千里	chàzhī háolí, shīzhī qiānlǐ	A miniscule off aim, a very long distance off target. *A miss is as good as a mile. *An inch, in a miss, is as good as an ell.
	拆东墙，补西墙	chāi dōngqiáng, bǔ xīqiáng	Take from the east wall to repair the west wall. *Rob Peter to pay Paul.
	长江后浪推前浪，世上新人赶旧人	Chángjiāng hòulàng tuī qiánlàng, shìshang xīnrén gǎn jiùrén	The waves of the Changjiang River push forth, and young people push out the old in this world. *One fire drives out another.

			*One nail drives out another.
	处处有路到长安	chùchùyǒulù dào Cháng'ān	Everywhere there are roads to Chang'an. *All roads lead to Rome.
	初生之犊不畏虎	chūshēngzhīdú búwèihǔ	A newborn calf does not fear the tiger. *As valiant as a calf. *Ignorance is bliss.
	村中无虎狗为王	cūnzhōngwúhǔ gǒuwéiwáng	When there are no tigers in the village, the dog is the king. *In the kingdom of the blind, the one-eyed man is king. *When the cat's away the mice will play.
D	打人别打脸，骂人别揭短	dǎrén biédǎliǎn, màrén biéjiēduǎn	Do not hit a person on the face, do not curse a person's shortcomings. (Do not attack people where they are vunerable.)
	大事化小，小事化了	dàshì huàxiǎo, xiǎoshì huàliǎo	Regard big troubles as small and small ones as nothing at all. (One should make mole-hills out of mountains.)

	刀不磨要生锈，水不流要发臭	dāobùmó yàoshēngxiù, shuǐ bùliú yàofāchòu	A knife will rust if it is not sharpened and stagnant water will turn foul. *Standing pools gather filth. *The best fish smell when they are three days old.
	道高一尺，魔高一丈	dàogāoyìchǐ, mógāoyízhàng	When virtue rises one foot, evil rises ten feet. *Where God has his church, the devil will have his chapel.
	到什么山上，唱什么歌	dào shénmeshānshang, chàng shénmegēr	Sing the songs of the mountain when you go there. *Do in Rome as the Romans do. *Go native.
	读万卷书，行万里路	dú wànjuànshū, xíng wànlǐlù	To be learned, one should read ten thousand books and travel ten thousand miles. *He that goeth far hath many encounters. *He that travels far knows much.
E	儿孙自有儿孙福，莫为儿孙作马牛	érsūn zìyǒu'érsūnfú, mòwèi érsūn zuòmǎniú	Children and grandchildren have their own fortune; don't work like horses and cows for them.

			(Let children take care of themselves.)
	耳听为虚，眼见为实	ěrtīngwéixū, yánjiànwéishí	What one hears is empty but what one sees is real. *One eye-witness is better than ten ear-witnesses. *Seeing is believing.
F	饭后百步走，活到九十九	fànhòu bǎibùzǒu, huódao jiǔshijiǔ	Walk one hundred steps after supper, and you will live to be ninety-nine. *After supper walk a mile.
G	各人自扫门前雪，休管他人瓦上霜	gèrén zìsǎo ménqiánxuě, xiūguǎn tārén wǎshangshuāng.	Each sweeps the snow in front of his/her own door. Never mind the frost on someone else's roof. *Attend to your own affairs. *Mind your own business.
	公说公有理，婆说婆有理	gōngshuō gōngyǒulǐ, póshuō póyǒulǐ	Grandpa says he is right and grandma says she is right. (Truth is relative.) *He says, she says.
	狗捉耗子，多管闲事	gǒu zhuōhàozi, duōguǎn xiánshì	A dog catching mice: much meddling in another's business.

			*Attend to your own affairs. *Mind your own business.
	官大有险， 树大招风	guāndà yǒuxiǎn, shùdà zhāofēng	High officials are in danger and big trees attract the wind. *Great winds blow upon high hills.
	光阴似箭， 日月如梭	guāngyīn sìjiàn, rìyuè rúsuō	Time flies like an arrow, and days and months pass as fast as a shuttle. *Time flies. *Time does sail. *Tempus fugit.
H	害人之心不 可有，防 人之心不 可无	hàirénzhīxīn bùkěyǒu, fángrénzhīxīn bùkěwú	One must not harbor bad intentions, but one must guard against the intentions of others.
	好汉不打 妻，好狗不 咬鸡	hǎohàn bùdǎqī, hǎogǒu bùyǎojī	A good man does not beat his wife; a good dog does not bite chickens. (One must not take advantage of the weak.)
	活到老，学 不了	huódàolǎo, xuébùliǎo	Live until old age, but there is always more to learn. *Live and learn.
J	己所不欲， 勿施于人	jǐ suǒbúyù, wùshīyú rén	What you do not want, do not inflict on others.

			(Do not force upon others what you do not want forced upon yourself.)
	家丑不可外扬	jiāchǒu bùkě wàiyáng	The ugly side of a family should not be revealed to outsiders. *Do not air your dirty linen in public. *Don't wash your dirty linen in public.
	家花不如野花香，家花倒比野花长	jiāhuā bùrú yěhuāxiāng, jiāhuā dàobǐ yěhuācháng	Flowers at home are not as fragrant as flowers in the wild, but they last longer than wild flowers. *Grass is greener on the other side of the fence.
	家家有本难念的经	jiājiā yǒuběn nánniàndejīng	Every family has a sutra that is hard to chant. *There is a skeleton in every closet.
	家有老，是个宝	jiāyǒulǎo, shìgebǎo	Having an old person in the house is a real treasure.
	江山易改，本性难移	jiāngshān yìgǎi, běnxìng nányí	Rivers and mountains can be easily moved, but a person's true nature cannot be changed. *Can the leopard change his spots?

107

			*Nature draws more than ten oxen. *What is bred in the bone will not be out of the flesh.
	今日有酒今日醉，明日愁来明日当	jīnrìyǒujiǔ jīnrìzuì, míngrìchóulái míngrìdāng	Drink today while you have wine; deal with tomorrow's problems when they come. *Seize the moment. *Seize the time. *Carpe diem.
	近水楼台先得月，向阳花木早逢春	jìnshuǐ lóutái xiāndéyuè, xiàngyáng huāmù zǎoféngchūn	The terrace closest to water gets the moon first and spring comes earlier to flowers and trees facing the sun. *A baker's wife may bite of a bun, a brewer's wife may drink of a tun. *The parson always christens his own child first.
	近朱者赤，近墨者黑	jìnzhūzhě chì, jìnmòzhě hēi	Near the vermillion, one turns red; near the ink, one turns black. *He that lives with cripples learns to limp.

			*Keep good men company and you shall be of the number. *One must howl with the wolves. *One who lies down with dogs, must rise with fleas. *The finger that touches rouge will be red. *Who keeps company with the wolf will learn to howl. *You cannot touch pitch without being defiled, and anyone who associates with a proud man will come to be like him.
	酒逢知己千杯少，话不投机半句多	jiǔféngzhījǐ qiānbēishǎo, huàbùtóujī bànjùduō	When with a bosom friend, a thousand cups of wine is too few; if they do not get along, half a sentence is too much. *Old friends and old wine are best. *Old wine and old friends are good provisions. *The company makes the feast.

K	开门七件事，柴米油盐酱醋茶	kāimén qījiànshì, chái mǐ yóu yán jiàng cù chá	Seven things one has to provide every day: firewood, rice, oil, salt, sauce, vinegar, and tea.
	孔子也有三分差	Kǒngzǐ yěyǒu sānfēnchà	Even Confucius can be a little off. *A good marksman may miss. *Even Homer sometimes nods. *No man is wise all times. *To err is human.
L	老王卖瓜，自卖自夸	lǎo Wáng màiguā, zìmài zìkuā	Old Wang selling melons: he brags about his own goods. *Every salesman boasts of his own wares.
	老虎不在山，猴子称大王	lǎohǔ búzàishān, hóuzi chēngdàwáng	When the tiger is not in the mountain, the monkey proclaims himself king. *When the cat's away, the mice will play.
	良药苦口利于病，忠言逆耳利于行	liángyào kǔkǒu lìyúbìng, zhōngyán nì'ěr lìyúxíng	Good medicine is bitter but beneficial for curing illness; sincere advice is hard on the ear but beneficial to conduct.

			*Bitter pills may have wholesome effects, good counsel never comes amiss.
	两虎相斗，必有一伤	liǎnghǔ xiāngdòu, bìyǒu yìshāng	When two tigers fight, one is sure to get wounded.
	留得青山在，不怕没柴烧	liúde qīngshānzài, búpà méicháishāo	As long as there is a mountain with trees, there will always be firewood. *Where there is life there is hope. *While there is life there is hope.
	龙生龙，凤生凤，老鼠生儿会打洞	lóngshēnglóng, fèngshēngfèng, lǎoshǔ shēng'ér huìdǎdòng	Dragon begets dragon, phoenix begets phoenix, and a mouse is born knowing how to dig holes. *It early pricks that will be a thorn. *Like begets like.
	路遥知马力，日久见人心	lùyáo zhīmǎlì, rìjiǔ jiànrénxīn	When the journey is long, you learn how strong the horse is; after a long time, you come to know a person's heart. *A friend is never known till needed. *A man knows his companion in a long journey and a little inn.

			*Before you make a friend, eat a bushel of salt with him. *Try before you trust. *Try your friend before you have need of him.
M	麻雀虽小， 五脏俱全	máquè suīxiǎo, wǔzàng jùquán	A sparrow may be small, but it has all five viscera. *Even a fly hath its spleen. *There is life in a mussel, though it be little.
	米已成饭， 木已成舟	mǐ yǐchéng fàn, mù yǐchéng zhōu	The rice is already cooked, the wood is already made into a boat. *It's no use crying over spilt milk. *The die is cast. *What's done cannot be undone.
	明枪易躲， 暗箭难防	míngqiāng yìduǒ, ànjiàn nánfáng	It is easier to avoid a spear in the open than an arrow from the back. *Better an open enemy than a false friend. *Better be stung by nettle than pricked by a rose.

			*With friends like that, who needs enemies?
	牡丹虽好，必要绿叶扶助。	mǔdān suīhǎo, bìyào lǜyè fúzhù	Peonies are beautiful, but their beauty is enhanced by green leaves. *No man is an island.
N	恼一恼，老一老，笑一笑，少一少	nǎoyìnǎo, lǎoyìlǎo, xiàoyíxiào, shàoyíshào	Get angry and you get older; laugh and you become younger. *Laugh and grow fat.
	泥菩萨过河，自身难保	nípúsa guòhé, zìshēn nánbǎo	A clay Buddha crossing a river: he may not even save himself. (One has enough trouble helping oneself, much less others.)
	宁为玉碎，不为瓦全	níngwéi yùsuì, bùwéi wǎquán	Rather be a piece of broken jade than a whole clay tile. *Better a glorious death than a shameful life. *Better to die in glory than live in dishonor.
	宁与千人好，不与一人仇	níngyǔ qiānrénhǎo, bùyǔ yìrénchóu	Better be friends with a thousand than an enemy of one.
P	旁观者清，当局者迷	pángguānzhě qīng, dāngjúzhě mí	The onlookers see clearly but those involved are in the dark.

			*Lookers-on see most of the game. *Standers-by see more than gamesters. *The darkest place is under the candlestick.
	胖子不是一口吃的	pàngzi búshi yìkǒu chīde	One mouthful does not a fat person make. *An oak is not felled at one stroke. *Rome was not built in a day. *The tree falls not at the first stroke.
	平生不做亏心事，半夜不怕鬼敲门	píngshēng búzuò kuīxīnshì, bànyè búpà guǐqiāomén	Never do a conscienceless deed and you won't fear a ghost knocking at the door at midnight. *A good conscience is a continual feast. *A quiet conscience sleeps in thunder. *A clean hand wants no washing.
Q	钱到手才算钱，肉到口才算吃	qiándàoshǒu cáisuànqián, ròudàokǒu cáisuànchī	Money is only good when it is in your hand, and meat is good only when it is in your mouth.

			*Do not count your chickens until they are hatched. *First catch your hare. *Gut no fish till you get them. *Never cackle till your egg is laid.
	前人种树，后人乘凉	qiánrén zhòngshù, hòurén chéngliáng	Forerunners plant trees and people after them enjoy the shade. *One man makes a chair, another man sits on it. *One man sows and another reaps.
	强中更有强中手，能人背后有能人	qiángzhōng gèngyǒu qiángzhōngshǒu, néngrén bèihòu yǒu néngrén	Among the strong there are stronger, and behind the capable there are more capable people. *Diamond cut diamond.
	巧媳妇煮不出没米的粥，巧嘴八哥说不过潼关去	qiǎoxífu zhǔbùchū méimǐdezhōu, qiǎozuǐbāger shuōbúguò Tóngguān qu	Even a skillful wife cannot cook without rice; even a myna bird cannot talk its way beyond the Tongguan Pass. (No one can create something out of nothing.)
	情人眼里出西施	qíngrén yǎnli chū Xīshī	Only her lover's eye sees her as a beautiful Xi Shi.

			*Beauty is in the eye of the beholder. *Beauty lies in a lover's eyes. *Love is blind.
	求人不如求己	qiúrén bùrú qiújǐ	Asking others for help is not as good as asking oneself. *Better spare to have thine own than ask of other men. *Let every tub stand on its own bottom.
R	人比人，气死人	rénbǐrén, qìsǐrén	One gets very angry when compared with others. *Comparison is odious.
	人不可貌相，海水不可斗量	rén bùkě màoxiàng, hǎishuǐ bùkě dǒuliáng	A person cannot be judged by looks alone; the sea cannot be measured by bushels. *A little body doth often harbor a great soul. *Appearances are deceptive. *It is not the hood that makes the monk. *Men are not to be measured by inches. *Never judge from appearance.

			*Never judge from appearances. *The cowl does not make the monk. *You cannot judge a book by its cover. *You cannot judge a tree by its bark.
	人过留名，雁过留声	rénguò liúmíng, yànguò liúshēng	A person leaves a name behind and a wild goose leaves a cry. *Where the horse lies down, there some hair will be found.
	人善被人欺，马善被人骑	rénshàn bèirénqī, mǎshàn bèirénqí	Nice people are taken advantage of; nice horses are ridden. *All lay the load on the willing horse.
	人往高处走，水往低处流	rén wàng gāochu zǒu, shuǐ wàng dīchu liú	People want to rise high; water flows down low. *No priestling, small though he may be, but wishes someday Pope to be.
	人无完人，金无足赤	rén wú wánrén, jīn wú zúchì	No one is perfect and no gold is pure. *A horse stumbles that has four legs. *Every bean has its black.

			*Every man has his faults. *He is lifeless that is faultless. *No man is wise at all times. *Nobody is perfect. *The peacock has fair feathers but foul feet. *There are lees to every wine.
	人心齐，泰山移	rénxīn qí, Tàishān yí	When everyone is of one mind, the great Taishan Mountain can be moved away. *A long pull, a strong pull, and a pull all together. *Unity is strength.
	人要衣装，佛要金装	rényào yīzhuāng, fóyào jīnzhuāng	A person needs fine clothes; a Buddha statue needs gilding. *Fine feathers make fine birds. *The tailor makes the man.
	人有失足，马有失蹄	rén yǒu shīzú, mǎ yǒu shītí	A person may slip and a horse may stumble. *A horse stumbles that has four legs.
	日有所思，夜有所梦	rìyǒusuǒsī, yèyǒusuǒmèng	What one thinks about during the day, one dreams about at night.

	入国问禁， 入乡从俗	rùguó wènjìn, rùxiāng cóngsú	When entering a country, ask about its taboos; when going into a village, follow its customs. *When in Rome, do as the Romans do.
	若要人不知，除非己莫为	ruòyào rénbùzhī, chúfēi jǐmòwéi	If one does not want people to know, one should not do the deed. *The day has eyes and the night has ears. *There is a witness everywhere. *What is done by night appears by day.
S	三百六十行，行行出状元	sānbǎiliùshi háng, hángháng chū zhuàngyuan	There are three hundred and sixty professions. In each profession, someone will excel.
	三个臭皮匠，顶个诸葛亮	sānge chòupíjiàng, dǐngge Zhūgě Liàng	Three leathersmiths can be as smart as Zhuge Liang. *Four eyes see more than two. *Many heads are better than one. *Three helping one another bear the burden of six. *Two heads are better than one.

119

			*Two eyes can see more than one.
	三人一条心，黄土变成金	sānrén yìtiáoxīn, huángtǔ biànchéngjīn	When three people are of one mind, they can turn dirt into gold. *Unity is strength.
	三十六计，走为上计	sānshiliùjì, zǒuwéishàngjì	Of the thirty-six strategies, the best is to run away. *He who fights and runs away lives to fight another day. *Seek safety in flight. *Take flight. *Take to one's legs.
	山不在高，有仙则名；水不在深，有龙则灵	shān búzàigāo, yǒuxiān zémíng; shuǐ búzàishēn, yǒulóng zélíng	A mountain does not have to be high to become famous when there is an immortal living on it. A river does not have to be deep to work wonders when there is a dragon living in it.
	善有善报，恶有恶报；不是不报，时机未到	shànyǒushànbào, èyǒu'èbào; búshibúbào, shíjīwèidào	Kindness will be rewarded, and evil will be punished. It is not that justice is not done, it is just that the time is not yet right. *Justice has long arms.

			*The mills of God grind slowly.
	上梁不正下梁歪	shàngliángbúzhèng, xiàliángwāi	If the upper beam is tilted, the lower beam will be crooked. *Fish begins to stink at the head. *A bad beginning makes a bad ending.
	少壮不努力，老大徒伤悲	shàozhuàng bùnǔlì, lǎodà túshāngbēi	If one does not work hard during one's prime, one will grieve during old age. *A lazy youth, a lousy age. *An idle youth, a needy age. *If you lie upon roses when young, you'll lie upon thorns when old. *Reckless youth makes rueful age.
	是非终日有，不听自然无	shìfēi zhōngrìyǒu, bùtīng zìránwú	There is gossip every day; if you don't listen to them, they will go away. *Were there no hearers, there would be no backbiters.
	十个指头，有长有短. 一棵果树，有酸有甜	shígezhítou, yǒucháng yǒuduǎn, yìkēguǒshù, yǒusuān yǒutián	Ten fingers: some are long and others short; one fruit tree: some fruits are sour, others sweet.

			*So many men, so many minds.
	十年树木， 百年树人	shínián shùmù, bǎinián shùrén	It takes ten years to grow a tree, but one hundred to educate a person. *A skill is not acquired in a matter of days. *Rome was not built in a day.
	世上没有不 散的宴席	shìshang méiyou búsànde yànxí	There is no feast that will not end. *All good things come to an end. *The best of friends must part. *The longest day must have an end.
	虱子多了 不痒	shīzi duōle bùyǎng	When one is infected with many lice, one does not feel the itch. (One more problem does not bother a person who has many.)
	树倒猢狲散	shùdǎo húsūn sàn	When a tree falls, all the monkeys scatter. *A rat leaving a sinking ship. *Rats desert a sinking ship.
T	天外有天， 人上有人	tiānwài yǒutiān, rénshàng yǒurén	There are heavens above heaven, and there are people above people.

			(There is always somewhere and someone better.)
	天无绝人之路	tiān wú juérénzhīlù	Heaven does not cut off roads for a person. *Every day brings its own bread. *When one door closes, another opens.
	天下乌鸦一般黑	tiānxià wūyā yìbānhēi	All crows under heaven are black. *All tarred with the same brush. *The same holds true everywhere. *The world is much the same everywhere.
	天下无难事，只怕有心人	tiānxià wúnánshì, zhǐpà yǒuxīnrén	There is nothing difficult, except for those who hesitate. *Nothing is difficult to a man who wills. *Nothing is impossible to a willing heart. *Nothing is impossible to a willing mind. *It is dogged that does it. *Where there is a will, there is a way.
	天下原来共一家，四海之内皆兄弟	tiānxià yuánlái gòngyìjiā, sìhǎizhīnèi jiēxiōngdì	The whole world is a family and all are siblings.

123

			*All are brothers within the four seas.
	天下兴亡，匹夫有责	tiānxià xīngwáng, pǐfū yǒuzé	Everyone is responsible for what the world becomes.
	天有不测风云，人有旦夕祸福	tiān yǒu búcèfēngyún, rén yǒu dànxīhuòfú	Nature brings unexpected weather and unexpected calamities and fortune. *A foul morn may turn to a fair day. *Here today and gone tomorrow.
W	万事开头难	wànshì kāitóunán	Everything is difficult at the start. *All things are difficult before they are easy. *The first blow is half the battle. *It is the first step which is troublesome.
	无风不起浪	wúfēng bùqǐlàng	Without wind, there are no waves. *Every bullet has its billet. *Every why has a wherefore. *There's no smoke without fire. *Where there is smoke there is fire.

X	瞎猫碰上死耗子	xiāmāo pèngshang sǐhàozi	A blind cat stumbles on a dead mouse. (Blind luck.)
	小时偷针，长大偷金	xiǎoshí tōuzhēn, zhǎngdà tōujīn	He who steals needles when young will steal gold when grown up. *Just as the twig is bent the tree is inclined.
Y	眼不见心不烦	yǎnbújiàn, xīnbùfán	What one cannot see one does not worry about. *Far from eye, far from heart. *Out of sight, out of mind. *What the eye doesn't see the heart doesn't grieve over.
	养儿防老，积谷防饥	yǎng'ér fánglǎo, jīgǔ fángjī	Raise sons for your old age, and store grain for times of hunger.
	羊毛出在羊身上	yángmáo chūzai yángshēnshang	Sheep's wool comes from the sheep's own body. (Nothing is free.)
	以贼捉贼，以毒攻毒	yǐzéi zhuōzéi, yǐdú gōngdú	Use a thief to catch a thief and attack poison with poison. *Set a thief to catch a thief.
	一寸光阴一寸金，寸金难买寸光阴	yícùnguāngyīn yícùnjīn, cùnjīn nánmǎi cùnguāngyīn	One inch of time is worth one inch of gold, but one inch of gold cannot buy one inch of time.

			*Take time by the forelock. *There is nothing more precious than time. *Time is money.
	一个和尚挑水吃，两个和尚抬水吃，三个和尚无水吃	yíge héshang tiāoshuǐchī, liǎngge héshang táishuǐchī, sānge héshang wúshuǐchī	One monk gets his own water; two monks fetch less water together; three monks will have no water. *Everybody's business is nobody's business.
	一个篱笆三个桩，一个好汉三个帮	yíge líba sānge zhuāng, yíge hǎohàn sānge bāng	One fence needs three posts. One successful person has the help of three. *No man is an island.
	一粒老鼠屎，坏了一锅粥	yílì lǎoshǔshǐ, huàile yìguōzhōu	One rat dropping spoils a whole pot of porridge. *One bad apple spoils the whole bunch. *One bad apple spoils the whole barrel. *One ill weed mars a whole pot of porridge. *The rotten apple spoils its neighbors.

	一年之计在于春，一日之计在于晨	yìniánzhījì zàiyúchūn, yírìzhījì zàiyúchén	The year's plan should be made in the spring, and the day's plan should be made in the morning. *An hour in the morning is worth two in the evening.
	一瓶子不响，半瓶子晃荡	yìpíngzi bùxiǎng, bànpíngzi huàngdang	A full bottle makes no noise, but half a bottle shakes and makes much noise. Making a great display of a little knowledge. *All asses wag their ears. *Empty vessels make the most sound.
	一人做事一人当，哪有嫂嫂替姑娘	yìrén zuòshì yìréndāng, nǎyǒu sǎosao tì gūniang	One should be responsible for one's own actions; how can she blame her sister-in-law? (One should take responsibility for one's own actions.)
	一日为师，终身为父	yírìwéishī, zhōngshēnwéifù	My teacher for one day is like my parent for life.
	一失足成千古恨，再回头是百年身	yìshīzú chéng qiāngǔhèn, zàihuítóu shi bǎiniánshēn	One slip of the foot brings eternal regret; in a blink of the eye, a whole life has passed.

			*Do wrong once and you'll never hear the end of it. *One wrong step may bring a great fall. *Short pleasure, long lament.
	以眼还眼，以牙还牙	yǐyǎn huányǎn, yǐyá huányá	An eye for an eye and a tooth for a tooth. *Eye for eye. *Like for like. *Measure for measure. *Tit for tat.
	一夜夫妻百夜恩，百夜夫妻百载情	yíyèfūqī bǎiyè'ēn, bǎiyèfūqī bǎizàiqíng	Husband and wife for one night, love for a hundred nights; husband and wife for a hundred nights, love for a hundred years.
	一言既出，驷马难追	yìyán jìchū, sìmǎ nánzhuī	Once a promise is made, a team of horses cannot bring it back. *A word and a stone let go cannot be recalled. *A word spoken is past recalling.
	一朝被蛇咬，十年怕草绳	yìzhāo bèi shéyǎo, shínián pà cǎoshéng	Once bitten by a snake, one fears ropes for ten years. *A burned child dreads the fire. *Once bit, twice shy.

			*Once bitten, twice shy. *The scalded cat fears cold water.
	一着不慎，满盘皆输	yìzhāo búshèn, mǎnpán jiēshū	One careless move, the whole chess game is lost. *One false move may lose the game. *One wrong move may lose the game.
	有借有还，再借不难	yǒujiè yǒuhuán, zàijiè bùnán	Borrow and return, and you can easily borrow again.
	有理走遍天下，无理寸步难移	yǒulǐ zǒubiàntiānxià, wúlǐ cùnbùnányí	You can go anywhere if you're upright. Otherwise, you cannot move an inch.
	有钱能使鬼推磨	yǒuqián néngshǐ guǐtuīmò	Money can make a demon push the grinder. *Gold goes in at any gate except heaven's. *Money makes the mare go. *Money talks. *Wage will get a page.
	又要马儿走得好，又要马儿不吃草	yòuyào mǎ'er zǒudehǎo, yòuyào mǎ'er bùchīcǎo	You want the horse to run well, but do not want it to eat hay. *You cannot eat your cake and have it too.

			*You cannot have your cake and eat it too. *You cannot sell the cow and drink the milk. *You can't have it both ways.
	有缘千里来相会，无缘对面不相逢	yǒuyuán qiānlǐ láixiānghuì, wúyuán duìmiàn bùxiāngféng	If you are so destined, you will meet though a thousand miles apart; if not destined, you will not meet even though facing each other. (People will not get together if they are not meant for each other.)
	欲加之罪，何患无词	yùjiāzhīzuì, héhuànwúcí	If you want to accuse someone of a crime, you can easily find a reason. *A stick is quickly found to beat a dog with. *Give a dog a bad name and hang him. *He that wants to hang a dog is sure to find a rope. *If you want a pretence to whip a dog, say that he ate the frying-pan.

	远水不救近火，远亲不如近邻	yuǎnshuǐ bújiù jìnhuǒ, yuǎnqīn bùrú jìnlín	Distant water cannot put out a nearby fire, a distant relative is not as good as a close neighbor. *Better is a neighbor that is near than a brother far off. *Water afar off quencheth not fire. *We can live without our friends, but not without our neighbors.
	月满则亏，水满则溢	yuèmǎnzékuī, shuǐmǎnzéyì	When the moon is full, it will wane; when water is full, it will spill. (Don't be too full of yourself.)
Z	这山望着那山高	zhèshān wàngzhe nàshān gāo	From this mountain, the other mountain looks higher. *Grass is greener on the other side of the fence.
	知己知彼，百战百胜	zhījǐ zhībǐ, bǎizhàn bǎishèng	Understand yourself and understand your opponents and you will never be defeated.
	只要工夫深，铁杵磨成针	zhǐyào gōngfushēn, tiěchǔ móchéngzhēn	If one puts in effort, an iron rod can be ground into a needle.

			*Constant dropping wears away the stone. *Feather by feather the goose is plucked. *Little strokes fell great oaks. *Many strokes fell great oaks. *With time and patience the leaf of the mulberry becomes satin.
	种瓜得瓜，种豆得豆	zhòngguādéguā, zhòngdòudédòu	Plant melons, you shall reap melons; plant beans, you shall reap beans. *As the call, so the echo. *As you sow, so will you reap. *You must reap what you have sown.
	坐吃山空	zuòchī shānkōng	Sitting around and eating, one will use up all the mountain's resources. *Always taking out of the meal-tub, and never putting in, soon comes to the bottom. *Dig one's grave with one's teeth. *Hair and hair makes the carle's head bare.

2.12   Punning allusion

One of the most enjoyable, and puzzling for the novice, aspects of
using modern Chinese is the "punning allusion, 歇后语 xiéhòuyǔ,"
which is so rare in modern English as to be practically non-existent.
We say "practically" because we have on occasion heard allegorical
puns spoken by monolingual English speakers, whom we know to
have been uninfluenced by Chinese language usage. An example is:
"These jeans fit like a cheap hotel – no ball room." This captures
almost perfectly the form and spirit of the Chinese xiéhòuyǔ, which
are used when one wants to display wit or humor, often disparagingly
when describing a person, a thing, or a situation. The basic structure
of the typical xiéhòuyǔ is quite simple: the speaker makes a concise
description of a scene, an action or situation that would appear
on the surface to be unrelated to the topic of discussion. The fact
that the utterance appears unrelated to the topic at hand makes
the listener search for a metaphorical analogy that would be more
appropriate in the current context. The metaphorical analogy is often
triggered through a pun. If the xiéhòuyǔ is well known, then the
speaker will not even verbalize the "punch line," because the listener
will make the connection and start laughing or nodding approval.
Structurally, the xiéhòuyǔ shares much in common with the riddle.
The best way to appreciate the punning allusion is through selected
examples. In the following examples, the first part is the "riddle" that
describes the situation and the second part is the "punch line" or the
intended answer.

半天空里挂口袋 – 装风
bàntiānkōnglǐ guà kǒudài – zhuāngfēng
Hanging a bag in mid-air – packaging the wind.

It is easier to understand this mechanism if we review the line of
thought in reverse order of its expression. We wish to say that a
person is "feigning madness." The Chinese expression for feigning
madness is "装疯 zhuāngfēng." If we grope around for a pun on
"madness," the nearest common word is "wind, 风 fēng." As it
happens, the Chinese word for "to package" also means "to adorn,"
"to apply makeup," and "to feign," as in "装傻 zhuāngshǎ, to feign
stupidity." What would be an example of trying to "package the
wind"? Obviously, holding or hanging a bag up in mid-air. So the
allusive pun's creative thought process is expressed in reverse.

电线杆上绑鸡毛 –   好大的掸子
diànxiàngānshang bǎng jīmáo – hǎodàde dǎnzi
Tie chicken feathers on a power line pole – very big duster.

The word for "feather duster, 掸子" is homophonous with the word
for "guts, 胆子," although written with a different character. This
pun is a roundabout way of saying that someone has "a lot of guts."

棺材里伸手 – 死要钱
guāncaili shēnshǒu – sǐ yàoqián
Stretching out the hand from inside the coffin – persistently
  wanting money.

The colloquial expression for "persistently" doing something, or
"persistently wanting" something, is: sǐ + verb phrase, or sǐ yào +
noun, similar to "just dying" to do something in English. Here,
"dying" is expressed by "in the coffin," and "wanting money" by
"stretching out the hand."

和尚打伞 – 无发无天
héshang dǎsǎn – wúfǎ wútiān
A monk using a parasol – hairless and heavenless.

"Hairless and heavenless" is a pun on "lawless and heavenless," i.e.,
defying all laws, of mankind and of nature. The pun is on "发
fǎ, hair" and "法 fǎ, law." The parasol obscures the view of the "sky
(heaven), 天 tiān."

茅坑里丢炸弹 – 激起公粪
máokènglǐ diū zhàdàn – jīqǐ gōngfèn
A grenade tossed into the outhouse – the shit's going to fly.

The expression "公愤 gōngfèn, public indignation" sounds like "公
粪 gōngfèn, public shit."

没弦的琵琶 – 从哪儿弹起
méixiánde pípā – cóngnǎr tánqǐ
A stringless lute – where to start strumming?

"弹起 tánqǐ, start strumming" is a pun on "谈起 tánqǐ, start talking
about something." Used when we don't know where to start talking
about a complex matter.

铁公鸡 – 一毛不拔
tiěgōngjī – yìmáo bùbá
An iron rooster – not a single feather can be plucked.

"毛, máo" in the context of birds means "feather," and in the context
of money means "dime, ten cents." Used to describe a "tightwad," a
stingy person who won't spend a dime to help you.

万岁爷的茅厕 – 没有你的粪
wànsuìyéde máocè – méiyǒu nǐde fèn
His Majesty's toilet – no room for your shit.
There is nothing for you.

The Chinese words "粪 fèn, shit" and "份 fèn, share" are
homophones.

蚊子放屁 – 小气
wénzi fàngpì – xiǎoqì
A mosquito fart – tiny air.

Stingy.
"小气 xiǎoqì" means "stingy," literally "tiny air."

小葱拌豆腐 – 一青二白
xiǎocōng bàndòufu – yìqīng èrbái
Shallots mixed with beancurd – one clearly green, the other clearly
   white.
   "Shallots mixed with beancurd – perfectly clear."

This one plays on the homophony between "green, 青 qīng" and
"pure, 清 qīng," so that "shallots mixed with beancurd" means
"completely clear and understandable."

2.13   Metaphorical allusion

The metaphorical allusion type of 歇后语 xiéhòuyǔ is somewhat
easier to understand, because the metaphor is only once removed
from the person or situation being described, as it involves no
punning. A near-equivalent English expression might be "between a
rock and a hard place – no way out." Some examples in Chinese:

财神爷敲门 – 福从天降；天大的好事
cáishényé qiāomén – fú cóngtiānjiàng; tiāndàde hǎoshì
The God of Wealth rapping at the door – a blessing from heaven,
   a colossal boon.

狗咬刺猬 – 无处下口
gǒu yǎo cìwei – wúchù xiàkǒu
A dog trying to bite a hedgehog – no place to sink his teeth into.
Used to describe a situation in which one has no idea where to
   start to accomplish anything.

老鼠过街 – 人人喊打
lǎoshǔ guòjiē – rénrén hǎndǎ
A rat running across the street – everybody shouts: "Get it!"
Used to describe a person universally recognized as bad, and
   reviled by everyone.

老王卖瓜 – 自卖自夸
lǎowáng màiguā – zìmài zìkuā
Old Wang selling melons – he's praising them because he's selling
   them.
Used to indicate that someone is exaggerating the virtues of
   something in which they have a vested interest.

蚂蚁吃萤火虫 – 亮在肚里
mǎyǐ chī yínghuǒchóng – liàng zài dùli
An ant swallows a firefly – the brightness is inside.

蚂蚁关在鸟笼里 – 门道很多
mǎyǐ guānzai niǎolóngli – méndào hěnduō
Ants locked inside a birdcage – there are many ways out.

蚂蚁喝水 – 点滴就够啦

mǎyǐ hēshuǐ – diǎndī jiùgòu la

An ant takes a drink of water – just a drop will do.

蚂蚁进牢房 – 自有出路

mǎyǐ jìn láofáng – zìyǒu chūlù

Ants in a jail cell – they have a way out.

蚂蚁抓上牛角尖 – 自以为上了高山

mǎyǐ zhuāshang niújiǎojiān – zìyǐwéi shàngle gāoshān

An ant has climbed to the tip of an ox horn – to him it's a mountain peak.

蚂蚱斗公鸡 – 自不量力

màzha dòu gōngjī – zì bùliánglì

Locust attacking a rooster – he hasn't gauged his own strength.

卖棺材的咬牙 – 恨人不死

màiguāncaide yǎoyá – hèn rén bùsǐ

The coffin salesman grits his teeth – wishing someone would die.

卖水的看大河 – 尽是钱

màishuǐde kàn dàhé – jìnshì qián

The water seller looking at the mighty river – all he sees is money!

猫不吃鱼 – 假斯文

māo bùchī yú – jiǎsīwén

A cat pretending not to eat fish – faked refinement.

猫哭老鼠 – 假慈悲

māo kū lǎoshǔ – jiǎ cíbēi

A cat crying over a mouse's misfortune – feigned mercy.

Used to describe someone showing false sympathy to another, or to a cause for which one has no sympathy.

猫捉老鼠 – 靠自己的本事

māo zhuō lǎoshǔ – kào zìjǐde běnshì

A cat catching mice – relying on its own abilities.

茅坑里放玫瑰花 – 显不出香味

máokèngli fàng méiguìhuā – xiǎnbuchū xiāngwèi

Roses placed inside the outhouse – the fragrance won't be noticed.

猫儿教老鼠 – 留一手

māor jiāo lǎoshǔ – liú yìshǒu

A cat teaching lessons to mice – withholding a trick or two.

猫儿捉老鼠，狗看门 – 各守本分

māor zhuō lǎoshǔ, gǒu kān mén – gèshǒu běnfèn

The cat catches mice and the dog guards the house – each doing his own thing.

煤球放在石灰里 – 黑白分明

méiqiú fàngzai shíhuīli – hēibái fēnmíng

A lump of coal in the lime – distinctions as clear as black and
white.

门缝里看天 – 目光狭小

ménfèngli kàntiān – mùguāng xiáxiǎo

Looking at the sky through a crack in the door – a narrow view of
things.

梦里讲的话 – 不知是真是假

mèngli jiǎngdehuà – bùzhī shìzhēn shìjiǎ

Something spoken in a dream – can't tell if it's true or false.

弥勒佛 – 笑口常开

mílèfó – xiàokǒu chángkāi

The Maitreya Buddha – always a big smile on the face.

米筛装水 – 漏洞多

mǐshāi zhuāng shuǐ – lòudòng duō

Trying to carry water in a rice sieve – too many loopholes.

米汤洗头 – 糊涂到顶

mǐtāng xǐtóu – hútudàodǐng

A rice-gruel shampoo – the head is muddled.

棉花槌打鼓 – 没音

miánhuachúi dǎgǔ – méi yīn

Drumming with a cotton drumstick – not a sound.

Used to describe a useless effort.

棉花里藏针 – 柔中有刚

miánhuali cáng zhēn – róuzhōng yǒugāng

A needle in a wad of cotton – soft on the outside, tough inside.

庙中的五百罗汉 – 各有各的一定的地位

miàozhōngde wǔbǎi luóhàn – gè yǒu gède yídìngde dìwei

Five hundred Arhat statues in the temple – a place for everyone
and everyone in his place.

泥菩萨过河 – 自身难保

nípúsa guòhé – zìshēn nánbǎo

A clay Buddha trying to cross the river – can hardly save himself,
much less others.

Used to explain that "I'd love to be able to help you, but you see
I'm…"

肉包子打狗 – 有去无回

ròubāozi dǎgǒu – yǒuqù wúhuí

A meat bun thrown at a dog – an irretrievable loss.

Used to describe an investment of resources for which there surely
will be no return – a wasted use of resources.

娃娃看魔术 – 莫明其妙

wáwa kàn móshù – mòmíngqímiào

Baby watching a magic show – not a clue what's going on.

娃娃骑木马 – 不进不退

wáwa qí mùmǎ – bújìn bútuì

Baby riding a hobbyhorse – neither progressing nor regressing.

娃娃下棋 – 胸无全局

wáwa xiàqí – xiōngwúquánjú

Baby playing chess – no long-range plan in mind.

歪锅配扁灶 – 一套配一套

wāiguō pèi biǎnzào – yítào pèi yítào

Slanted frying-pan on a lopsided stove – a perfect fit.

歪嘴和尚念经 – 说不出一句正经话

wāizuǐ héshang niànjīng – shuōbuchū yíjù zhèngjinghuà

A crooked-mouth monk chanting scriptures: can't get a straight line out of him.

网里的鱼，笼中的鸟 – 跑不了

wǎnglǐde yú, lóngzhōngde niǎo – pǎobuliǎo

A fish in the net, a bird in the cage – no way to escape.

王七的兄弟 – 王八

Wáng Qī de xiōngdi – Wáng Bā

Wang Number Seven's younger brother = Wang Number Eight = a turtle = a bastard.

围着火炉吃西瓜 – 心上甜丝丝，身上暖烘烘

wéizhe huǒlú chīxīguā – xīnshang tiánsīsī, shēnshang nuǎnhōnghōng

Eating watermelon by the stove – feeling sweet inside, and warm outside.

蚊子叮菩萨 – 认错了人

wénzi dīng Púsa – rèncuòle rén

Mosquito bites a Buddha – misrecognized the person.
Used to describe an ill-advised attack on a benevolent personage.

蚊子飞过能认公母 – 好眼力

wénzi fēiguò néngrèn gōngmǔ – hǎo yǎnlì

Able to tell the sex of a mosquito flying by – good eyesight.
Discerning eyes.

蚊子找蜘蛛 – 自投罗网

wénzi zhǎo zhīzhu – zìtóu luówǎng

Mosquito hunting for a spider – looking for a trap to fall into.
One voluntarily falls in a trap.

屋顶上的王八 – 上不着天，下不着地

wūdǐngshangde wángba – shàngbuzháo tiān, xiàbuzháo dì

A turtle on the rooftop – can't climb any higher and can't climb
   back down.
In a quandary.

蜈蚣吃蝎子 – 以毒攻毒
wúgōng chī xiēzi – yǐdúgōngdú
Centipede eating a scorpion – fighting poison with poison.
Tit for tat.

屋檐下躲雨 – 不长久
wūyánxià duǒyǔ, bùchángjiǔ
Avoid rain under the eaves – not long.
Ducking under the eaves in the rain – this won't last long.

2.14 Onomatopoeia

Onomatopoeia, 拟声词 nǐshēngcí, is a word or string of syllables
that imitates the sound it is describing. Examples in English
are: "bang," "clang," "oink," "arf, arf," and "meow, meow." Such
expressions are used more commonly by Chinese speakers than by
English speakers.

2.14.1 Animal sounds

呱呱	guāguā	quack-quack, croak-croak, caw-caw
呼噜呼噜	hūlūhūlū	snorting sound of a pig; sound of snoring
唧唧	jījī	sound of a monkey chattering
叽叽喳喳	jījīzhāzhā	chirping, twittering sound
咪咪	mīmī	"here, kitty-kitty" (sound used to call a cat)
喵	miāo	meow
咩咩	miēmiē	baa-baa (sound of a sheep)
汪汪	wāngwāng	bow-wow, arf-arf (barking sound)
嗡嗡	wēngwēng	buzz-buzz (sound of a mosquito flying)
喔喔	wōwō	cock-a-doodle-doo
吱吱	zīzī	peeping sound of a mouse; chirping of a bird
吱吱	zhīzhī	creaking sound

2.14.2 Human, inanimate, and mechanical sounds

吧嗒吧嗒	bādābādā	chit-chatty
叮当	dīngdāng	clinking sound, tinkling sound
咚咚	dōngdōng	thump-thump-thump, sound of drums

嘟嘟	dūdū	toot-toot (the sound of a horn)
嘎吱嘎吱	gāzhīgāzhī	crunching sound, creaking sound
咕噜咕噜	gūlūgūlū	gurgle, gurgle (sound of liquid pouring out of a vessel, or stomach growling)
轰隆	hōnglōng	sound of thunder, machinery, or artillery
呼呼	hūhū	soughing sound of wind
哗啦	huālā	the sound of crashing or rustling
哗啦哗啦	huālāhuālā	crashing sound, splashing sound, sound of heavy rainfall
哗啦啦	huālālā	crashing sound
叽里咕噜	jīlīgūlū	gabble-gabble (incessant talking)
叽里呱啦	jīlīguālā	hullabaloo
劈里啪啦	pīlīpālā	cracking or crackling sound
乒零乓啷	pīnglingpānglāng	banging and clanging
乒乓	pīngpāng	sound of gunfire, sound of a ping-pong ball
扑通	pūtōng	kerplunk (sound of something falling into water)
飕飕	sōusōu	soughing sound of the wind
淅沥哗啦	xīlihuālā	rustling sound, splashing sound; swish, swish
嘘	xū!	shh! hush! hissing sound
牙牙	yāyā	babbling (of a baby)

2.14.3 Other onomatopoeic expressions

哒	dā	gee-up, giddup
叨咕	dáogu	grumble
喋喋不休	diédiébùxiū	incessant chattering
呱呱叫	guāguājiào	tip-top, top knotch
咕噜咕噜	gūlūgūlū	grumble; sound of stomach growling
咕哝	gūnong	grumble
哈哈笑	hāhā xiào	to laugh out loud
笑哈哈	xiàohāhā	laughing (out loud)

2.15 Mimetopoeia

Mandarin speakers make much use of imitative sounds in ordinary conversation. Speech sounds that imitate other sounds are called "onomatopoeia," and these are such English expressions as "bang," "burp" or "guzzle." There is another kind of imitative speech, which we might call "mimetopoeia," 拟态词 nǐtàicí, which imitates not sounds, but mannerisms, airs, or "vibes" of people, animals, and even inanimate objects or weather. We have a few mimetopoeic words in English, like "higgledy-piggledy" and "helter-skelter," but far fewer than we find used in everyday Chinese speech.

Selected examples follow:

大不咧咧	dàbuliēliē	casual, careless; arrogant
灰不溜丢	huībuliūdiū	very grey, dreary
凉飕飕	liángsōusōu	chilly (in a wind)
慢腾腾	màntēngtēng	ever so slow
迷迷糊糊	mímihūhū	dazed, confused, muddle-headed
磨磨蹭蹭	mómócèngcèng	walk dragging the feet, slow and tardy
蔫不唧唧	niānbujījī	(of a person) in low spirits
扭扭捏捏	niǔniuniēniē	diffident(ly), timorous(ly), unwillingly
胖咚咚	pàngdōngdōng	fat, chubby
胖嘟嘟	pàngdūdū	fat, plump
七叱夸叉	qīchīkuāchā	doing something at a whizzing speed
傻乎乎	shǎhūhū	simple-minded, naive
瘦伶仃	shòulíngdīng	skinny as a rail
笑呵呵	xiàohēhē	smilingly, laughing happily
笑哈哈	xiàohāhā	happily laughing aloud
笑咪咪	xiàomīmī	smilingly, with a gentle smile
笑嘻嘻	xiàoxīxī	smilingly, with a smile
笑吟吟	xiàoyínyín	smilingly, with a dainty smile
摇摇晃晃	yáoyáohuànghuàng	wobbly, falteringly
直不楞噔	zhíbulēngdēng	straight as an arrow

There is an interesting category of colloquial adjectival expression, which is composed of neither ordinary adjectives nor clearly imitative supplements, but which share some of the feeling of mimetopoeic expressions. In this type of expression, we may take an adjective such as "傻 shǎ, silly," "土 tǔ, rustic," or "粗 cū, coarse," reduplicate it (傻傻 shǎshǎ, 土土 tǔtǔ，粗粗 cūcū), and add a "里 li, used as a filler" after the first syllable and a "气 qì, air, atmosphere, manner" after the repeated syllable, to form the expressions 傻里傻气 shǎlishǎqì, 土里土气 tǔlitǔqì, and 粗里粗气 cūlicūqì, adding a "physical feel" to the simple adjective. A somewhat similar pattern is seen when we take a disyllabic adjective like "糊涂 hútu, muddle-headed" or "慌张 huāngzhang, flurried, flustered," add a "里 li" after the first syllable and repeat the original word to form "糊里糊涂 húlihūtū" and "慌里慌张 huānglihuāngzhāng," making it more colorful than the original adjective.

2.16   Riddles

Riddling has been a favorite pastime of Chinese speakers for many centuries. There are riddles of all kinds. Guessing the answers to riddles, 谜语 míyǔ, is a popular game at festive gatherings, often at dinner parties, where the first person to answer a riddle correctly may receive a prize. There are also many different kinds of riddles involving Chinese characters. Usually they are closely connected with (1) the shape, (2) the constituent elements, (3) the pronunciation, or (4) the meaning of a Chinese character. Following are samples of riddles that illustrate the four types of riddle involving Chinese characters mentioned above and samples of other types of riddles:

(1)   Riddles referring to the shape of Chinese characters:

Riddle: 远看似我爹，近看非我爹，脱下帽子看，真的是我爹
yuǎnkàn sì wǒdiē, jìnkàn fēi wǒdiē, tuōxia màozi kàn, zhēndeshì wǒdiē.

From a distance, it looks like my dad; on closer look, it's not my dad; taking off the hat, I see it really is my dad.

Answer: 谜底 mǐ dǐ: 交 jiāo, cross over, give over, intersect

Explanation: The character 交, originally a pictograph of a person with legs crossed, is composed of two elements: the top part being "亠 lid, cover" and the bottom being "父 fù, father." From a distance, the character does indeed resemble "父," but upon closer examination it is not "父" but "交." If, however, the "hat," i.e., the "lid" or "cover" element on top is removed, the character is indeed "父," or "father."

(2)   Riddles referring to the constituent elements of Chinese characters:

Riddle: 米老鼠
mǐ lǎo shǔ
Mickey Mouse

Answer: 籽 zǐ, seed

Explanation: The character 籽 is composed of two structural elements – "米" meaning "rice" but pronounced "mǐ," which represents the sound of "Mickey," and "子," which means "child" or "son," but is also the first of the "Twelve Earthly Branches, 地支 dìzhī," representing the "mouse" or "rat" among the "Twelve Zodiacal Animals, 十二生肖 shí'èr shēngxiào." Therefore 米老鼠 alludes to "mǐ + mouse" = "籽."

Riddle: 水落石出
shuǐ luò shí chū
When the river waters recede, the rocks will emerge.

Answer: 泵 bèng, pump

Explanation: The proverb "When the river waters recede, the rocks will emerge," means that "conditions will evolve so that the truth will be seen." The character 泵 is composed of the character for "water 水" below the character for "rock 石," which together form the word for "pump 泵."

Riddle: 人有它大，天无它大
rén yǒutā dà, tiān wútā dà
With it, a person becomes great; without it, heaven becomes great.

Answer: 一 yī, one

Explanation: The answer being "one, 一" (a horizontal stroke). If a person, 人, has "it" (一), then "person, 人" becomes "great, 大"; if "Heaven, 天" lacks "it" (一), then "Heaven, 天" becomes "great, 大."

(3) Riddles referring to the pronunciation of Chinese characters (often a pun):

Riddle: 笼中之鸟
lóng zhōng zhī niǎo
A caged bird

Hint: 国名 guómíng, name of a country.

Answer: 南非 Nánfēi, South Africa (pun: from 难飞 nán fēi, "hard to fly")

Explanation: A bird in a cage finds it hard to fly, 难飞. The character "难" is homophonous with the character for "south, 南 nán," while "飞 fēi" is homophonous with "非 fēi," the first syllable of "非洲 Fēizhōu, Africa." Therefore, "hard to fly" is the same pronunciation as the abbreviated reference to "South Africa."

Riddle: 金银铜铁
jīn yín tóng tiě
gold, silver, copper, iron

Hint: 地名 dìmíng, place name in China

Answer: 无锡 Wúxī, a city not far from Shanghai

Explanation: "金银铜铁锡 jīn yín tóng tiě xī, gold, silver, copper, iron and tin " is a set phrase in Chinese, referring to "the Five Metals." If we say only "gold, silver, copper, iron," then "tin" is missing, i.e., "there is no tin." The characters for the city of Wúxī mean "without tin."

(4) Riddles referring to the meaning of Chinese characters:

Riddle: 双喜临门
shuāng xǐ lín mén
Double Happiness arrives at the door.

Hint: 地名 dìmíng, a place name

Answer: 重庆 Chóngqìng, a city in Sichuan Province

Explanation: The character "重 chóng" means "repeated" or "doubled," and "庆 qìng" means "felicitations" or "celebrations."

(5) Some other types of riddles:

Riddle: 左一片，右一片，两片东西不见面。
zuǒyípiàn, yòuyípiàn, liǎngpiàn dōng xī bújiànmiàn.
One on the left; one on the right. They are just east and west of each other, but they never meet.

Answer: ears, 耳朵 ěrduo

Riddle: 上边毛，下边毛，中间一颗黑葡萄。
shàngbian máo, xiàbian máo, zhōngjiān yìkē hēipútao.
Hairs above, hairs below, and a dark grape in between.

Answer: eye, 眼睛 yǎnjing

Riddle: 五个兄弟，住在一起，名字不同，高矮不齐。
wǔge xiōngdì, zhùzai yìqǐ, míngzi bùtóng, gāo'ǎi bùqí.
Five brothers, living together: different names and different heights.

Answer: fingers, 手指头 shǒuzhítou

Riddle: 麻屋子，红帐子，里面坐个白胖子。
máwūzi, hóngzhàngzi, lǐmian zuò ge báipàngzi.
a pock-marked room, a red bed-curtain, sitting inside is a white chubby person.

Answer: peanut kernel, 花生米 huāshēng mǐ

2.17 Tongue twisters

Following are a few examples of commonly heard tongue twisters, 绕口令 ràokǒulìng, which are Chinese parallels to the English "Peter Piper picked a peck of pickled pepper":

妈妈骑马，马慢，妈妈骂马
māma qímǎ, mǎ màn, māma mà mǎ.
Mother rides a horse; the horse is slow; mother curses the horse.

四是四，十是十，十四是十四，四十是四十
sì shi sì, shí shi shí, shísì shi shísì, sìshí shi sìshí
Four is four, ten is ten, fourteen is fourteen, forty is forty.

老石和老史，天天去公司，一直是同事
lǎo Shí he lǎo Shǐ, tiāntiān qù gōngsī, yìzhí shi tóngshì
Old Shí and old Shǐ, go to the same company every day, have always been colleagues.

老石老是骗老史，老史说，老石实在不老实
lǎo Shí lǎoshi piàn lǎo Shǐ, lǎo Shǐ shuō, lǎo Shí shízài bù lǎoshi
Old Shí always tricks old Shǐ. Old Shǐ says: Old Shí is truly
  dishonest.

一个大嫂子，一个大小子，大嫂子和大小子，比赛包饺子
yíge dàsǎozi, yíge dàxiǎozi, dàsǎozi hé dàxiǎozi, bǐsài bāojiǎozi
A woman, a guy: the woman and the guy have a dumpling-
  making match.

大嫂子包的饺子，又大又多又好吃，大小子包的饺子，又小
又少又难吃
dàsǎozi bāode jiǎozi, yòudà yòuduō yòuhǎochī, dàxiǎozi bāode
  jiǎozi,
yòuxiǎo yòushǎo yòunánchī.
The dumplings the woman makes are big, numerous, and delicious.
  The dumplings the guy makes are small, few, and taste awful.

一只青蛙一张嘴, 两只眼睛四条腿, 扑通一声跳下水,
yìzhī qīngwā yìzhāngzuǐ, liǎngzhī yǎnjing sìtiáo tuǐ, pūtōng
  yìshēng tiàoxiashuǐ
One frog, one mouth, two eyes, and four legs: splash! It jumps
  into the water.

两只青蛙两张嘴, 四只眼睛八条腿, 扑通扑通两声跳下水,
liǎngzhī qīngwā liǎngzhāngzuǐ, sìzhī yǎnjing bātiáo tuǐ, pūtōng
  pūtōng liǎng shēng tiàoxiashuǐ.
Two frogs, two mouths, four eyes, and eight legs: splash! splash!
  They jump into the water.

三只青蛙三张嘴, 六只眼睛十二条腿, 扑通扑通扑通三声跳下
水
sānzhī qīngwā sānzhāngzuǐ, liùzhī yǎnjing shí'èrtiáo tuǐ, pūtōng
  pūtōng pūtōng sānshēng tiàoxiashuǐ.
Three frogs, three mouths, six eyes, and twelve legs: splash! splash!
  splash!
They jump into the water.

2.18 Colors

For the Chinese, red is an auspicious color but white is an
inauspicious color. Green is a very good color now because it implies
environmental friendliness.

  Some basic color words are monosyllabic:

红	hóng	red
黄	huáng	yellow
蓝	lán	blue
白	bái	white
黑	hēi	black

绿	lǜ	green
紫	zǐ	purple
灰	huī	grey

The above colors can be modified by 深 shēn, dark, deep, or 浅 qiǎn, light/淡 dàn, light, to make them a darker or lighter shade. Other colors are disyllabic:

大红	dàhóng	scarlet, bright
粉红	fěnhóng	pink, rosy
枣红	zǎohóng	burgundy
桃红	táohóng	peach, pink
橘红	júhóng	orange
米黄	mǐhuáng	beige, cream
杏黄	xìnghuáng	apricot, pinkish yellow
金黄	jīnhuáng	golden, golden yellow
翠蓝	cuìlán	bright blue
宝蓝	bǎolán	sapphire blue
天蓝	tiānlán	azure, sky blue
靛蓝	diànlán	indigo, indigo blue
草绿	cǎolǜ	grass green
翠绿	cuìlǜ	jade green, emerald green
嫩绿	nènlǜ	light green, soft green
青绿	qīnglǜ	dark green

Some colorful differences:

Same things expressed with different colors in English and Chinese:

Black tea	红茶 hóngchá, red tea
Black and blue	青一块紫一块 qīngyíkuài zǐyíkuài, a patch of blue and a patch of purple
Blue blood	贵族血统 guìzú xuètǒng, noble clan blood
Blue movies	黄色电影 huángsè diànyǐng, yellow movies
Brown bread	黑面包 hēimiànbāo, black bread
Brown sugar	红糖 hóngtáng, red sugar
Green-eyed, green with envy	眼红 yǎnhóng, eyes are red; 害红眼病 hài hóngyǎnbìng, infected with red-eye disease

Phrases with color in English, but equivalent phrases in Chinese have no color:

Black sheep	败家子 bàijiāzǐ, children who ruin the family; 害群之马 hàiqúnzhīmǎ, horses who ruin the herd

Greenhorn	生手 shēngshǒu, new hand; 没经验的人 méijīngyande rén, a person without experience
Greenhouse	温室 wēnshì, warm room
Green thumb	有园艺技能 yǒu yúanyì jìnéng, having gardening skills
Grey matter	大脑 dànǎo, brain; 智力 zhìlì, intelligence
In a blue mood	情绪低沉 qíngxù dīchén, emotions are low
Once in a blue moon	千载难逢的机会 qiānzǎi nánféngde jīhui, a chance in a thousand years
Out of the blue	意想不到的 yìxiǎng búdàode, unexpected
In the black	赢利 yínglì, profit
Lily-livered or yellow-bellied person	胆小鬼 dǎnxiǎoguǐ, coward
Pink slip	解雇通知 jiěgù tōngzhī, firing notice
In the red	亏损 kuīsǔn, loss
Not a red cent	不名一文 bùmíng yìwén, not having one cent to one's name
Red-letter day	大喜的日子 dàxǐde rìzi, great happy day
Red tape	烦琐的事 fánsuǒde shì, tedious things
Roll out the red carpet	隆重欢迎贵宾 lóngzhòng huānyíng guìbīn, welcoming honored visitors in a grand manner
White elephant	昂贵无用的东西 ángguì wúyòngde dōngxi, expensive and useless things
White lies	无恶意的谎言 wú èyìde huǎngyán, lies without any evil intentions
White sale	大减价 dàjiǎnjià, big reduction in prices
Yellow pages	分类电话簿 fēnlèi diànhuàbù, classified telephone book

Phrases with no color in English, but with color in Chinese:

Boiled water	白开水 bái kāishuǐ, white boiled water, plain boiled water
Dividend	红利 hónglì, red profit

147

Enjoy extreme popularity and fame	红得发紫 hóngdefāzǐ, so red it is turning purple
Funeral	白事 báishì, white event
Go-between (female), matchmaker (female)	红娘 hóngniáng, red lady
Good luck	红运 hóngyùn, red fortune
To be a cuckold (said of married men)	戴绿帽子 dài lǜmàozi, to wear a green hat
Wedding	红事 hóngshì, red event
Weddings and funerals	红白喜事 hóngbái xǐshì, red and white happy events

2.19   Opposites

Opposites are always expressed in the following order, and never in reverse. For example: 胖 pàng – 瘦 shòu, 大 dà – 小 xiǎo, etc.

悲 bēi, sad	喜 xǐ, joyful
长 cháng, long	短 duǎn, short (not for people's height)
粗 cū, thick (circumference)	细 xì, thin (circumference)
大 dà, large, big, older (age)	小 xiǎo, little, small, younger (age)
单 dān, single	双 shuāng, double
动 dòng, moving	静 jìng, still
多 duō, many, much	少 shǎo, few, little
肥 féi, fat (animal, meat)	瘦 shòu, thin; lean (animal, meat)
干 gān, dry	湿 shī, wet
高 gāo, high	低 dī, low
高 gāo, tall	矮 ǎi, short (person)
好 hǎo, good	坏 huài, bad
黑 hēi, black	白 bái, white
厚 hòu, thick	薄 báo, thin
呼 hū, breathe out	吸 xī, breathe in
开 kāi, open; turn on	关 guān, close; turn off
哭 kū, cry	笑 xiào, laugh
快 kuài, fast	慢 màn, slow
宽 kuān, wide	窄 zhǎi, narrow
老 lǎo, old (age)	少 shào, young (age)
冷 lěng, cold	热 rè, hot (temperature)
里 lǐ, inside	外 wài, outside

买 mǎi, buy	卖 mài, sell
美 měi, beautiful	丑 chǒu, ugly
难 nán, difficult	易 yì, easy
胖 pàng, fat (person)	瘦 shòu, thin (person)
前 qián, front	后 hòu, back
强 qiáng, strong	弱 ruò, weak
勤 qín, diligent	懒 lǎn, lazy
轻 qīng, light	重 zhòng, heavy
软 ruǎn, soft	硬 yìng, hard
上 shàng, up, above	下 xià, down, below
深 shēn, deep; dark (color)	浅 qiǎn, shallow; light (color)
生 shēng, live, life	死 sǐ, die, death
松 sōng, loose	紧 jǐn, tight
天 tiān, heaven, sky	地 dì, earth, land
直 zhí, straight	弯 wān, winding, curved
先 xiān, first (in order)	后 hòu, next, last (in order)
新 xīn, new	旧 jiù, used
左 zuǒ, left	右 yòu, right

Some opposites can be combined to become nouns:

长短 chángduǎn	length
粗细 cūxì	thickness
大小 dàxiǎo	size
动静 dòngjing	movement
多少 duōshǎo	amount, number
肥瘦 féishòu	size (of clothes); the proportion of fat and lean (of meat)
高低 gāodī	height (of mountains, cliffs); sense of propriety
高矮 gāo'ǎi	height (persons, trees), stature
好坏 hǎohuài	good and bad (quality)
黑白 hēibái	black and white; right and wrong
厚薄 hòubáo	thickness (surfaces)
呼吸 hūxī	breathing; to breathe
开关 kāiguān	switch
快慢 kuàimàn	speed
宽窄 kuānzhǎi	width, breadth, size (of clothes)
买卖 mǎimai	business, trade, transaction
前后 qiánhòu	order (of lining up); around; from beginning to the end
轻重 qīngzhòng	weight; relative importance
软硬 ruǎnyìng	the softness or hardness (of some object)
上下 shàngxià	high and low; old and young; from top to bottom; up and down
生死 shēngsǐ	life and death
深浅 shēnqiǎn	depth; shade (of color)

松紧　sōngjǐn	degree of tightness, elasticity
天地　tiāndì	heaven and earth, the world, universe
先后　xiānhòu	priority, order
新旧　xīnjiù	the newness (of something)
左右　zuǒyòu	around (for approximate number); control; to master

2.20 Figurative expressions

Sometimes people like to use different words to express the same idea, that is, they may use "figurative" terms, 委婉语 wěiwǎnyǔ or 隐语 yǐnyǔ. These terms are used to say things in a roundabout way, to avoid being too direct, to avoid embarrassment or to express things in a more colorful manner. "Death or to die, 死 sǐ" has to be the most widely tabooed word, and there are about 500 different ways of saying "sǐ" in Chinese without actually using the word.

The following are samples of figurative expressions:

English and Chinese	Figurative expression
argue 争论 zhēnglùn, 吵架 chǎojià	红脸 hóngliǎn, redden the face
bathroom 厕所 cèsuǒ	卫生间 wèishēngjiān, hygiene room 洗手间 xǐshǒujiān, wash hand room 一号 yíhào, number one
blind 瞎 xiā	失明 shīmíng, lose brightness
brag, boast 夸大 kuādà	吹牛 chuīniú, blow a cow 说大话 shuōdàhuà, speak big words
break up (a relationship) 分手 fēnshǒu	吹 chuī, to blow it 蹬 dēng, to kick 掰 bāi, to break into two
change jobs 换单位 huàndānwèi	跳槽 tiàocáo, to jump to another trough
chaperone (derogatory) 伴随者 bànsuízhě	灯泡 dēngpào, light bulb 电灯泡 diàndēngpào, electric light bulb
chase women, find a girlfriend 追女人 zhuīnǚren	嗅蜜 xiùmì, sniff for honey

commit suicide 自杀 zìshā	寻短见 xúnduǎnjiàn, seek short view
	抹脖子 mǒbózi, slash neck
	轻生 qīngshēng, make light of life
	厌世 yànshì, sick of the world
	自尽 zìjìn, self finish
	自寻短见 zìxún duǎnjiàn, self seek short view of life
cuckold (a man) 奸妇的丈夫 jiānfùde zhàngfu	戴绿帽子 dài lǜmàozi (wear a green hat; in ancient times, such a person had to wear a green hat or turban) 乌龟 wūguī, tortoise
death, die 死 sǐ	安眠 ānmián, peaceful sleep
	安息 ānxī, peaceful rest
	不在了 búzàile, no longer here
	长眠 chángmián, long sleep
	长逝 chángshì, left forever
	辞世 císhì, quit the world
	蹬腿 dēngtuǐ, kick legs
	断气 duànqì, break off breath
	故世 gùshì, pass away from the world
	归天 guītiān, return to heaven
	归西 guīxī, return to the western heaven where paradise is
	裹尸 guǒshī, wrap up the corpse, to die on the battlefield
	过去 guòqu, pass away
	见上帝 jiànshàngdì, to meet with God
	见马克思 jiàn Mǎkèsī, to meet with Karl Marx
	捐躯 juānqū, donate one's body to the country

	没世 mòshì, to disappear from the world
	没有了 méiyǒule, no more, no longer here
	涅盘 nièpán, death of a monk or nun
	气绝 qìjué, breath terminated
	弃世 qìshì, abandon the world
	去 qù, go, leave, depart
	去世 qùshì, go away from the world
	升天 shēngtiān, rise up to heaven
	伸腿 shēntuǐ, stretch out legs
	逝世 shìshì, disappear from the world
	寿终正寝 shòuzhōng zhèngqǐn, finish life for a proper sleep
	玩儿完 wánrwán, finish playing
	呜呼哀哉 wūhu āizai, alas, how sad
	牺牲 xīshēng, sacrifice oneself for one's country
	殉国 xùnguó, die for one's country
	殉教 xùnjiào, die for religion
	殉情 xùnqíng, die for love
	殉职 xùnzhí, die on duty
	咽气 yànqì, swallow up the breath
	夭逝 yāoshì, disappear young
	夭折 yāozhé, broken young
	一病不起 yíbìngbùqǐ, once sick, never get up
	永别 yǒngbié, part forever
	永逝 yǒngshì, disappear forever
	与世长辞 yǔshì chángcí, bid farewell to the world forever
	葬身鱼腹 zàngshēnyúfù, buried in a fish belly
	走了 zǒule, left, gone, departed

	作古 zuògǔ, become a person of the past
deaf	耳背 ěrbèi, ear out of the way
聋 lóng	失聪 shīcōng, lose faculty of hearing
	失听 shītīng, lose hearing
diarrhea	拉肚子 lādùzi, evacuate the tummy
泻肚 xièdù	拉稀 lāxī, evacuate watery
	闹肚子 nào dùzi, belly stirs
	跑肚子 pǎodùzi, belly runs
divorce	分手 fēnshǒu, part hands
离婚 líhūn	
drug addict	瘾君子 yǐnjūnzǐ, addicted personage
吸毒者 xīdúzhě	
flirt (with women), to tease (women)	吃豆腐 chī dòufu, eat beancurd (which is soft)
调情 tiáoqíng	
foolish, stupid person	笨蛋 bèndàn, dumb egg
笨人 bènren	蠢货 chǔnhuò, dumb goods
	二百五 èrbǎiwǔ, two hundred and fifty: no full understanding of things
	傻瓜 shǎguā, silly melon
	傻帽儿 shǎmàor, silly hat
foreigner	老外 lǎowài, old outsider
外国人 wàiguorén	
funerals	白事 báishì, white event (white is the color of mourning)
葬礼 zànglǐ	白喜 báixǐ, white happiness, especially an old person's funeral
	后事 hòushì, event afterwards
go to the washroom	大便 dàbiàn, big convenience
上厕所 shàng cèsuǒ	方便 fāngbian, convenience
	解手 jiěshǒu, loosen hands
	净手 jìngshǒu, clean hands
	去洗手 qùxǐshǒu, go wash hands

	上洗手间 shàng xǐshǒujiān, go to the hand-washing room 上一号 shàngyíhào, go to number one 小便 xiǎobiàn, small convenience
have sex 性交 xìngjiāo	房事 fángshì, bedroom business: husband and wife 上床 shàngchuáng, go to bed 睡觉 shuìjiào, sleep 云雨 yúnyǔ, clouds and rain 作爱 zuò'ài, make love
homosexual 同性恋 tóngxìngliàn	同志 tóngzhì, comrade 兔儿 tùr, rabbit
jealous 忌妒 jìdu	吃醋 chīcù, eat vinegar 眼红 yǎnhóng, eyes red 犯红眼病 fàn hóngyǎnbìng, suffer red eye disease 害红眼病 hài hóngyǎnbìng, suffer red eye disease
lay off 解雇 jiěgù lose one's job, to be fired 失业 shīyè	下岗 xiàgǎng, leave sentry duty 炒鱿鱼 chǎoyóuyú, fry squid, fried squid (fried squids roll up like the bedroll a fired person has to carry) 砸饭碗 záfànwǎn, smash the rice bowl
make things difficult for 使不快 shǐbúkuài (a subordinate)	穿小鞋 chuān xiǎoxié, wear tight shoes
marriage 婚姻 hūnyīn, 结婚 jiéhūn	成家 chéngjiā, establish home 大事 dàshì, great event 喜事 xǐshì, happy event 终身大事 zhōngshēn dàshì, great event of the whole life
menstruation, period 月经 yuèjīng	例假 lìjià, regular holiday 小朋友 xiǎopéngyou, little friend
old age	白首 báishǒu, white head

老年 lǎonián	薄暮 bómù, early evening
	末暮 mòmù, late evening
	暮景 mùjǐng, evening scene
	上年纪 shàngniánji, move up in age
	霜发 shuāngfà, frosted hair
pickpocket 扒手 páshǒu	三只手 sānzhǐshǒu, three hands
pornographic movie 色情电影 sèqíng diànyǐng	黄色电影 huángsè diànyǐng, yellow movie
pornographic video 色情片 sèqíngpiān	毛片 máopiān, fuzz film
poor 穷 qióng	揭不开锅 jiēbukāi guō, cannot open the cooking pot
poverty-stricken person 穷人 qióngrén	穷光蛋 qióngguāngdàn, poor as a smooth egg
	困难户 kùnnánhù, difficult household
pregnant 怀孕 huáiyùn	抱娃娃 bào wáwa, hold baby
	怀身 huáishēn, harbor a body
	怀喜 huáixǐ, harbor happiness
	有了身子 yǒule shēnzi, have a body
	有喜 yǒuxǐ, have happiness
prison 监狱 jiānyù	铁窗 tiěchuāng, iron window
refused entry 被拒进入 bèijù jìnrù	吃闭门羹 chī bìméngēng, eat close-door soup
shoot the breeze, chat 闲谈 xiántán	砍大山 kǎndàshān, chop big mountain
	聊天 liáotiānr, chat about the day
	闲磕牙 xiánkēyá, leisurely click teeth
sick 病 bìng	不安 bù'ān, not at ease
	不快 búkuài, not happy
	不适 búshì, not fit
	不舒服 bùshūfu, not comfortable

	欠安　qiàn'ān, lack wellness
	欠爽　qiànshuǎng, lack well-being
thief 贼 zéi, 小偷 xiǎotōu	梁上君子　liángshàng jūnzǐ, gentleman on the beams
tidy up someone else's mess 收拾 shōushi	擦屁股　cā pìgu, wipe bottom
weddings 婚礼 hūnlǐ	红事 hóngshì, red event (red being the color of happiness)

2.21   Vulgar sayings and insulting words

For cursing and/or insulting someone, besides the obvious direct
insults, the Chinese speaker often resorts to cursing or insulting
the person's ancestors or casting doubt upon the legitimacy of that
person's lineage. Another way is to challenge that person's sanity or
moral fibre.

Here are some examples:

笨蛋	bèndàn	stupid, dumb ass
别狗眼看人低	bié gǒuyǎn kànrén dī	How dare you look down on me!, Do I look like a fool ?
别装傻	bié zhuāngshǎ	Stop playing the fool. Don't act stupid.
操你妈	cào nǐmā	f*ck your mother
操你祖宗	cào nǐzǔzōng	f*ck your ancestors
吹牛	chuī niú	You're bragging!
呆头呆脑的	dāitóu dāinǎode	dull, slow-witted
什么德行	shénme déxing	disgusting, shameful
放屁	fàngpì	fart, nonsense
该死	gāisǐ	damn! damn it!
狗屁	gǒupì	dog fart, nonsense
鸡巴	jība	jerk, pr*ck
他妈的	tāmāde	his mother's, damn it
王八	wángba	turtle, a cuckolded husband
王八蛋	wángbadàn	turtle egg, bastard
有病	yǒubìng	crazy, nuts

Some of these expressions are in four-character format:

不得好死	bùdéhǎosǐ	die a terrible death
不伦不类	bùlúnbúlèi	neither fish nor fowl

不学无术	bùxuéwúshù	ignorant, not learned
大惊小怪	dàjīngxiǎoguài	fuss over something small, a storm in a teacup
对牛弹琴	duìniútánqín	cast pearls before swine
多管闲事	duōguǎnxiánshì	busybody, meddler
鬼鬼祟祟	guǐguǐsuìsuì	secretive, stealthy
好吃懒做	hàochīlǎnzuò	good for nothing, gluttonous and lazy
胡说八道	húshuōbādào	talk nonsense, stuff and nonsense
邋里邋遢	lālilātā	sloppy, slovenly
狼心狗肺	lángxīngǒufèi	wolf's heart and dog's lungs: heartless
狼狈为奸	lángbèiwéijiān	in cahoots
乱七八糟	luànqībāzāo	messy, chaotic, topsy-turvy
罗里罗嗦	luōliluōsuō	fussy, nagging
明知故犯	míngzhīgùfàn	violate knowingly, do something wrong knowingly
莫名其妙	mòmíngqímiào	ridiculous, baffling
旁若无人	pángruòwúrén	So arrogant!, act as if no one else mattered
岂有此理	qíyǒucǐlǐ	sheer nonsense
惹是生非	rěshìshēngfēi	meddlesome
太过分了	tàiguòfènle	That's going too far!
贪得无厌	tāndéwúyàn	greedy, avaricious
挑拨离间	tiǎobōlíjiàn	pit one against another
心猿意马	xīnyuányìmǎ	restless, fickle-minded
行尸走肉	xíngshīzǒuròu	an utterly useless person, one who vegetates
幸灾乐祸	xìngzāilèhuò	gloat over other people's disasters
又怎么样	yòuzěnmeyàng	So what? What are you going to do about it?
愚昧无知	yǔmèiwúzhī	stupid and ignorant
杂乱无章	záluànwúzhāng	without pattern or order, confused and disorderly
执迷不悟	zhímíbúwù	refuse to come to one's senses
自欺欺人	zìqīqīrén	deceive oneself as well as others, self-deceit
自私自利	zìsīzìlì	very selfish
自讨苦吃	zìtǎokǔchī	ask for trouble and get it
作茧自缚	zuòjiǎnzìfù	caught in one's own trap, stew in one's own juice
做贼心虚	zuòzéixīnxū	have a guilty conscience

2.22 Issues in translation

We are not truly "competent" in a language until we can "think in it," which means that we have formed the habit of using a "Chinese mindset" when engaging in Chinese discourse. To get there, we should aim to transcend thinking about what we want to say first in English, then translating the English into Chinese. Rather, we should aim to see situations and their relationships as Chinese-speaking people are expected to see them (this is what "culture" means in practice), and describe them or engage them as a Chinese speaker would. Remember, if we think in English, then directly translate what we think into equivalent Chinese words and grammatical structures, we may very well come across as saying or writing something totally inappropriate. Having said this, it is sometimes necessary to translate English and Chinese sentences back and forth – newspaper articles, journal articles, novels, poems, subtitles for films, consecutive or simultaneous interpreting for speeches, and other important and culturally significant forms. One of the first concerns must always be the "unit of translation," that is, should one focus on words, phrases, sentences, or larger units of meaning? The classical philologist may well tell us to focus first on finding precisely equivalent words, then using equivalent grammatical structures in the target language, perhaps using footnotes to explain any difference in nuance, metaphorical reference, or subtle allusion. If the source text is modern fiction, poetry, drama, or feature film screenplay, perhaps the focus should be on "functional equivalence" or "pragmatic equivalence." For example, the common phrase "晚安 wǎn ān" would be translated at the word level as "evening calm," but its pragmatic equivalent would be "good night" (not "good evening," which would be "wǎnshang hǎo!"). When one friend greets another for the first time in the morning with "Chīfànle ma?," the literal meaning of "Have you eaten?" should be rendered into its pragmatic equivalent: "Good morning! How are you?." When considering fundamental strategies for translation, some people think in terms of polarities such as "domestication" (finding in the target language a functionally equivalent way of representing a foreign concept or object that does not exist in the target language) or "alienation" (using a direct translation or transliteration of the source language object or concept for which there is no functional equivalent in the target language). One common example might be the Chinese word/ thing/concept called "龙 lóng." Mostly for the sake of convenience, we usually translate "龙 lóng" as "dragon," since Euro-American mythic traditions do have a large reptile-like beast with four legs, a long neck and a long tail, but that is where the resemblance ends. The Western dragon usually has a pair of wings, may sometimes spout fire, may stand on the ground, and is often seen as a malevolent beast. The Chinese 龙 lóng, however, usually resembles a huge snake with four short legs and sharp talons, no wings, always either in the air or in water, and is usually viewed as a benevolent power and a symbol of the emperor. The "domestication/alienation" issue here is whether there is enough similarity between the Euro-American "dragon" and the Chinese "lóng" to justify representing one as the other. The most commonly used Chinese–English and English–Chinese dictionaries define "dragon" as "lóng" and vice versa. Perhaps "Chinese dragon" would be an optimal accommodation.

Specific examples such as "dragon" are too numerous to list here, but perhaps the following contrastive features of Chinese and English may be useful in the struggle to find pragmatic equivalence in translation:

1. Chinese speakers usually focus first on the forest, then on specific trees; English speakers often begin with specific details first, then broaden the focus. This sometimes poses a challenge for structuring a natural paragraph in the target language.
2. Chinese speakers tend to use more metaphorical expressions, such as proverbs, maxims, analogies, and allusions, than would be the norm for English speakers. This may require creative means to naturalize a passage in the target language.
3. Chinese utterances are often characterized by "parataxis," in which the relationship between the surface elements of a sentence may be loose and unclear. Natural English utterances may be characterized by "hypotaxis," in which greater importance is attached to the formal cohesion of sentence elements.

Most Chinese people who know anything at all about translation theory know that the most often quoted rule for high-quality translation was proposed by 严复 Yán Fù (1853–1921), one of the greatest translators of the late Qing Dynasty and early Republican period. He wrote, in his Chinese translation of *Evolution and Ethics*, 天演论 Tiānyǎnlùn, that there are three fundamental challenges to overcome when translating: fidelity, 信 xìn, to the source text; clarity, 达 dá, of the target text; and elegance, 雅 yǎ. Though highly abstract and generalized, Yan's "three challenges" do seem to cover the main points that are still the subject of scholarly debate in the twenty-first century.

2.23   Transliteration vs. translation

The process of "alienation-to-domestication" is clearly observable in the history of Chinese translation. As early as the medieval period of Chinese history, we see monumental translation projects undertaken to render the major Buddhist sutras into Chinese from their original Pali and Sanskrit texts. Extremely talented and disciplined translators came up with the following strategies for rendering foreign things, names, titles, and concepts into Chinese, all of which are still used when dealing with neologisms from English and other languages. Roughly, they are:

1. Pure transliteration:
   chocolate = 巧克力 qiǎokèlì; clone = 克隆 kèlóng; sofa = 沙发 shāfā

2. Part transliteration, part translation:
   beer = 啤酒 pí (beer) jiǔ (alcoholic beverage); AIDS = 艾滋病 àizī (AIDS) bìng (illness)

3. Pure translation:
   democracy = 民主 mín (people) zhǔ (sovereign); web page = 网页 wǎng (web) yè (page)

4. Transliteration with added meaning:
   Coca-Cola = 可口可乐 kěkǒu (delicious) kělè (enjoyable); Pepsi-Cola = 百事可乐 bǎishì (all occasions) kělè (enjoyable)

5. Inventing a new Chinese character for a new foreign term:
   germanium = 锗 zhě; mendelevium = 钔 mén; radon = 氡 dōng.

3 Functional language

3.1 Proper names

3.1.1 Surnames

A Chinese name is expressed with the 姓 xìng, surname/last name/
family name, followed by the 名 míng, personal/first/given name.
A married woman usually keeps her own surname. Children usually
inherit their father's surname, although it is legal to take on their
mother's surname. And, indeed, some do take their mother's surname.

In 2006, a study which used the names of 296 million people
of the entire 1.3 billion population, found that there are 4,100
surnames. It found that 129 surnames account for 87% of the whole
population. The three most widely used surnames are 李 Lǐ (7.4%),
王 Wáng (7.2%), and 张 Zhāng (6.8%).

Most of the surnames are monosyllabic, 单姓 dānxìng, but some
are also disyllabic, 复姓 fùxìng. Chinese usually ask other people's
names by first asking their surnames: 您贵姓? Nín guìxìng?
People normally respond by giving their surname: 我姓 X, Wǒ
xìng X. Sometimes this may be followed by a verbal explanation or
description of the character used for the surname by dividing it up
into its constituent parts or by using a famous person's surname as an
illustration. Sometimes, people may use their index finger to write
the character in the air or on their palm for people to see.

The following are some major surnames and some examples of
their conventional explanations.

Ten major surnames:

Character	Pinyin	Explanation
李	Lǐ	木 mù 子 zǐ 李 Lǐ
王	Wáng	三 sān 横 héng 王 Wáng
张	Zhāng	弓 gōng 长 cháng 张 Zhāng

Character	Pinyin	Explanation
刘	Líu	刘 Líu 备 Bèi de 刘 Líu
陈	Chén	耳 ěr 东 dōng 陈 Chén
杨	Yáng	木 mù 易 yì 杨 Yáng
黄	Huáng	黄 huáng 颜色 yánsè de 黄 Huáng
赵	Zhào	赵 Zhào 钱 Qián 孙 Sūn 李 Lǐ de 赵 Zhào
周	Zhōu	周朝 Zhōucháo de 周 Zhōu
吴	Wú	口 kǒu 天 tiān 吴 Wú

Next ten surnames:

徐	Xú
孙	Sūn
朱	Zhū
马	Mǎ
胡	Hú
郭	Guō
林	Lín
何	Hé
高	Gāo
梁	Liáng

Double surnames:

公孙	Gōngsūn
欧阳	Ōuyáng
上官	Shàngguān
司马	Sīmǎ
司徒	Sītú
西门	Xīmén
诸葛	Zhūgě

Rare surnames:

汗	Hàn
老	Lǎo
难	Nán
宿	Sù
图	Tú
危	Wēi
宰	Zǎi

3.1.2 Personal names

There are no set Chinese personal or first names. Han Chinese
personal names are usually either disyllabic, 双名 shuāngmíng, or
monosyllabic, 单名 dānmíng. In the past half a century, there has
been a tendency for more and more people to have monosyllabic
personal names in China. This may increase the possibility of more
people having the same names by coincidence. Traditionally, and still
observed by some families, in disyllabic names, one of the characters
is a generation name. Usually the first one is the generation name
which all the children, especially males, will have, for example: 富贵
Fùguì, 富祥 Fùxiáng. Some may have the second as their generation
name, for example: 富祥 Fùxiáng, 贵祥 Guìxiáng. Children are
usually given names which have good meanings, or impressive words
from classical writings. Generally speaking, males are given names
which express or imply strength, high aspirations, glorification of the
ancestors, or goodwill; female names express or imply gentleness,
beauty, colors, or preciousness. In any case, people usually try to
avoid a combination of surnames and personal names that could
sound funny or ridiculous. For example: 吴能 Wú Néng, which
sounds like: 无能 wúnéng, meaning "incompetent," or 吴理 Wú Lǐ
which sounds like 无理 wúlǐ, meaning "unreasonable." It is almost
a taboo to name children after their parents, relatives, ancestors, or
friends.

According to statistics, in 1984 the ten most frequently used
characters appearing in first names were:

英	yīng	flower, outstanding person
华	huá	magnificent, splendid
玉	yù	jade, beautiful
秀	xiù	elegant, beautiful
明	míng	bright, brilliant
珍	zhēn	precious, valuable
文	wén	civil, refined

芳	fāng	fragrant, virtuous
兰	lán	orchid
国	guó	nation, state

3.1.3 Continents

The seven continents are:

Asia	亚洲	Yàzhōu
Africa	非洲	Fēizhōu
North America	北美洲	Běiměizhōu
South America	南美洲	Nánměizhōu
Antarctica	南极洲	Nánjízhōu
Europe	欧洲	Ōuzhōu
Oceania/Australia	大洋洲 / 澳洲	Dàyángzhōu/Àozhou

3.1.4 Highest peaks in the world

The following peaks are all over 8,000 meters high.

Peak	Chinese	Pinyin	Location
Everest	珠穆朗玛峰	Zhūmùlǎngmǎfēng	Nepal, Tibet
K-2	乔戈里峰	Qiáogélǐfēng	Pakistan
Kangchenjunga	干城章嘉峰	Gānchéngzhāngjiā fēng	Nepal, India
Lhortse	洛子峰	Luòzǐfēng	Nepal
Makalu	马卡鲁峰	Mǎkǎlǔfēng	Nepal, Tibet
Cho Oyu	卓奥友峰	Zhuó'àoyǒufēng	Nepal, Tibet
Dhaulagiri	道拉吉里峰	Dàolājílǐfēng	Nepal
Manaslu	马拉斯鲁峰	Mǎlāsīlǔfēng	Nepal
Manga Parbat	南伽峰	Nángāfēng	Pakistan
Annapurna	安纳布尔纳峰	Ānnàbù'ěrnàfēng	Nepal
Gasherbrum I	加舒尔布鲁木I峰	Jiāshū'ěrbùlǔmù I Fēng	China, Pakistan
Broad Peak	布洛阿特峰	Bùluò'ātèfēng	China, Pakistan

Peak	Chinese	Pinyin	Location
Gasherbrum II	加舒尔布鲁木II峰	Jiāshū'ěrbùlǔmù II Fēng	Pakistan
Xixiabangma Peak/Gosainthan Peak	希夏邦马峰 / 高僧赞峰	Xīxiàbāngmǎfēng/ Gāosēngzànfēng	China, Nepal

3.1.5   Major mountain ranges in China

Name	Chinese	Pinyin	Location
Himalayan Mountains	喜玛拉雅山脉	Xǐmǎlāyǎ Shānmài	China, India, Nepal
Kunlun Mountains	昆仑山脉	Kūnlún Shānmài	Pamir Plateau
Tianshan Mountains	天山山脉	Tiānshān Shānmài	Xinjiang
Tanggula Mountains	唐古拉山脉	Tánggǔlā Shānmài	Qinghai, Tibet
Qinling Mountains	秦岭山脉	Qínlǐng Shānmài	Gansu
Greater Hinggan Mountains	大兴安岭山脉	Dàxīng'ānlǐng Shānmài	Heilongjiang
Taihang Mountains	太行山山脉	Tàiháng Shānmài	The Loess Plateau
Qilianshan Mountain Range	祁连山山脉	Qǐliánshān Shānmài	Tibet
Hengduanshan Mountain Range	横断山山脉	Héngduànshān Shānmài	Tibet, Sichuan, Yunnan
Taiwan Mountain Range	台湾山脉	Táiwān Shānmài	Taiwan

3.1.6   Oceans

There are five oceans on earth. They cover about 70% of the earth's surface and contain almost 97% of the earth's water supply.

The five oceans recognized since the year 2000

Pacific Ocean	太平洋	Tàipíngyáng
Atlantic Ocean	大西洋	Dàxīyáng

Indian Ocean	印度洋	Yìndùyáng
Southern Ocean	南极洋 / 南冰洋 / 南大洋	Nánjíyáng/ Nánbīngyáng/ Nándàyáng
Arctic Ocean	北冰洋	Běibīngyáng

3.1.7 Seas

It is said that there are ninety-five seas in the world. The table lists some of the better known seas:

The better known seas

Aegean Sea	爱琴海	Aìqínhǎi
Andaman Sea	安达曼海	Āndámànhǎi
Baltic Sea	波罗的海	Bōluódìhǎi
Bering Sea	白令海	Báilìnghǎi
Black Sea	黑海	Hēihǎi
Bohai Sea	渤海	Bóhǎi
Caribbean Sea	加勒比海	Jiālèbǐhǎi
Coral Sea	珊瑚海	Shānhúhǎi
East China Sea	东海	Dōnghǎi
Greenland Sea	格林兰海	Gélínlánhǎi
Gulf of Mexico	墨西哥湾	Mòxīgēwān
Hudson Bay	赫德逊湾	Hèdéxùnwān
Japan Sea	日本海	Rìběnhǎi
Mediterranean Sea	地中海	Dìzhōnghǎi
North Sea	北海	Běihǎi
Okhotsk Sea	鄂霍次克海	Èhuòcìkèhǎi
Red Sea	红海	Hónghǎi
South China Sea	南海	Nánhǎi
Yellow Sea	黄海	Huánghǎi

3.1.8 Major rivers in the world

River	Chinese	Pinyin	Location
Nile	尼罗河	Níluóhé	Africa
Amazon	亚马孙河	Yàmǎsūnhé	South America
Changjiang/ Yangtze	长江 / 扬子江	Chángjiāng/ Yángzǐjiāng	China
Huanghe/ Yellow	黄河	Huánghé	China
Ob/Obi	鄂华河	Èhuáhé	Russia
Heilongjiang/ Amur	黑龙江	Hēilóngjiāng	China
Lena	勒拿河	Lènáhé	Russia
Congo	刚果河	Gāngguǒhé	Africa
Mackenzie	马更些河	Mǎgèngxiēhé	Canada
Mekong	湄公河	Méigōnghé	Southeast Asia
Niger	尼日尔河	Nírì'ěrhé	Africa
Yenisey	叶尼塞河	Yènísàihé	Russia
Parana	巴拉那河	Bālānàhé	South America
Mississippi	密西西比河	Mìxīxībǐhé	USA
Missouri	密苏里河	Mìsūlǐhé	USA
Volga	伏尔加河	Fú'ěrjiāhé	Russia
Purus	普鲁斯河	Pǔlǔsīhé	Brazil
Madeira	马代腊河	Mǎdàilàhé	Brazil
Yukon	育空河	Yùkōnghé	Canada
Rio Grande	格兰德河	Gélándéhé	USA, Mexico
Brahmaputra	布拉马普特拉河	Bùlāmǎpǔtèlāhé	China, India
Indus	印度河	Yìndùhé	Pakistan
Danube	多瑙河	Duōnǎohé	Germany
St. Lawrence	圣劳伦斯河	Shèngláolúnsīhé	Canada
Euphrates	幼发拉底河	Yòufālādǐhé	Turkey, Iraq, etc.

River	Chinese	Pinyin	Location
Tigris	底格里斯河	Dǐgélǐsīhé	Turkey, Iran, Iraq
Ganges	恒河	Hénghé	Himalayas
Saskatchewan	萨斯喀切温河	Sāsīkāqièwēnhé	Canada
Don	顿河	Dùnhé	Russia
Peace	和平河	Hépínghé	Canada

3.1.9 Rivers in China

There are more than 1,500 rivers in China, each of which drains 1,000 or more square kilometers. The Changjiang River is the longest and the Huanghe River the second longest. The Zhujiang River is the longest in the south. The Changjiang River is also the third longest in the world.

The table lists rivers longer than 1,000 kilometers:

Rivers longer than 1,000 kilometers

Changjiang River/ Yangtze River	长江 / 扬子江	Chángjiāng/ Yángzǐjiāng
Huanghe River/ Yellow River	黄河	Huánghé
Heilongjiang River/ Amur River	黑龙江	Hēilóngjiāng
Zhujiang River/Pearl River	珠江	Zhūjiāng
Lancang River	澜沧江	Láncāngjiāng
Talimu River	塔里木河	Tǎlǐmùhé
Yaluzangbu River	雅鲁藏布江	Yǎlǔzàngbùjiāng
Nu River/Salween River	怒江	Nùjiāng
Songhua River/ Sungari River	松花江	Sōnghuājiāng
Han River	汉水	Hànshuǐ
Yalong River	雅砻江	Yǎlóngjiāng
Liao River	辽河	Liáohé

Yu River	郁江	Yùjiāng
Jialing River	嘉陵江	Jiālíngjiāng
Hai River	海河	Hǎihé
Hetian River	和田河	Hétiánhé
Nen River/Nonni River	嫩江	Nènjiāng
Dadu River	大渡河	Dàdùhé
Yuan River	沅江	Yuánjiāng
Wu River	乌江	Wūjiāng
Huai River	淮河	Huáihé

3.1.10 Major lakes in the world

Lake	Chinese	Pinyin	Location
Caspian Sea	里海	Lǐhǎi	Russia, Iran
Superior	苏必利湖	Sūbìlìhú	USA, Canada
Victoria	维多利亚湖	Wéiduōlìyàhú	Africa
Huron	休伦湖	Xiūlúnhú	USA, Canada
Michigan	密西根湖	Mìxīgēnhú	USA
Tanganyika	坦葛尼喀湖	Tǎngěníkāhú	Africa
Baikal	贝加尔湖	Bèijiā'ěrhú	Russia
Great Bear	大熊湖	Dàxiónghú	Canada
Nyasa	尼亚萨湖	Níyàsāhú	Africa
Great Slave	大奴湖	Dànúhú	Canada
Chad	乍得湖	Zhàdéhú	Africa
Erie	伊利湖	Yīlìhú	USA, Canada
Winnipeg	温尼伯湖	Wēnníbóhú	Canada
Ontario	安大略湖	Āndàluèhú	USA, Canada
Ladoga	拉多加湖	Lāduōjiāhú	Russia

Lake	Chinese	Pinyin	Location
Oniga	奥涅加湖	Àonièjiāhú	Russia
Titicaca	的的喀喀湖	Dìdìkākāhú	South America
Nicaragua	尼加拉瓜湖	Níjiālāguāhú	Nicaragua
Athabaska	阿撒巴斯卡湖	Āsābāsīkǎhú	Canada
Turkana/Rudolf	图尔卡纳湖 / 卢多尔夫湖	Tú'ěrkǎnàhú/ Lúduō'ěrfūhú	Kenya
Reindeer	伦迪尔湖	Lúndí'ěrhú	Canada
Eyre	埃尔湖	Āi'ěrhú	South Australia
Urmia	乌米亚湖	Wūmǐyàhú	Iran
Vänern	维纳恩湖	Wéinà'ēnhú	Sweden
Great Salt	大盐湖	Dàyánhú	USA
Qinghai	青海湖	Qīnghǎihú	China

3.1.11 Lakes in China

According to published statistics, there are around 2,600 lakes which are one square kilometer or over, in China. They include fresh and saltwater lakes.

Some important lakes in China:

Name	Chinese	Pinyin	Province
Poyang Lake	鄱阳湖	Póyánghú	Jiangxi
Dongting Lake	洞庭湖	Dòngtínghú	Hunan
Taihu Lake	太湖	Tàihú	Jiangsu
Hongze Lake	洪泽湖	Hóngzéhú	Jiangsu
Lake Chaohu	巢湖	Cháohú	Anhui
Nantian Lake	南田湖	Nántiánhú	Shandong
Lake Dianchi	滇池	Diānchí	Yunnan
Erhai Lake	洱海	Ěrhǎi	Yunnan
Lake Jingpo	镜泊湖	Jìngpōhú	Heilongjiang
Sun Moon Lake	日月潭	Rìyuètán	Taiwan

Name	Chinese	Pinyin	Province
Qinghai Lake/ Koko Nor	青海湖	Qīnghǎihú	Qinghai
Namtso Lake	纳木错	Nàmùcuò	Tibet
Lake Honghu	洪湖	Hónghú	Hubei
West Lake	西湖	Xīhú	Zhejiang

3.1.12 Countries and their capitals

Depending on the point of view and who is counting, the number of countries in the world may range from 186 to well over 200. The more accurate number, however, is believed to be 193, that is, 192 members of the United Nations plus Vatican City. The following table includes most of the countries.

Asia	亚洲	**Yàzhōu**			
Country	*Chinese*	*Pinyin*	*Capital*	*Chinese*	*Pinyin*
Afghanistan	阿富汗	Āfùhàn	Kabul	喀布尔	Kābù'ěr
Azerbaijan	阿塞拜疆	Āsàibàijiāng	Baku	巴库	Bākù
Bangladesh	孟加拉国	Mèngjiālāguó	Dacca	达卡	Dákǎ
Bhutan	不丹	Bùdān	Thimphu	廷布	Tíngbù
Brunei	文莱	Wénlái	Bandar Seri Begawan	斯里巴加湾市	Sīlǐbājiāwān shì
Burma/ Myanmar	缅甸	Miǎndiàn	Rangoon	仰光	Yǎngguāng
Cambodia	柬埔寨	Jiǎnpǔzhài	Phnom Penh	金边	Jīnbiān
China	中国	Zhōngguó	Beijing	北京	Běijīng
Georgia	乔治亚	Qiáozhìyà	Tbilisi	提比里西	Tíbǐlǐxī
India	印度	Yìndù	New Delhi	新德里	Xīndélǐ
Indonesia	印度尼西亚	Yìndùníxīyà	Djakarta	雅加达	Yǎjiādá
Japan	日本	Rìběn	Tokyo	东京	Dōngjīng
Kazakstan	卡扎克斯坦	Kǎzhákèsītǎn	Astana	阿斯坦纳	Āsītǎnnà
Korea (South)	韩国	Hánguó	Seoul	汉城	Hànchéng
Laos	老挝	Lǎowō	Vientiane	万象	Wànxiàng
Malaysia	马来西亚	Mǎláixīyà	Kuala Lumpur	吉隆坡	Jílóngpō

Country	Chinese	Pinyin	Capital	Chinese	Pinyin
Mongolia	蒙古	Měnggǔ	Ulan Bator	乌兰巴托	Wūlánbātuō
Nepal	尼泊尔	Nípō'ěr	Katmandu	加德满都	Jiādémǎndū
North Korea	朝鲜	Cháoxiǎn	Pyongyang	平壤	Píngrǎng
Pakistan	巴基斯坦	Bājīsītǎn	Islamabad	伊斯兰堡	Yīsīlánbǎo
Philippines	菲律宾	Fēilùbīn	Manila	马尼拉	Mǎnílā
Russia	俄罗斯	Éluósī	Moscow	莫斯科	Mòsīkē
Saudi Arabia	沙特阿拉伯	Shātè Ālābó	Riyadh	利雅得	Lìyǎdé
Singapore	新加坡	Xīnjiāpō	Singapore	新加坡	Xīnjiāpō
Sri Lanka	斯里兰卡	Sīlǐlánkǎ	Colombo	科伦坡	Kēlúnpō
Tajikistan	塔吉克斯坦	Tǎjíkèsītǎn	Dushanbe	杜尚别	Dùshàngbié
Thailand	泰国	Tàiguó	Bangkok	曼谷	Màngǔ
Turkey	土耳其	Tǔ'ěrqí	Ankara	安卡拉	Ānkǎlā
Uzbekistan	乌兹别克	Wūzībiékè	Tashkent	塔什干	Tǎshígān
Vietnam	越南	Yuènán	Hanoi	河内	Hénèi

Africa	非洲	**Fēizhōu**			
Country	Chinese	Pinyin	Capital	Chinese	Pinyin
Algeria	阿尔及利亚	Ā'ěrjílìyà	Algiers	阿尔及尔	Ā'ěrjí'ěr
Angola	安哥拉	Āngēlā	Luanda	罗安达	Luó'āndá
Benin	贝宁	Bèiníng	Porto Novo	波多诺伏	Bōduōnuòfú
Botswana	博兹瓦纳	Bózīwǎnà	Gaborone	加博罗内	Jiābóluónèi
Cameroon	喀麦隆	Kāmàilóng	Yaoundé	雅温得	Yǎwēndé
Cape Verde	佛得角	Fódéjiǎo	Praia	普拉亚	Púlāyà
Central Africa Republic	中非共和国	Zhōngfēi Gònghéguó	Banjul	班吉	Bānjí
Chad	乍得	Zhàdé	N'Djamena	恩贾梅纳	Ēnjiǎméinà
Comoros	科摩罗	Kēmóluó	Moroni	莫罗尼	Mòluóní
Congo	刚果	Gāngguǒ	Brazzaville	布啦柴维尔	Bùlācháiwéi'ěr
Cote d'ivoire	象牙海岸	Xiàngyáhǎi'àn	Abidjan	阿比让	Ābǐràng

Country	Chinese	Pinyin	Capital	Chinese	Pinyin
Egypt	埃及	Āijí	Cairo	开罗	Kāiluó
Equatorial Guinea	赤道几内亚	Chìdàojǐnèiyà	Malabo	马拉博	Mǎlābó
Ethiopia	埃塞俄比亚	Āisài'ébǐyà	Addis Ababa	亚的斯亚贝巴	Yàdìsīyàbèibā
Gambia	冈比亚	Gāngbǐyà	Banjul	班珠尔	Bānzhū'ěr
Ghana	加纳	Jiānà	Accra	阿克拉	Ākèlā
Guinea	几内亚	Jǐnèiyà	Conakry	科纳克里	Kēnàkèlǐ
Guinea-Bissau	几内亚比绍	Jǐnèiyàbǐshào	Bissau	比绍	Bǐshào
Kenya	肯尼亚	Kěnníyà	Nairobi	内罗毕	Nèiluóbì
Lesotho	莱索托	Láisuǒtuō	Maseru	马塞卢	Mǎsàilú
Liberia	利比里亚	Lìbǐlǐyà	Monrovia	蒙罗维亚	Méngluówéiyà
Libya	利比亚	Lìbǐyà	Tripoli	的黎波里	Dìlíbōlǐ
Madagascar	马达加斯加	Mǎdájiāsījiā	Tananarive	塔那那利佛	Tǎnànàlìfó
Malawi	马拉维	Mǎlāwéi	Lilongwe	利隆圭	Lìlóngguī
Mali	马里	Mǎlǐ	Bamako	巴马科	Bāmǎkē
Morocco	摩洛哥	Móluògē	Rabat	拉巴特	Lābātè
Mozambique	莫桑比克	Mòsāngbǐkè	Maputo	马普托	Mǎpǔtuō
Namibia	纳米比亚	Nàmǐbǐyà	Windhoek	温得和克	Wēndéhékè
Nigeria	尼日利亚	Nírìlìyà	Lagos	拉各斯	Lāgèsī
Rwanda	卢旺达	Lúwàngdá	Kigali	基加利	Jījiālì
Sao Tomé and Principe	圣多美和普林西比	Shèngduōměi hé Pǔlínxībǐ	Sao Tomé	圣多美	Shèngduōměi
Senegal	塞内加尔	Sàinèijiā'ěr	Dakar	达喀尔	Dákā'ěr
Seychelles	塞舌尔	Sàishé'ěr	Victoria	维多利亚	Wéiduōlìyà
Sierra Leone	塞拉利昂	Sàilālì'áng	Freetown	佛里敦	Fólǐdūn
Somalia	索马里	Suǒmǎlǐ	Mogadishu	摩加迪沙	Mójiādíshā
South Africa	南非	Nánfēi	Pretoria	比勒陀利亚	Bǐlètuólìyà
Sudan	苏丹	Sūdān	Khartoum	喀土穆	Kātǔmù
Swaziland	斯威士兰	Sīwēishìlán	Mbabane	姆巴巴纳	Mǔbābānà

Country	Chinese	Pinyin	Capital	Chinese	Pinyin
Tanzania	坦桑尼亚	Tǎnsāngníyà	Dar es Salaam	达累斯萨拉姆	Dálèisīsālāmǔ
Togo	多哥	Duōgē	Lomé	洛美	Luòměi
Tunisia	突尼斯	Tūnísī	Tunis	突尼斯	Tūnísī
Uganda	乌干达	Wūgāndá	Kampala	坎帕拉	Kǎnpàlā
Western Sahara	西撒哈拉	Xīsāhālā	N/A		
Zambia	赞比亚	Zànbǐyà	Lusaka	卢萨卡	Lúsākǎ
Zimbabwe	津巴布韦	Jīnbābùwéi	Salisbury	索尔兹伯里	Suǒ'ěrzībólǐ

Central America	中美洲	**Zhōngměizhōu**			
Country	Chinese	Pinyin	Capital	Chinese	Pinyin
Belize	伯里兹	Bólǐzī	Belmopan	贝尔莫潘	Bèi'ěrmòpān
Costa Rica	哥斯达黎加	Gēsīdálíjiā	San Jose	圣约瑟	Shèngyuēsè
El Salvador	萨尔瓦多	Sà'ěrwǎduō	San Salvador	圣萨尔瓦多	Shèngsà'ěrwǎduō
Guatemala	危地马拉	Wēidìmǎlā	Guatemala City	危地马拉市	Wēidìmǎlāshì
Honduras	洪都拉斯	Hóngdūlāsī	Tegucigalpa	特古西加尔巴	Tègǔxījiā'ěrbā
Nicaragua	尼加拉瓜	Níjiālāguā	Managua	马那瓜	Mǎnàguā
Panama	巴拿马	Bānámǎ	Panama City	巴拿马城	Bānámǎ chéng

Caribbean	加勒比	**Jiālèbǐ**			
Country	Chinese	Pinyin	Capital	Chinese	Pinyin
Antigua and Barbuda	安提瓜和巴布达	Āntíguā hé Bābùdá	St. John's	圣约翰	Shèngyuēhàn
Bahamas, The	巴哈马	Bāhāmǎ	Nassau	拿骚	Násāo
Barbados	巴巴多斯	Bābāduōsī	Bridgetown	布里奇顿	Bùlǐqídùn
Cuba	古巴	Gǔbā	Havana	哈瓦那	Hāwǎnà
Dominica	多米尼克	Duōmǐníkè	Roseau	罗索	Luósuǒ
Dominican Republic	多米尼加共和国	Duōmǐníjiā Gònghéguó	Santo Domingo	圣多明各	Shèngduō mínggè

Country	Chinese	Pinyin	Capital	Chinese	Pinyin
Grenada	格林纳达	Gélínnàdá	St. George	圣乔治	Shèngqiáozhì
Haiti	海地	Hǎidì	Port-au-Prince	太子港	Tàizǐgǎng
Jamaica	牙买加	Yámǎijiā	Kingston	金斯敦	Jīnsīdūn
Saint Kitts and Nevis	圣基茨和尼维斯	Shèngjīcī hé Níwéisī	Basseterre	巴斯特尔	Bāsītè'ěr
Saint Lucia	圣卢西亚	Shènglúxīyà	Castries	卡斯特里	Kǎsītèlǐ
Saint Vincent and the Grenadines	圣文森特和格林纳丁斯	Shèngwénsēntè hé Gélínnàdīngsī	Kingstown	金斯敦	Jīnsīdūn
Trinidad and Tobago	特立尼达和多巴哥	Tèlìnídá hé Duōbāgē	Port of Spain	西班牙港	Xībānyágǎng

North America	北美洲	**Běiměizhōu**			
Country	Chinese	Pinyin	Capital	Chinese	Pinyin
Canada	加拿大	Jiānádà	Ottawa	渥太华	Wòtàihuá
Mexico	墨西哥	Mòxīgē	Mexico City	墨西哥城	Mòxīgēchéng
United States	美国 / 美利坚合众国	Měiguó/ Měilìjiān Hézhòngguó	Washington D.C.	华盛顿	Huáshèngdùn

Europe	欧洲	**Ōuzhōu**			
Country	Chinese	Pinyin	Capital	Chinese	Pinyin
Albania	阿尔巴尼亚	Ā'ěrbāníyà	Tirana	地拉那	Dìlānà
Andorra	安道尔	Āndào'ěr	Andorra	安道尔	Āndào'ěr
Austria	奥地利	Àodìlì	Vienna	维也纳	Wéiyěnà
Belgium	比利时	Bǐlìshí	Brussels	布鲁塞尔	Bùlǔsài'ěr
Bosnia and Herzegovina	波斯尼亚和黑塞哥维那	Bōsīníyà hé Hēisàigēwéinà	Sarajevo	萨拉热窝	Sālārèwō
Bulgaria	保加利亚	Bǎojiālìyà	Sofia	索非亚	Suǒfēiyà
Czech Republic	捷克	Jiékè	Prague	布拉格	Bùlāgé
Denmark	丹麦	Dānmài	Copenhagen	哥本哈根	Gēběnhāgēn

Country	Chinese	Pinyin	Capital	Chinese	Pinyin
England/ United Kingdom	英国 / 联合 王国	Yīngguó/Liánhé Wángguó	London	伦敦	Lúndūn
Finland	芬兰	Fēnlán	Helsinki	赫尔辛基	Hè'ěrxīnjī
France	法国	Fǎguó	Paris	巴黎	Bālí
Germany	德国	Déguó	Berlin	柏林	Bólín
Greece	希腊	Xīlà	Athens	雅典	Yǎdiǎn
Hungary	匈牙利	Xiōngyálì	Budapest	布达佩斯	Bùdápèisī
Iceland	冰岛	Bīngdǎo	Reykjavik	雷克雅未克	Léikèyǎwèikè
Ireland	爱尔兰	Ài'ěrlán	Dublin	都柏林	Dūbólín
Italy	意大利	Yìdàlì	Rome	罗马	Luómǎ
Liechtenstein	列支敦士登	Lièzhīdūnshìdēng	Vaduz	瓦杜兹	Wǎdùzī
Luxembourg	卢森堡	Lúsēnbǎo	Luxembourg	卢森堡	Lúsēnbǎo
Monaco	摩纳哥	Mónàgē	Monaco-Ville	摩纳哥	Mónàgē
Netherlands	荷兰	Hélán	Amsterdam	阿姆斯特丹	Āmǔsītèdān
Norway	挪威	Nuówēi	Oslo	奥斯陆	Àosīlù
Poland	波兰	Bōlán	Warsaw	华沙	Huáshā
Portugal	葡萄牙	Pútáoyá	Lisbon	里斯本	Lǐsīběn
Romania	罗马尼亚	Luómǎníyà	Bucharest	布加勒斯特	Bùjiālèsītè
Russia	俄罗斯	Éluósī	Moscow	莫斯科	Mòsīkē
San Marino	圣马力诺	Shèngmǎlìnuò	San Marino	圣马力诺	Shèngmǎlìnuò
Spain	西班牙	Xībānyá	Madrid	马德里	Mǎdélǐ
Sweden	瑞典	Ruìdiǎn	Stockholm	斯德格尔摩	Sīdégé'ěrmó
Switzerland	瑞士	Ruìshì	Berne	伯尔尼	Bó'ěrní
Vatican/Holy See	梵蒂冈 / 教廷	Fándìgāng/ Jiàotíng			

Middle East	中东	Zhōngdōng			
Country	*Chinese*	*Pinyin*	*Capital*	*Chinese*	*Pinyin*
Iran	伊朗	Yīlǎng	Tehran	德黑兰	Déhēilán
Iraq	伊拉克	Yīlākè	Baghdad	巴格达	Bāgédá
Israel	以色列	Yǐsèliè	Jerusalem	耶路撒冷	Yélùsālěng
Jordan	约旦	Yuēdàn	Amman	安曼	Ānmàn
Kuwait	科威特	Kēwēitè	Kuwait	科威特	Kēwēitè
Lebanon	黎巴嫩	Líbānèn	Beirut	贝鲁特	Bèilǔtè
Oman	阿曼	Āmàn	Muscat	马斯喀特	Mǎsīkātè
Qatar	卡塔尔	Kǎtǎ'ěr	Doha	多哈	Duōhā
Saudi Arabia	沙特阿拉伯	Shātè'ālābó	Riyadh	利雅得	Lìyǎdé
Syria	叙利亚	Xùlìyà	Damascus	大马士革	Dàmǎshìgé
United Arab Emirates	阿拉伯联合酋长国	Ālābóliánhé qiúzhǎngguó	Abu Dhabi	阿布扎比	Ābùzhābǐ
Yemen	也门	Yěmén	Sana	萨那	Sānà

Oceania	大洋洲	Dàyángzhōu			
Country	*Chinese*	*Pinyin*	*Capital*	*Chinese*	*Pinyin*
Australia	澳大利亚	Àodàlìyà	Canberra	堪培拉	Kānpéilā
Cook Islands	库克群岛	Kùkèqúndǎo	Avarua	阿瓦鲁阿	Āwǎlǔ'ā
Fiji	斐济	Fěijì	Suva	苏瓦	Sūwǎ
Marshall Islands	马绍尔群岛	Mǎshào'ěr qúndǎo	Majuro	马朱罗	Mǎzhūluó
Federated States of Micronesia	蜜克罗尼西亚	Mìkèluóníxīyà	Palikir	帕利基尔	Pàlìjī'ěr
Nauru	瑙鲁	Nǎolǔ	Nauru	瑙鲁	Nǎolǔ
New Zealand	新西兰	Xīnxīlán	Wellington	惠灵顿	Huìlíngdùn
Palau	帕劳	Pàláo	Koror	科罗尔	Kēluó'ěr
Samoa	萨摩亚	Sāmóyà	Apia	阿皮亚	Āpíyà
Solomon Islands	所罗门群岛	Suǒluómén qúndǎo	Honiara	霍尼亚拉	Huòníyàlā

Country	Chinese	Pinyin	Capital	Chinese	Pinyin
Tonga	汤加王国	Tāngjiā Wángguó	Nuku'alofa	努库阿洛法	Núkù'āluòfǎ
Vanuatu	瓦努阿图	Wǎnú'ātú	Port Vila	维拉港	Wéilāgǎng

South America 南美洲 Nánměizhōu					
Country	Chinese	Pinyin	Capital	Chinese	Pinyin
Argentina	阿根廷	Āgēntíng	Buenos Aires	布宜诺斯艾利斯	Bùyínuòsī'àilìsī
Bolivia	玻利维亚	Bōlìwéiyà	La Paz	拉巴斯	Lābāsī
Brazil	巴西	Bāxī	Brasilia	巴西利亚	Bāxīlìyà
Chile	智利	Zhìlì	Santiago	圣地亚哥	Shèngdìyàgē
Colombia	哥伦比亚	Gēlúnbǐyà	Bogotá	波哥大	Bōgēdà
Ecuador	厄瓜多尔	Èguāduō'ěr	Quito	基多	Jīduō
Guyana	圭亚那	Guīyànà	Georgetown	乔治敦	Qiáozhìdūn
Paraguay	巴拉圭	Bālāguī	Asuncion	亚松森	Yàsōngsēn
Peru	秘鲁	Bìlǔ	Lima	利马	Lìmǎ
Uruguay	乌拉圭	Wūlāguī	Montevideo	蒙得维的亚	Méngdéwéidìyà
Venezuela	委内瑞拉	Wěinèiruìlā	Caracas	加拉加斯	Jiālājiāsī

3.1.13 Administrative divisions in China: municipalities, autonomous regions, provinces and their capitals, and special administrative regions

Administratively, there are four municipalities, 直辖市 zhíxiáshì, that function directly under the central government, five autonomous regions, 自治区 zìzhìqū, twenty-two provinces, 省 shěng and Taiwan, and two special administrative regions (SAR), 特别行政区 tèbié xíngzhèngqū, in China. Each of the above has its own abbreviated name, 简称 jiǎnchēng.

Municipalities			
Municipality	Pinyin	Abbreviation	Pinyin
北京	Běijīng	京	Jīng
上海	Shànghǎi	沪	Hù
天津	Tiānjīn	津	Jīn
重庆	Chóngqìng	渝	Yú

Special administrative regions				
Region	*Pinyin*	*English*	*Abbreviation*	*Pinyin*
香港	Xiānggǎng	Hong Kong	港	Gǎng
澳门	Àomén	Macau	澳	Ào

Autonomous regions and their capitals					
Region	*Pinyin*	*Abbreviation*	*Pinyin*	*Capital*	*Pinyin*
广西壮族自治区	Guǎngxī Zhuàngzú Zìzhìqū	桂	Guì	南宁	Nánníng
内蒙古自治区	Nèiměnggǔ Zìzhìqū	蒙	Měng	呼和浩特	Hūhéhàotè
宁夏回自治区	Níngxià Huí Zìzhìqū	宁	Níng	银川	Yínchuān
西藏自治区	Xīzàng Zìzhìqū	藏	Zàng	拉萨	Lāsā
新疆维吾尔自治区	Xīnjiāng Wéiwú'ěr Zìzhìqū	新	Xīn	乌鲁木齐	Wūlǔmùqí

Provinces and their capitals					
Province	*Pinyin*	*Abbreviation*	*Pinyin*	*Capital*	*Pinyin*
安徽	Ānhuī	皖	Wǎn	合肥	Héféi
福建	Fújiàn	闽	Mǐn	福州	Fúzhōu
甘肃	Gānsū	甘 / 陇	Gān/Lǒng	兰州	Lánzhōu
广东	Guǎngdōng	粤	Yuè	广州	Guǎngzhōu
贵州	Guìzhōu	黔 / 贵	Qián/Guì	贵阳	Guìyáng
海南	Hǎinán	琼	Qióng	海口	Hǎikǒu
河北	Héběi	冀	Jì	石家庄	Shíjiāzhuāng
河南	Hénán	豫	Yù	郑州	Zhèngzhōu
黑龙江	Hēilóngjiāng	黑	Hēi	哈尔滨	Hā'ěrbīn
湖北	Húběi	鄂	È	武汉	Wǔhàn
湖南	Húnán	湘	Xiāng	长沙	Chángshā
吉林	Jílín	吉	Jí	长春	Chángchūn

179

Province	Pinyin	Abbreviation	Pinyin	Capital	Pinyin
江苏	Jiāngsū	苏	Sū	南京	Nánjīng
江西	Jiāngxī	赣	Gàn	南昌	Nánchāng
辽宁	Liáoníng	辽	Liáo	沈阳	Shěnyáng
青海	Qīnghǎi	青	Qīng	西宁	Xīníng
山东	Shāndōng	鲁	Lǔ	济南	Jǐnán
山西	Shānxī	晋	Jìn	太原	Tàiyuán
陕西	Shǎnxī	陕 / 秦	Shǎn/Qín	西安	Xī'ān
四川	Sìchuān	川 / 蜀	Chuān/Shǔ	成都	Chéngdū
云南	Yúnnán	滇 / 云	Diān/Yún	昆明	Kūnmíng
浙江	Zhèjiāng	浙	Zhè	杭州	Hángzhōu
（台湾）*	Táiwān	台	Tái	台北	Táiběi
*China considers Taiwan to be part of the PRC, but Taiwan does not.					

3.2 Festivals

Spring Festival is the most widely celebrated and most important festival in China, and people generally get three days off from work. Students begin their winter vacation during this period. Various minority nationalities also have their own festivals.

The following are major traditional Han Chinese festivals and they are generally based on the Lunar calendar:

春节 chūnjié, Spring Festival, also known as traditional Chinese New Year: the first day of the first month of the lunar calendar, usually falling between early January and late February on the solar calendar. This is celebrated by family reunion, visiting friends and relatives, setting off firecrackers, wearing new clothes, and eating plenty of food. It is often compared to Christmas in the West.

元宵节 yuánxiāojié, Lantern Festival: the fifteenth day of the first lunar month. This festival is celebrated by making lanterns to parade or display, and by eating 圆宵/元宵 yuánxiāo, sweet rice dumplings.

清明节 qīngmíngjié, Tomb Sweeping Festival, also known as Clear and Bright Festival: usually in the third lunar month, or around April 5th. Activities include making offerings at family grave sites and going on spring outings.

端午节 duānwǔjié, Dragon Boat Festival: the fifth day of the fifth month of the lunar calendar. There are dragon boat races on this day and generally people eat 粽子 zòngzi, sweet rice dumplings wrapped in bamboo leaves.

中元节 zhōngyuánjié, Festival of the Ghosts, also known as 鬼节 guǐjié, Festival of the Hungry Ghosts: the fifteenth day of the seventh month of the lunar calendar. This is a day on which people burn paper money and/or make offerings to the souls of ancestors and others.

中秋节 zhōngqiūjié, Mid-Autumn Festival, also known as the Moon Festival: the fifteenth day of the eighth month of the lunar calendar. This is a day to celebrate the harvest and have family reunions. People also take advantage of the occasion to view and appreciate the harvest moon. Special food for the day is the moon cake, 月饼 yuèbǐng.

重阳节 chóngyángjié, Double-Ninth Festival: the ninth day of the ninth month of the lunar calendar. People take advantage of cool weather to make autumn outings and go mountain climbing.

腊八节 làbājié, Eighth of the Twelfth Month Festival: the eighth day of the twelfth lunar month. For some, this is an important day in the twelfth month of the lunar calendar. It is a day to pay respects to ancestors. It is said that this was the day on which Buddha achieved enlightenment. People eat congee cooked with mixed grains, nuts and dried fruits, known as 腊八粥 làbāzhōu.

3.3 Holidays

A new policy on public holidays came into effect on January 1, 2008. According to this new policy, there are a total of eleven days of official public holiday, 法定节日 fǎdìng jiérì. They are:

New Year's Day, 元旦 yuándàn	1 day
Spring Festival, 春节 chūnjié	3 days
Tomb Sweeping Festival, 清明节 qīngmíngjié	1 day
May 1st International Labor Day, "五一"国际劳动节 wǔyī guójì láodòngjié	1 day
Dragon Boat Festival, 端午节 duānwǔjié	1 day
Mid-Autumn Festival, 中秋节 zhōngqiūjié	1 day
National Day, 国庆节 guóqìngjié	3 days

The Spring Festival holiday starts on the day before the first day of the Lunar New Year. Linked together with the preceding or following weekends, it works out that there are two seven-day holidays: Spring Festival and National day. The other five usually become three-day holidays in practice.

3.4 Family relationships

The family is the most important unit in Chinese society so it is very important to know how the members of a family are related to each other and how the relationships are named. The following shows how the members of a family are named from the great grandparents' generation to the grandchildren's generation:

Great grandparents' generation	
Relation to self	*Chinese*
Paternal great grandfather	曾祖父 zēngzǔfù
Paternal great grandmother	曾祖母 zēngzǔmǔ
Maternal great grandfather	外曾祖父 wài zēngzǔfù
Maternal great grandmother	外曾祖母 wài zēngzǔmǔ

Grandparents' generation	
Relation to self	*Chinese*
Paternal grandfather	祖父 zǔfù/爷爷 yéye
Paternal grandmother	祖母 zǔmǔ/奶奶 nǎinai
Maternal grandfather	外祖父 wài zǔfù/老爷 lǎoye
Maternal grandmother	外祖母 wài zǔmǔ/外婆 wàipó/姥姥 lǎolao

Parents' generation	
Relation to self	*Chinese*
Uncle, father's elder brother	伯父 bófù/大爷 dàye
His wife	伯母 bómǔ/大娘 dàniáng
Aunt, father's elder sister	姑妈 gūmā
Her husband	姑丈 gūzhàng
Father	父亲 **fùqin**/爸爸 **bàba**
Father-in-law, father of wife	岳父 yuèfù
Father-in-law, father of husband	公公 gōnggong

Relation to self	Chinese
Uncle, father's younger brother	叔父 shūfù/叔叔 shūshu
His wife	叔母 shūmǔ/婶子shěnzi
Aunt, father's younger sister	姑姑 gūgu
Her husband	姑父 gūfu
Uncle, mother's elder brother	舅父 jiùfu/舅舅 jiùjiu
His wife	舅母 jiùmu/舅妈 jiùmā
Aunt, mother's elder sister	姨母 yímǔ/ 姨妈 yímā
Her husband	姨父 yífù
Mother	母亲 **mǔqin**/妈妈 **māma**
Mother-in-law, mother of wife	岳母 yuèmǔ
Mother-in-law, mother of husband	婆婆 pópo
Uncle, mother's younger brother	舅父 jiùfu/舅舅 jiùjiu
His wife	舅母 jiùmu/舅妈 jiùmā
Aunt, mother's younger sister	姨妈 yímā/姨 yí
Her husband	姨父 yífù

One's own generation	
Relation to self	Chinese
Brother, elder	哥哥 gēge
Sister-in-law, his wife	嫂子 sǎozi/嫂嫂 sǎosao
Sister, elder	姐姐 jiějie
Brother-in-law, her husband	姐夫 jiěfu
Cousin, paternal older male cousin	堂兄 tángxiōng
His wife	堂嫂 tángsǎo
Cousin, paternal older female cousin	堂姐 tángjiě
Her husband	堂姐夫 tǎngjiěfu
Cousin, maternal older male cousin	表哥 biǎogē

183

Relation to self	Chinese
His wife	表嫂 biǎosǎo
Cousin, maternal older female cousin	表姐 biǎojiě
Her husband	表姐夫 biǎojiěfu
Self	**自己 zìjǐ/我 wǒ**
Husband	丈夫 zhàngfu/先生 xiānsheng/爱人 àiren
Wife	妻子 qīzi/太太 tàitai/爱人 àiren
Brother, younger	弟弟 dìdi
Sister-in-law, his wife	弟妹 dìmèi
Sister, younger	妹妹 mèimei
Brother-in-law, her husband	妹夫 mèifu
Cousin, paternal younger male cousin	堂弟 tángdì
His wife	堂弟妹 tángdìmèi
Cousin, paternal younger female cousin	堂妹 tángmèi
Her husband	堂妹夫 tángmèifu
Cousin, maternal younger male cousin	表弟 biǎodì
His wife	表弟媳 biǎodìxí
Cousin, maternal younger female cousin	表妹 biǎomèi
Her husband	表妹夫 biǎomèifu

Children's generation	
Relation to self	Chinese
Nephew, brother's son	侄子 zhízi/侄儿 zhí'er
His wife	侄媳妇 zhíxífu
Niece, brother's daughter	侄女 zhínü
Her husband	侄女婿 zhínǚxu

Relation to self	Chinese
Son	儿子 **érzi**
Daughter-in-law, his wife	媳妇 xífu
Daughter	女儿 **nǚ'er**
Son-in-law, her husband	女婿 nǚxu
Nephew, sister's son	外甥 wàisheng
His wife	外甥媳妇 wàishēng xífu
Niece, sister's daughter	外甥女 wàishēngnǚ
Her husband	外甥女婿 wàishēng nǚxu

Grandchildren's generation	
Relation to self	Chinese
Grandson, son's son	孙子 **sūnzi**
His wife	孙媳妇 sūnxífu
Granddaughter, son's daughter	孙女 **sūnnü**
Her husband	孙女婿 sūnnǚxu
Grandson, daughter's son	外孙 wàisūn
His wife	外孙媳妇 wàisūn xífu
Granddaughter, daughter's daughter	外孙女 wàisūnnǚ
Her husband	外孙女婿 wàisūn nǚxu

When there is more than one person of a generation, then "大 dà," "二 èr," "三 sān," etc. can be added to name them. For example, the eldest sister is "大姐 dàjiě," the next is "二姐 èrjiě," etc.

A stepfather is "后父 hòufù or 继父 jìfù" and a stepmother is "后母 hòumǔ or 继母 jìmǔ," while a stepson is "义子 yìzǐ" and a stepdaughter is "义女 yìnǚ."

3.5   Forms of address

It is important to use an appropriate term to address a person. It shows that one is cultivated and knows how to show respect to the other person, and it clarifies the relationship between the people concerned.

The following are different forms of addressing people:

1. Using family relationship:
Unlike common usage in English, one should not address a family member using just the first name. One addresses them using their family relationship (refer to family relationship section) terms. For different aunts: 姑姑 gūgu, 姨妈 yímā, etc. For different uncles: 伯伯 bóbo, 叔叔 shūshu, 舅舅 jiùjiu, etc. For the same generation: 大哥 dàgē, 二姐 èrjiě, 堂哥 tánggē, 表妹 biǎomèi, etc. Husband and wife address each other using first names or 老伴儿 lǎobànr, old companion, if they are older.

2. Using family relationship terms in a social situation:
If the speaker is younger, he/she might address people as: 叔叔 shūshu, uncle; 阿姨 āyí, aunt; 爷爷 yéye, grandpa; 奶奶 nǎinai, grandma, etc.

3. More polite:
Surname + one of the following: 先生 xiānsheng, Mr.; 夫人 fūren, madam; 太太 tàitai, Mrs.; 女士 nǔshì, Ms.; 小姐 xiǎojie, Miss. For example: 张先生 Zhāng xiānsheng; 田夫人 Tián fūren, etc.

4. Using names:
Full names or personal names are generally used among colleagues and people who know each other well, as in the following variations: (1) using full name; (2) for both sexes: 老 lǎo (older), 大 dà (similar age) or 小 xiǎo (younger) + surname. For example: 老张 Lǎo Zhāng, 大李 Dà Lǐ, 小王 Xiǎo Wáng; (3) using only first name: generally only used among the same sex, older to younger, husband and wife, close friends, schoolmates and neighbors.

5. Surname + lǎo:
For socially respected and accomplished persons of both sexes: 周老 Zhōu Lǎo, 田老 Tián Lǎo.

6. Using the person's profession:
Only using the name of the profession or surname + profession. These can be: 教授 jiàoshòu, professor; 博士 bóshì, Dr. (Ph.D.), 老师 lǎoshī, teacher or someone accomplished in a field of endeavor; 大夫 dàifu/医生 yīshēng, medical doctor; 会计 kuàiji, accountant; 律师 lùshī, lawyer; 大使 dàshǐ, ambassador; 参赞 cānzàn, counsellor; 总领事 zǒnglǐngshì, consul general; 领事 lǐngshì, consul; 总经理 zǒngjīnglǐ, president (of a company), etc.

7. Using position titles:
(1) using only position title; (2) surname + position title; (3) full name + position title. Here are some position titles: 部长 bùzhǎng, Minister (of a government department); 省长 shěngzhǎng, Governor/Premier; 市长 shìzhǎng, Mayor; 处长 chùzhǎng, Bureau Chief/Director; 校长 xiàozhǎng, President/Principal; 院长 yuànzhǎng, Dean; 主任 zhǔrèn, Director.

8. Addressing strangers:
(1) For a young person to address an older person: 老大爷 lǎodàye, "grandpa"; 老大娘 lǎodàniáng, "grandma"; (2) to address a store

clerk, a taxi driver, etc.: 师傅 shīfu, "master worker"; (3) to address young children: 小朋友 xiǎo péngyou, little friend (s); 小姑娘 xiǎo gūniang, young girl; 小伙子 xiǎo hǔozi, young chap.

3.6 Social interaction

3.6.1 Greetings

(1) general:

你好！
Nǐ hǎo!
How are you?; Good morning/afternoon/evening!

您好！
Nín hǎo!
(polite form of above)

你们早！
Nǐmen zǎo!
Good morning everybody!

早上好！
Zǎoshang hǎo!
Good morning!

晚安。
Wǎn ān.
Good night.

好久不见，您身体好吗？
Hǎojiǔ bújiàn, nín shēnti hǎo ma?
Long time no see. How are you doing?

欢迎欢迎！
Huānyíng, huānyíng!
Welcome!

(2) more famliar, intimate, more casual, or when running into each other:

吃饭了吗？
Chīfànle ma?
(Have you eaten?); How are you doing?

上班去？
Shàngbānqu?
Going to work?

下班啦？
Xiàbān la?
Just off work?

上课去？
Shàngkè qu?
Going to classes?

上哪儿去？
Shàng nǎr qu?
Where to?/Hello!

工作忙吧？
Gōngzuò máng ba?
Busy with your work?

家里都好吧？
Jiāli dōu hǎo ba?
Everybody fine in your family?

身体好吧？
Shēnti hǎo ba?
How are you doing?/Are you doing well?

(3) by addressing a person, 称呼 chēnghu:

周老师！
Zhōu lǎoshī!
Professor Zhōu!

老王！
Lǎo Wáng!
Hi! Wang!
Responses: smile, nod, or ask the same question in return.

3.6.2 Introductions

(1) introducing others:

我给您介绍一下儿，这位是大为。
Wǒ gěi nín jièshaoyixiar, zhèwei shi Dàwèi.
Let me introduce you. This is David.

您好。认识你，很高兴。
Nín hǎo. Rènshi nǐ, hěn gāoxìng.
How do you do? I'm happy to know you.

(2) self-introduction:

我叫玛利。您贵姓？
Wǒ jiào Mǎlì. Nín guìxìng?
My name is Mary. What is your honorable surname?

免贵，我姓唐。
Miǎn guì, wǒ xìng Táng.
Please do not say 'honorable'. It is Tang.

幸会！ 幸会！
Xìnghuì! xìnghuì!
So fortunate to have met you!

3.6.3   Farewells

(1)   general:

再见！
Zàijiàn!
Goodbye!

再会！
Zàihuì!
(another form of above)

明天见。
Míngtian jiàn.
See you tomorrow.

回头见。
Huítóu jiàn.
See you later.

一会儿见。
Yìhuǐr jiàn.
See you shortly.

再见，一路平安！
Zàijiàn, yílùpíng'ān!
Goodbye, bon voyage!

(2)   when seeing off a guest:

慢走！
Mànzǒu!
Take it easy./Drive safe!/Drive safely.

有空儿再来玩儿。
Yǒukòngr, zài lái wánr.
Come to visit again when you have time.

Responses:

请留步。
Qǐng liúbù.
Please do not walk me any farther.

请回。
Qǐng huí.
Please go back.

3.6.4   Apologies

对不起。
Duìbuqǐ.
Sorry.

太对不起了。
Tài duìbuqǐle.
So sorry.

真对不起。
Zhēn duìbuqǐ.
Really sorry.

真抱歉。
Zhēn bàoqiàn.
Truly sorry.

对不起，我插一句，好吗？
Duìbuqǐ, wǒ chā yíjù, hǎo ma?
I'm sorry. May I interrupt?

请原谅。
Qǐng yuánliàng.
I beg your pardon./Please forgive me.

Responses:

没关系。
Méi guānxi.
That's all right.

不要紧。
Bú yàojǐn.
No problem.

可以。
Kěyi.
Fine.

3.6.5 Requests

请问，厕所在那儿？
Qǐng wèn, cèsuǒ zài nǎr?
May I ask, where is the washroom?

请慢点儿说。
Qǐng màndiǎnr shuō.
Please speak more slowly.

请帮帮忙，好吗？
Qǐng bāngbang máng, hǎo ma?
Can you help me, please?

劳驾，我看看那件大衣。
Láojià, wǒ kànkan nàjiàn dàyī.
May I trouble you? I'd like to take a look at that coat.

我们是不是最好别打扰他？
Wǒmen shìbushi zuìhǎo bié dǎrǎo tā?
Would it be better if we do not disturb him?

我能不能看一下儿这个新电脑？
Wǒ néngbunéng kànyixiar zhège xīn diànnǎo?
May I have a look at this new computer?

明天才去，可以不可以？
Míngtian cái qù, kěyibukěyi?
Is it all right if we don't go until tomorrow?

麻烦你，请转告她一下儿，行吗？
Máfan ni, qǐng zhuǎngào tā yixiàr, xíng ma?
May I trouble you to tell her?

3.6.6 Refusals

(1) more direct:

不行。
Bùxíng.
No, not all right.

不好。
Bùhǎo.
No, it's not fine.

不可以。
Bùkěyǐ.
No, you may not.

不成。
Bùchéng.
No, can't do it.

没有。
Méiyou.
No, we do not have any.

(2) more roundabout:

对不起，今天不行。
Duìbuqǐ, jīntian bùxíng.
Sorry. It won't do today.

我再想想
Wǒ zài xiǎngxiang.
Let me think it over.

考虑考虑。
Kǎolǜ, kǎolǜ.
Let me think it over.

再研究研究。
Zài yánjiu yánjiu.
Let me think about it some more.

这个， 恐怕不好办。
Zhège, kǒngpà bùhǎo bàn.
Well, this won't be easy.

真不巧，我不能去，下次再说吧。
Zhēn bùqiǎo, wǒ bùnéng qù, xiàcì zài shuō ba.
Unfortunately I cannot go. Perhaps next time.

3.6.7 Invitations

(1) informal:

星期六，请您一家到我们家来吃晚饭，好吗？
Xīngqīliù qǐng nín yìjiā dào wǒmen jiā lái chīwǎnfàn, hǎo ma?
We would like to invite you and your family to come for dinner
on Saturday. How about it?

那，太麻烦了吧？
Nà, tài máfanle ba?
But, that's a lot of trouble for you, isn't it?

不麻烦。六点来，好吗？
Bù máfan. Liùdiǎn lái, hǎo ma?
No trouble. How about coming at six?

好吧。
Hǎo ba.
Fine.

(2) more formal:

星期三晚上七点，我们有个餐会，请您和夫人光临。
Xīngqisān wǎnshang qīdiǎn, wǒmen yǒu ge cānhuì, qǐng nín he
fūren guānglín.
We are having a dinner party at seven in the evening on
Wednesday. We would like you and your wife to join us.

您太客气了。
Nín tài kèqi le.
That's so nice of you.

恭候您。
Gōnghòu nín.
We'll look forward to seeing you then.

3.6.8 Compliments

真漂亮！
Zhēn piàoliang!
So beautiful.

真棒！
Zhēn bàng!
Great!

太棒了！
Tài bàngle!
Marvellous!

好极了！
Hǎojíle!
Excellent!

真不错！
Zhēn búcuò!
Really good!

太流利了！
Tài liúlì le!
So fluent!

3.6.9   Self-deprecating responses

哪里哪里。
Nǎli, nǎli.
Not at all (reply to a compliment).

不敢当。
Bùgǎndāng.
(similar to above)

不好意思。
Bùhǎoyìsi.
I'm embarrassed (by the compliment).

我说得没有你好。
Wǒ shuōde méiyou nǐ hǎo.
I do not speak as well as you do.

还不好，我还得多学习。
Hái bùhǎo, wǒ háiděi duō xuéxí.
Not so good yet. I need to study more.

过奖过奖。
Guòjiǎng, guòjiǎng.
You flatter me.

3.6.10   Regrets

真糟糕！
Zhēn zāogāo!
That's awful!

太可惜了！
Tài kěxī le!
It's such a pity!, That's too bad!

真遗憾!
Zhēn yíhàn!
Really unfortunate!, That's really regrettable!

真不巧!
Zhēn bù qiǎo!
That's a pity!, What a shame!

3.6.11   Thanks

谢谢!
Xièxie!
Thank you!

太谢谢了!
Tài xièxie le!
Thank you so much!

非常感谢!
Fēicháng gǎnxiè!
I'm very grateful!

太麻烦您了!
Tài máfan nín le!
I have troubled you so much!

Responses:

不谢。
Bú xiè.
Not at all.

不客气。
Bú kèqi.
You're welcome.

没什么。
Méi shénme.
That's nothing.

没关系。
Méi guānxi.
No problem.

不麻烦
Bù máfan.
No trouble at all.

3.6.12   Polite expressions

请坐。
Qǐng zuò.
Please sit down.

请喝茶。
Qǐng hēchá.
Please have some tea.

请吃。
Qǐng chī.
Please have (eat) some.

请等一等。
Qǐng děngyìděng.
Please wait for a while.

请稍候。
Qǐng shāohòu.
Please wait a bit.

多多保重。

Duōduō bǎozhòng.
Please take care.

3.6.13   Emergency expressions

小心！
Xiǎoxīn!
Be careful!

快快！
Kuài, kuài!
Hurry up!

来人啊！
Láirén a!
Help!/Somebody help!

找医生！
Zhǎo yīshēng!
Get a doctor!

叫警察！
Jiào jǐngchá!
Call the police!

火！
Huǒ!
Fire!

救火！
Jiù huǒ!
Fire!

救命啊！
Jiùmìng a!
Help!/Somebody save me!

我的钱包不见了！
Wǒde qiánbāo bújiàn le!
My wallet is gone!

有小偷！
Yǒu xiǎotōur!
Thief!

有贼！
Yǒuzéi!
Thief!

捉贼！
Zhuōzéi!
Catch the thief!

3.7 Directions

Compass direction words in Chinese:

English	Chinese	Pinyin
East	东	dōng
South	南	nán
West	西	xī
North	北	běi
Northeast	东北	dōngběi
Southeast	东南	dōngnán
Northwest	西北	xīběi
Southwest	西南	xīnán

The conventional way of saying the cardinal directions is "dōng, nán, xī, běi" and the other way is "dōng, xī, nán, běi."

3.8 Measurements

The metric system is the official system of measurement in China. However, the traditional market system, 市制 shìzhì, is still in common use.

The following shows equivalent units in the market, metric, and British systems:

3.8.1 Length

Length 长度 chángdù	Market 市制 shìzhì	Metric 公制 gōngzhì	British 英制 yīngzhì
毫 háo		0.0033 cm 公分 gōngfēn	0.0013 inches 英寸 yīngcùn
厘 lí	10 háo	0.0333 cm	0.0131 inches
分 fēn	10 lí	0.3333 cm	0.1312 inches
寸 cùn	10 fēn	3.3333 cm	1.3123 inches
尺 chǐ	10 cùn	0.3333 meters 公尺 / 米 gōngchǐ/mǐ	1.0936 feet 英尺 yīngchǐ
丈 zhàng	10 chǐ	3.3333 meters	3.6454 yards 码 mǎ
里 lǐ	150 zhàng	500 meters	0.3107 mile 英里 yīnglǐ
2 里 lǐ	300 zhàng	1 kilometer 公里 gōnglǐ	0.6214 miles

3.8.2 Area

1 square kilometer = 100 hectares = 4 square lǐ = 0.386 square miles
1 square meter = 9 square chǐ = 10.764 square feet

Area 面积 miànjī	Market	Metric	British
平方厘 píngfāng lí	100 平方毫 píngfāng háo	0.0011 cm^2 平方公分 píngfāng gōngfēn	0.00017 in^2 平方英寸 píngfāng yīngcùn
平方分 píngfāng fēn	100 píngfāng lí	0.1110 cm^2	0.0172 in^2
平方寸 píngfāng cùn	100 píngfāng fēn	11.1108 cm^2	1.7216 in^2
平方尺 píngfāng chǐ	100 píngfāng cùn	0.1111 m^2 平方公尺 / 平方米 píngfāng gōngchǐ/ píngfāng mǐ	1.1960 ft^2 平方英尺 píngfāng yīngchǐ

Area 面积 miànjī	Market	Metric	British
平方丈 píngfāng zhàng	100 píngfāng chǐ	11.1111 m²	13.2888 yd² 平方码 píngfāng mǎ
平方里 píngfāng lǐ	22500 píngfāng zhàng	0.25 km² 平方公里 píngfāng gōnglǐ	0.0965 mi² 平方英里 píngfāng yīnglǐ

3.8.3 Land Area

Land Area 地积 dìjī	Market	Metric	British
分 fēn	6 píngfāng zhàng	66.6666 m²	79.732 yd²
亩 mǔ	10 fēn	6.6666 ares 公亩 gōngmǔ	0.1647 acres 英亩 yīngmǔ
顷 qǐng	100 mǔ	6.6666 hectares 公顷 gōngqǐng	16.4737 acres

3.8.4 Weight

1 kilogram = 2 jīn = 2.205 lb

Weight 重量 zhòngliang	Market	Metric	British
钱 qián	10 fēn	5 grams 克 kè	0.1764 oz 盎司 àngsī
两 liǎng	10 qián	50 grams	1.7637 oz
斤 jīn	10 liǎng	0.5 kilogram 公斤 gōngjīn	1.1023 lb 磅 bàng
担 dàn	100 jīn	0.5 quintal 公担 gōngdàn	110.2310 lb

3.8.5   Volume

Volume 体积 tǐjī	Market	Metric	British
立方寸 lìfāngcùn	1000 立方分 lìfāngfēn		
立方尺 lìfāngchǐ	1000 lìfāng cùn	0.0370 m³ 立方公尺 lìfāng gōngchǐ	1.3080 ft³ 立方英尺 lìfāng yīngchǐ
立方丈 lìfāngzhàng	1000 lìfāng chǐ	37.0370 m³	1308 ft³

3.8.6   Capacity

Capacity 容量 róngliàng	Market	Metric	British
合 hé	10 勺 sháo	1 deciliter 分公升 fēngōngshēng	0.1750 pint 品脱 pǐntuō
升 shēng	10 hé	1 liter 公升 gōngshēng	0.2200 gallon 加仑 jiālún
斗 dǒu	10 shēng	10 liters	2.1997 gallons
石 dàn	10 dǒu	100 liters	2.7497 bushels 蒲式耳 púshì'ěr

3.9 Temperature

In China temperature is told in Celsius, 摄氏 Shèshì, although Fahrenheit, 华氏 Huáshì, is also taught in schools. Therefore, the normal human body temperature 36.8° C is expressed as: 摄氏 36.8 度 Shèshì sānshiliù diǎn bā dù, but it is 98.2° F which is expressed as: 华氏 98.2 度 Huáshì jiǔshibā diǎn èr dù. A temperature of −10° C is: 摄氏零下10度 Shèshì língxià shí dù.

3.10 Calendar

There are two kinds of calendars in use in China: the official calendar is the Gregorian calendar, but the traditional lunar calendar is also commonly used.

The Gregorian calendar is used for day-to-day purposes. The Gregorian calendar is called "西历 xīlì , Western calendar," "公历 gōnglì, public calendar," "阳历 yánglì, solar calendar" or "新历 xīnlì, new calendar." In recent history, the Gregorian calendar was officially adopted in 1912 which is the first year of the Republic of China. It was in disuse for a while but was readopted officially on January 1, 1929. Since 1949, all the years, months, days, and days of the week are named according to the Gregorian calendar, in line with the international standard.

When China was still an agrarian society, it was and still is, important to help farmers plan their activities and the solar calendar system is more accurate than the lunar calendar system. As a result, the twenty-four solar-based seasonal terms were devised and called "二十四节气 èrshísì jiéqì, twenty-four solar terms." This way, both the farmers and other people can plan their seasonal activities accordingly. The dates are fairly close to those of the Gregorian calendar. The starting dates of the four seasons are according to the Chinese solar calendar system and are different from those of the Gregorian calendar.

A list of 24 节气 jiéqì, 24 solar terms:

	Chinese name	**English name**	**Date**	**Meaning**
1	立春 Lìchūn	Start of spring	February 4/5	begins to get warm
2	雨水 Yǔshuǐ	Rain water	February 18/19	rain starts
3	惊蛰 Jīngzhé	Awakening of insects	March 5/6	animals come out of hibernation
4	春分 Chūnfēn	Vernal equinox	March 20/21	day and night equal length
5	清明 Qīngmíng	Clear and bright	April 4/5	clear and warm
6	谷雨 Gǔyǔ	Grain rain	April 20/21	rain increases
7	立夏 Lìxià	Start of summer	May 5/6	gets warmer
8	小满 Xiǎomǎn	Ripening grain	May 21/22	wheat ripens
9	芒种 Mángzhǒng	Grain in ear	June 5/6	other grains ripen
10	夏至 Xiàzhì	Summer solstice	June 21/22	longest day

	Chinese name	English name	Date	Meaning
11	小暑 Xiǎoshǔ	Minor heat	July 7/8	becomes hot
12	大暑 Dàshǔ	Major heat	July 22/23	hottest
13	立秋 Lìqiū	Start of autumn	August 7/8	starts cooling down
14	处暑 Chǔshǔ	Limit of heat	August 23/24	heat will be over
15	白露 Báilù	White dew	September 7/8	cool at night
16	秋分 Qiūfēn	Autumn equinox	September 23/24	day and night equal length
17	寒露 Hánlù	Cold dew	October 8/9	temperature drops
18	霜降 Shuāngjiàng	Hoar frost	October 23/24	frosty
19	立冬 Lìdōng	Start of winter	November 7/8	cold begins
20	小雪 Xiǎoxuě	Light snow	November 21/22	begins to snow
21	大雪 Dàxuě	Heavy snow	December 7/8	heavier snow
22	冬至 Dōngzhì	Winter solstice	December 21/22	longest night
23	小寒 Xiǎohán	Minor cold	January 5/6	fairly cold
24	大寒 Dàhán	Great cold	January 20/21	coldest

The traditional lunar calendar is based on the moon's waxing and waning cycles which take about a month. A greater month consists of 30 days and a lesser month consists of 29 days. There are also 12 months in a year, with an intercalary month, 闰月 rùnyuè, added every few years, in which case there will be 13 months in the year. Depending on where it is inserted, the intercalary month is called "rùn X yuè." For example, if an intercalary month is inserted after the third month of the lunar calendar, it is called "闰 三月 rùnsānyuè." The names of the months are: "一月 yīyuè, 二月 èryuè...十二月 shí'èryuè," with the first month also known as "正 月 zhēngyuè" and the twelfth month also known as "腊月 làyuè." The traditional Chinese calendar, known as "农历 nónglì, agrarian calendar," "阴历 yīnlì, lunar calendar" or "旧历 jiùlì, old calendar," is used for dating the traditional festivals such as the Spring Festival, Mid-Autumn Festival, etc. Some people also use the traditional Chinese calendar to choose auspicious dates for weddings, the opening of a business or the inauguration of a new building. Chinese artists also tend to date their paintings or calligraphy using traditional calendar dates. Many Chinese calendars now denote the year, month, and day using both the Gregorian and traditional systems.

The years in the traditional calendar are not continuous, but are expressed in sixty-year cycles. They are arranged by matching the ten heavenly stems and twelve earthly branches. For example, the year 2000 was 庚辰年 gēngchén nián, and the year 2007 was 丁亥年 dīnghài nián. After each cycle of sixty years, another cycle of matching will begin, and so on. Each of the heavenly stems corresponds to one of the Five Elements, 五行 wǔxíng: wood, fire, earth, metal, and water. Each of the earthly branches is represented by one animal and together they are known as: 十二生肖 shí'èr shēngxiào, the twelve zodiacal animals. A person born in a given year is said to "属 shǔ, belong to" the animal of that year, modified by the matching element. For example, a person born in the year of the dragon is said to "属 龙 shǔ lóng." If he/she was born in the year 2000 which is a 庚辰 gēngchén year, that person is a 金龙 jīnlóng, metal dragon.

The ten heavenly stems and their corresponding elements:

Heavenly stem	Element	Heavenly stem	Element
1 甲 jiǎ	木 mù wood	6 己 jǐ	earth
2 乙 yǐ	wood	7 庚 gēng	金 jīn metal
3 丙 bǐng	火 huǒ fire	8 辛 xīn	metal
4 丁 dīng	fire	9 壬 rén	水 shuǐ water
5 戊 wù	土 tǔ earth	10 癸 guǐ	water

The twelve earthly branches and the animals representing each year:

Earthly branch	Animal	English
1 子 zǐ	鼠 shǔ	rat
2 丑 chǒu	牛 niú	ox
3 寅 yín	虎 hǔ	tiger
4 卯 mǎo	兔 tù	rabbit
5 辰 chén	龙 lóng	dragon
6 巳 sì	蛇 shé	snake

Earthly branch	Animal	English
7 午 wǔ	马 mǎ	horse
8 未 wèi	羊 yáng	sheep
9 申 shēn	猴 hóu	monkey
10 酉 yǒu	鸡 jī	rooster
11 戌 xū	狗 gǒu	dog
12 亥 hài	猪 zhū	pig

3.10.1 Year

The year is expressed in numbers as in the West and followed by the word: 年 nián. Some examples:

1911: yījiǔyīyī nián
2000: èrlínglíngling nián or liǎngqiān nián
2008: èrlínglíngbā nián or liǎngqiānlíngbā nián

If it is "BC" or "BCE," the word "公元前 gōngyuánqián" or "纪元前 jìyuánqián" precedes the year. The use of "gōngyuánqián" is more common. For example, "221 BC" is "公元前221年 gōngyuánqián èr'èryī nián."

There is no specific word for "decade" which is simply "十年 shínián," so "three decades" is "三十年 sānshi nián." The word for "century" is "世纪 shìjì" and "three centuries" is "三个世纪 sānge shìjì." "Twentieth century" is "二十世纪 èrshi shìjì" and "third century BC" is "公元前第三世纪 gōngyuánqián dìsān shìjì."

3.10.2 Month

The months are numbered rather than named. To say how many months, one only has to insert the measure word "个 ge" between the number and the word "月 yuè." For example, eight months is "八个月 bāge yuè" and twelve months is "十二个月 shí'èrge yuè."

Month	Pinyin	English
一月	yīyuè	January
二月	èryuè	February
三月	sānyuè	March
四月	sìyuè	April
五月	wǔyuè	May
六月	liùyuè	June

Month	Pinyin	English
七月	qīyuè	July
八月	bāyuè	August
九月	jiǔyuè	September
十月	shíyuè	October
十一月	shíyīyuè	November
十二月	shí'èryuè	December

3.10.3   Week

The days of the week are numbered rather than named as in English and Monday is considered the first day of the week. "One week" is "一星期 yìxīngqī," "一个星期 yíge xīngqī" or "一周 yìzhōu." The other term for week, which is older and is still used often orally, is "礼拜 lǐbài," and "one week" is "一个礼拜 yíge lǐbài." "Weekend" is "周末 zhōumò."

Day of week	Pinyin	English
星期一 / 礼拜一	xīngqīyī/lǐbàiyī	Monday
星期二 / 礼拜二	xīnqī'èr/lǐbài'èr	Tuesday
星期三 / 礼拜三	xīngqīsān/lǐbàisān	Wednesday
星期四 / 礼拜四	xīngqīsì/lǐbàisì	Thursday
星期五 / 礼拜五	xīngqīwǔ/lǐbàiwǔ	Friday
星期六 / 礼拜六	xīngqīliù/lǐbàiliù	Saturday
星期日 / 星期天 / 礼拜天	xīngqīrì/ xīngqītiān/ lǐbàitiān	Sunday

3.10.4   Time of day

In telling time, the following units are used:

Time	Consists of	English
点 diǎn	60 fēn	o'clock
刻 kè	15 fēn	quarter
分 fēn	60 miǎo	minute
秒 miǎo		second

Time is told from larger units to smaller units. Therefore, "8 o'clock, 45 minutes, 8 seconds" is:

"八点四十五分（or 三刻）八秒 bādiǎn sìshiwǔfēn (or sānkè) bāmiǎo."

When telling time on the hour, the alternative to "点 diǎn" is "点钟 diǎnzhōng." For example, 11 o'clock is "十一点钟 shíyī diǎnzhōng."

3.10.5 Duration of Time

The duration of time is expressed with the larger units first, followed successively by smaller units. Thus, "8 days, 8 hours, 15 minutes, and 8 seconds" is:

"八天八小时十五分 （or 一刻）八秒 bātiān bāxiǎoshí shíwǔfēn (or yíkè) bāmiǎo."

The units for duration of time

Time	Duration	English
日 rì/天 tiān	24 xiǎoshí/24 ge zhōngtóu	day
小时 xiǎoshí/ 钟头 zhōngtóu	60 fēn	hour
刻 kè	15 fēn	quarter, 15 minutes
分 fēn	60 miǎo	minute
秒 miǎo		second

3.11 Currency

The official currency in China is 人民币 Rénmínbì, People's Currency. The abbreviation for Rénmínbì is RMB. The basic unit of RMB is the 元 yuán, a dollar. Next is 角 jiǎo which is 1/10 of a yuán and is like a dime or ten cents. One tenth of a jiǎo is 分 fēn, a cent. This set of units is usually a written form but is also used by some as an oral form. There is another set that is used more often orally. The two sets cannot be mixed.

More written	More oral
元 yuán	块 kuài
角 jiǎo	毛 máo
分 fēn	分 fēn

Thus, three dollars and thirty-three cents is 三元三角三分 sānyuán sānjiǎo sānfēn, which is usually expressed orally as 三块三毛三分 sānkuài sānmáo sānfēn.

All numerals can be put in front of the units to count money, except "two" which can also be spoken as "liǎng." For example, two dollars is 二元 èryuán (but not èrkuài) or 两元 liǎngyuán or 两块 liǎngkuài; twenty-two thousand two hundred and twenty-two dollars is 二万二千二百二十二 元 èrwàn èrqiān èrbǎi èrshi'èr yuán (or kuài) or 两万两千两百二十二元 liǎngwàn liǎngqiān liǎngbǎi èrshi'èr yuán (or kuài). Twenty-two dollars is only expressed as 二十二元 èrshi'èr yuán (or kuài), and twenty dollars is 二十元 èrshi yuán (or kuài).

Paper money is 纸币 zhǐbì and coins are 硬币 yìngbì.

3.12 Numbers

3.12.1 Numerals

There are three ways of writing numbers in Chinese: the Arabic numerals which are used in general practice and in mathematics; a set of numbers in Chinese characters; and a more formal set of numbers in Chinese characters which are used to prevent unauthorized changes, much like spelling out "3" as "three." The basic numbers are one to ten. Eleven is "ten one," nineteen is "ten nine," twenty-one is "two ten one," etc. until ninety-nine which is "九十九 jiǔshíjiǔ" (nine ten nine). "Zero," líng, is written as "0" and "零." The written character for "zero" is the same in both the simpler set of Chinese characters and the formal set of Chinese characters.

Arabic	1	2	3	4	5	6	7	8	9	10
Pinyin	yī	èr	sān	sì	wǔ	liù	qī	bā	jiǔ	shí
Chinese	一	二	三	四	五	六	七	八	九	十
Formal	壹	贰	叁	肆	伍	陆	柒	捌	玖	拾

Another way of looking at numbers and the way the larger numbers are formed:

English	Arabic	Pinyin	Simpler	Formal
One	1	yī	一	壹
Ten	10	shí	十	拾
One hundred	100	yì bǎi	一 百	壹 佰
One thousand	1,000	yì qiān	一 千	壹 仟

English	Arabic	Pinyin	Simpler	Formal
Ten thousand	10,000	yí wàn	一 万	壹 万
One hundred thousand	100,000	shí wàn	十万	拾万
One million	1,000,000	yì bǎiwàn	一 百万	壹百万
Ten million	10,000,000	yì qiānwàn	一 千万	壹仟万
One hundred million	100,000,000	yí yì	一 亿	壹亿

Symbolic values attached to some numbers

Some numbers have taken on symbolic meanings, notably:

1. The odd numbers are considered to be 阳 yáng numbers and are viewed as more dynamic or potent. Therefore, "jiǔ, nine" which is the highest single digit yáng number is considered the most potent. The 九龙壁 jiǔlóngbì, nine dragon wall, in the Palace Museum is a symbol of the Emperor.
2. The even numbers are considered to be 阴 yīn numbers which are less dynamic but more stable.
3. "Sì, four" is considered by many to be an unlucky number, because it sounds like "死 sǐ, death."
4. "Bā, eight" is recently considered to be a very lucky number because it sounds like "发 fā, to prosper."

A special numeral: 俩 liǎ

"俩 liǎ, two" is a contraction of 两个 liǎngge. It is only used for people. For example:

他们俩是很好的朋友。
Tāmen liǎ shi hěnhǎode péngyou.
The two of them are very good friends.

3.12.2 Ordinals

Ordinal numbers in Chinese are formed by adding "第 dì" in front of numerals. For example: "2nd" is "第二 dì èr," "3rd" is "第三 dì sān," "99th" is "第九十九 dì jiǔshijiǔ" and "1,001st" is "第一千零一 dì yìqiānlíngyī."

3.12.3   Decimals

A decimal point is called a "点 diǎn" in Chinese. For example: "0.03" is "零点零三 líng diǎn líng sān"; "99.99" is "九十九点九九 jiǔshíjiǔ diǎn jiǔjiǔ." Conventionally, the number or numbers after the diǎn are expressed by saying each number individually.

3.12.4   Percentages

Percentages are expressed by "百分之...bǎifēn zhī," that is, "of one hundred parts." Therefore, 89% is "百分之八十九 bǎifēn zhī bāshíjiǔ," that is, "of one hundred parts, eighty-nine"; and 100% is "百分之百 bǎifēn zhī bǎi," or "of one hundred parts, one hundred."

3.12.5   Fractions

Fractions are expressed by "分之...fēn zhī," that is, "of how many parts, how many."
    For example:

1. "8/9 (eight ninths)" is "九分之八 jiǔ fēn zhī bā."
2. "1/10 (one tenth)" is "十分之一 shí fēn zhī yī."
3. "1⅔ (one and two thirds) is "一又三分之二 yī yòu sān fēn zhī èr."

3.12.6   Multiples

Multiples are expressed by adding "倍 bèi" to a numeral. For example: 两倍 liǎngbèi, twice as; 十倍 shíbèi, ten times as.

3.12.7   Approximate numbers

Approximate numbers are expressed by stating the approximate numbers in sequence.
    For example: "five or six" is "5、6/ 五六 wǔ liù."
Here are some samples of approximate numbers:

1. 8 or 9 times/eight or nine times: 8、9次/八九次 bā jiǔ cì.
2. 16 or 17 students/sixteen or seventeen students: 16、7个学生/十六七个学生 shíliù qīge xuésheng."
3. 117 or 118 people/one hundred seventeen or one hundred eighteen people: 117、8个人; 一百十七八个人 yìbǎi shíqī bāge rén.
4. 1,300 or 1,400 dollars/one thousand three hundred or one thousand four hundred dollars: 13、400元; 一千三四百元 yìqiān sān sì bǎi yuán.

4 Letters

4.1 Addressing an envelope

Normal format for addressing an envelope

```
┌─────────────────────────────────────────────────────┐
│ 100002                                                │
│                                                  邮票 │
│                                                       │
│ 中国北京 海淀区学院路30号                              │
│              李甲仕教授收                              │
│                    加拿大比西省温哥华36街王寄          │
└─────────────────────────────────────────────────────┘
```

When addressing an envelope in Chinese, the receiver's postal code (zip code), 邮政编码 yóuzhèng biānmǎ or 邮编 yóubiān, is written at the top left corner of the envelope, followed by the receiver's address. The address is logically written from larger units to smaller units:

country + province/state + city + street + number.

The receiver's name follows the address and is written in the centre of the envelope with slightly larger characters to show respect. The order is: last name + first name + title of address + "receives." The title of address for the recipient may be: 先生 xiānsheng, Mr.; 女士 nǚshì, Ms.; 小姐 xiǎojiě, Miss; 校长 xiàozhǎng, President (of a university) or Principal (of a high school or elementary school); 系主任 xìzhǔrèn, Department Head or Chair; 主任 zhǔrèn, Director; 教授 jiàoshòu, Professor; 总经理 zǒngjīnglǐ, General Manager; 经理 jīnglǐ, Manager; 总裁 zǒngcái, President (of a company), etc. The last part on this line may be: 收 shōu, receive; 启 qǐ, open; 大启 dàqǐ, open (respectful term); 敬启 jìngqǐ, open (respectful term); 亲启 qīnqǐ, personally open/personal.

At the bottom, more to the right, is the sender's address and surname. Normally, the full name of the sender is not necessary. The last part is the word: 寄 jì, send or 缄 jiān, seal.

Points to remember when writing an envelope: (1) do not use red ink, which has negative connotations, and usually indicates breaking off a relationship; (2) do not use a pencil, because it may be erased and it does not show respect; (3) it is best to use black or blue ink.

4.2   General form of a letter

The figure shows the normal format for both informal and formal letters. In fact, it is a format for writing e-mails as well.

Normal format for letters

称呼 chēnghu, salutation:

正文 zhèngwén, text

祝语 zhùyǔ, a (good) wish,

                写信人 xiěxìnrén, name of the writer + 上 shàng, presented

                      日期 rìqī, date (year, month, day)

Note: The name of the writer and date can also be written on the left bottom corner, two or three lines down from the good wishes.

4.3   Informal letters

Salutation, 称呼 *chēnghu:*

Unlike in English letters, in Chinese letters the word "dear, 亲爱的 qīn'àide" and "my dear, 我亲爱的 wǒ qīn'àide" can only be used for people who are very close to the letter writer. There are many different ways to address the person or persons to whom the letter is written.

(1) For close family members, a name is not necessary: 敬爱的奶奶 jìng'àide nǎinai, respected grandmother; 亲爱的妈妈 qīn'àide māma, dear mother; 大哥 dàgē, oldest brother; 二姐 èrjiě, second older sister; 妹妹 mèimei, younger sister, etc. For the younger generation, if there is only one son or one daughter: 我儿 wǒ'ér, my son; 女儿 nǚ'er, my daughter. If there is more than one, then precede the relation with a name: 雄儿 Xióng ér, my son Xióng; 英女 Yīng nǚ, my daughter Yīng, etc.

(2) For other older relatives: first name + address. For example: 国雄叔 Guóxióng shū, uncle Guóxióng; 美丽姑 Měilì gū, aunt Měilì; 玲阿姨 Ling āyí, aunt Ling.

(3) For younger relatives or friends: name + relation or just names. For example: 小华侄 Xiǎohuá zhí, nephew Xiǎohuá; 小华 Xiǎohuá; 达华侄女 Dáhuá zhínü, niece Dáhuá; 达华 Dǎhuá; 晓明友 Xiǎomíng yǒu, friend Xiǎomíng; 晓明 Xiǎomíng; or 小李 Xiǎo Lǐ.

Good wishes, 祝语 *zhùyǔ:*

These can be: 敬祝安康 jìngzhù ānkāng, respectfully wishing you good health; 恭祝万事如意 gōngzhù wànshìrúyì, respectfully wishing that everything goes well with you; 祝身体健康 zhù shēntǐjiànkāng, wishing you good health; 祝暑安 zhù shǔ'ān, wishing you peace during the hot season; 祝新年好 zhù xīnniánhǎo, Happy New Year; 祝学业进步 zhù xuéyèjìnbù, wishing you progress in school work; 祝生日快乐 zhù shēngrìkuàilè, happy birthday, etc.

Note: Normally the words "敬祝," "恭祝" or "祝" are written on one line and the wish itself will follow in the next line or with a line of space in between.

Name of the writer, 写信人 *xiěxìnrén:*

This can be just the first name of the writer or a signature, but usually it should be clear enough that the reader would have no difficulty in deciphering the name. An expression identifying the writer's relation to the reader can also come before the name. For example: 孙 sūn, your grandson; 女儿 nǚ'er, your daughter; 弟 dì, your younger brother; 你的朋友 nǐde péngyou, your friend. After the name, a polite word or two often follows: 敬上 jìngshàng, respectfully presented; 谨上 jǐnshàng, carefully/solemnly presented; 上 shàng, presented.

Sample informal letter: In informal letters, the language can be more plain and the tone more personal.

爸、妈：

　　　　您两位好！

　　　　谢谢您的来信！收到您的信，我真高兴，也非常多谢您对我的关心。

　　　　我来英国读书不知不觉已经六个月了。时间过得真快。这六个月来，我的英文已进步了不少。基本上听课和应对进退已经没什么大问题了。教授们也觉得我有进步。在英国的生活我也比较习惯了。同时，我也认识了几个新朋友。我们除了一起做功课、练习英文和锻炼以外，还有时去听音乐和看电影。我的生活也比较规律。希望您两位放心。

　　　　最近这里的天气很好，很舒服。希望您那里的天气也好。

　　　　我得做些研究，然后写文章。

　　　　下次再谈。

　　　　请代问爷爷、奶奶好！

敬祝

安康！

　　　　　　　　　　儿
　　　　　　　　　　　小明
　　　　　　　　　　　　敬上
　　　　　　　　　　四月八日

Translation:

Dad and Mom:

　　Greetings to both of you!

　　Thank you for your letter! I am so very happy to have received your letter and I thank you very much for your concern about me.

　　Suddenly it has been six months since I came to study in England. How time flies. My English has improved a lot in these six months. Basically I do not have much problem listening to lectures and for my daily life. My professors also think I have made progress. I am also more used to life in England now. At the same time, I have made a few friends. Besides doing homework, practicing English and doing physical exercises together, we also go to concerts and movies sometimes. My life has become more routine too. I hope you will not worry about me.

　　The weather has been nice and comfortable. I hope your weather is nice too.

　　I have to do some research and then write a paper.

　　I will write to you again.

Please give my best regards to Grandpa and Grandma!
I wish you
Best of health!

Your son, Xiaoming
April 8

4.4 Formal letters

Salutation，称呼 *chēnghu:*

To address a person in a formal letter, we may use: (1) 先生 xiānsheng, Mr.; 夫人 fūren, Madam; 太太 tàitai, Mrs.; 女士 nǚ shì, Ms.; 小姐 xiǎojiě, Miss, etc.; or (2) if a person's official position is known: surname + official position title. These are some official titles: 院长 yuànzhǎng, Dean; 教授 jiàoshòu, Professor; 博士 bóshì, Dr. (Ph.D.); 董事长 dǒngshìzhǎng, President of a board; 总裁 zǒngcái, President; 总经理 zǒngjīnglǐ, General Manager; 经理 jīnglǐ, Manager; 主任 zhǔrèn, Director, etc.; (3) If the letter is written to an organization whose specific recipient is unknown, one may start the letter by saying: 敬启者 jìngqǐzhě, the respected person who opens this letter (equivalent to: Dear Sir or Madam).

Good wishes, 祝语 *zhùyǔ:*

The good wishes are more formal: 敬祝新春快乐 jìngzhù xīnchūnkuàilè, wishing you a Happy Chinese New Year; 祝工作顺利 zhù gōngzuòshùnlì, wishing everything goes smoothly with your work; 恭祝大安 gōngzhù dà'ān, respectfully wishing you peace; 恭祝事业兴隆 gōngzhù shìyèxīnglóng, respectfully wishing your work will prosper; 诚祝生意兴隆 chéngzhù shēngyìxīnglóng, sincerely wishing your business will prosper; 顺致敬意 shùnzhì jìngyì, taking the opportunity to show my respect; 此致真诚的谢意 cǐzhì zhēnchéngde xièyì, here I send you my sincerest thanks, etc.

Name of the writer, 写信人 *xiěxìnrén:*

The writer usually identifies himself/herself by giving an official title, for example: 剑桥大学教授 Jiànqiáo Dàxué jiàoshòu, Professor at Cambridge University; 美国达克公司经理 Měiguó Dákègōngsī jīnglǐ, Manager of Daker Company in the USA, etc. As with informal letters, the name is followed by 敬上 jìngshàng, respectfully presented, or 谨上 jǐnshàng, solemnly presented.

Sample letter:

Vocabulary used in a formal letter is usually more "literary" and the tone is more impersonal, for example: 贵校 guìxiào, your honorable school/university; 我校 wǒxiào, our school/university; 贵公司 guì gōngsī, your honorable company; 我公司 wǒ gōngsī, our company;

贵厂 guìchǎng, your honorable factory; 我厂 wǒchǎng, our factory, etc. If the letter is a very important one, in addition to being written on official letterhead, an official seal, 公章 gōngzhāng, should be stamped at the end of the letter.

Sample formal letter

张经理：

　　您好！
　　贵公司最近登广告招聘推销员。我看到此广告后，觉得这件工作是我喜欢做的工作，也应该是有资格可以胜任的。所以决定申请。
　　我是去年商学系毕业的学生。在大学曾经学过三年的中文。毕业后，去北京又学了一年的中文。现在能说、能看，也能写。
　　随信付上我的简历，请查收。您如需要推荐人的姓名或推荐信，也请告知。我会尽快寄去。

盼望着您的回音。

恭祝
大安！

　　　　晚
　　　　　陆杰利(Jerry Lucas)敬上
　　　　　2008年8月8日

Translation:
Manager Zhang:
　Greetings!
　Your company has recently advertised a position for a salesperson. When I read your advertisement, I felt that this is a job I would like and I think I am well qualified for it. Therefore I have decided to apply for it.
　I graduated from the Department of Commerce last year. I studied Chinese for three years at university. After graduation, I went to Beijing and studied Chinese for another year. I can speak, read and write Chinese now.
　Attached please find my resumé. If you need any names or reference letters, please let me know and I will send them to you as soon as possible.
　I look forward to your reply.
　Respectfully wishing you
　Great Peace!

Sincerely,
Jerry Lucas
August 8, 2008

5 Grammar

The first Modern Standard Chinese grammar book: *Ma's Basic Principles for Writing* (1898), 马氏文通 Mǎshìwéntōng, was written just over a century ago by 马建忠 Mǎ Jiànzhōng (1845–1900), who was strongly influenced by grammars published for European languages. Of course this does not mean that Chinese were unaware that they were speaking in accordance with shared grammatical rules. It may never have occurred to them that rules should be systematically compiled, categorized and described for purely structural analysis apart from rhetorical effect. Similarly, it was about one and a half millennia ago that the Chinese scholar 沈约 Shěn Yuē (441–513) wrote the first treatise, *On the Four Tones* 四声谱 Sìshēngpǔ, describing the four tones of the Chinese language, even though speakers had been pronouncing the same syllables in four different tones for many centuries before he wrote his treatise. It was the challenge of translating Buddhist sutras into Chinese from Sanskrit and Pali, particularly transliterating untranslatable names such as Avalokiteshvara Bodhissatva into pronounceable Chinese syllables, that caused scholars to pay more attention to the structure of their own language than they had for centuries before. In the nineteenth century, it was increased contact with Westerners and their languages that made some Chinese feel the need to systematize the rules for speaking well-formed sentences in their own tongue.

5.1 The main features of Chinese grammar

5.1.1 Absence of morphological change

Perhaps the most salient feature of Chinese grammar is the absence of fixed rules for changing the form of words when their grammatical function changes. There is no change in the form of a verb expressing a present, past, or future action, and no change for subjunctive expressions; there is no gender differentiation among nouns, and no difference between singular and plural nouns. This feature was illustrated earlier in this volume.

5.1.2   Frequent ellipsis

China's "high context culture," as defined by E.T. Hall in *Beyond Culture*, is reflected most clearly in language usage. Once the subject, topic, or even the verb is understood by both speaker and listener, it is commonly omitted. As long as the topic, subject, object, or the verb is understood, it may be omitted in subsequent utterances until the topic, subject, object or verb is changed.

Elliptical sentences are usually responses to questions and they are context-dependent and therefore do not stand alone without a context.

(1)   There is no single word for "yes" or "no" in Chinese as there is in English. The shortest possible "yes" or "no" response to a question is to repeat or negate the verb or auxiliary verb used in the question. Therefore such short answers are elliptical sentences.

他们是法国人吗?	是。 / 不是。
Tāmen shi Fǎguórén ma?	Shì./Bú shi.
Are they French?	Yes./No.
他们明年去不去法国旅游?	去。 / 不去。
Tāmen míngnián qùbuqu Fǎguo lǚyóu?	Qù./Bú qù.
Will they visit France next year?	Yes./No.
他们会不会说法语?	会。 / 不会。
Tāmen huìbuhui shuō Fǎyǔ?	Huì./Bú huì.
Can they speak French?	Yes./No.

(2)   Short answers to questions with question words:

谁请他们去饭馆吃饭?	她。
Shéi qǐng tāmen qù fànguǎnr chīfàn?	Tā.
Who invited them to eat in a restaraunt?	She.
那本英文杂志是谁的?	我们的。
Nàběn Yīngwén zázhì shi shéide?	Wǒmende.
Whose English magazine is that?	Ours.
我看不清，那张纸上写的是什么?	人名字。
Wǒ kàn buqīng, nàzhāng zhǐshang xiěde shi shénme?	Rén míngzi.
I can't see clearly. What is written on that piece of paper?	Someone's name.
你知不知道他们下星期去哪儿?	德国。
Nǐ zhībuzhīdao tāmen xiàxīngqi qù nǎr?	Déguo.
Do you know where they are going next week?	Germany.
明天早上几点见面?	十点。
Míngtian zǎoshang jǐdiǎn jiànmiàn?	Shídiǎn.
When are we meeting tomorrow morning?	Ten o'clock.

你的朋友要在你家住多久？	五、六天。
Nǐde péngyou yào zài nǐjiā zhù duōjiǔ?	Wǔ、liù tiān.
How long are your friends going to stay in your house?	Five or six days.
他们今年几月毕业？	七月。
Tāmen jīnnian jǐyuè bìyè?	Qīyue.
When do they graduate this year?	July.

5.1.3   Mutual influence of monosyllabic and disyllabic words

Although each monosyllabic Chinese character is meaningful, there is a tendency in Modern Standard Chinese to use disyllabic words, which we may call "binomes." For example, the English title of this book, *Using Chinese*, could be translated into Chinese as "用汉语 Yòng Hànyǔ," but that would sound less natural than "使用汉语 Shǐyòng Hànyǔ," which consists of two binomes. Similarly, we could translate "Chinese cuisine" directly into "中国餐 Zhōngguocān," but the preferred expression is "中餐 Zhōngcān." A Chinese could say "扫街道 sǎo jiēdào, sweep the streets," or "打扫街 dǎsǎo jiē, sweep the streets," but surely would prefer "打扫街道 dǎsǎo jiēdào" as a balanced pair of binomes, or even the single binome "扫街 sǎo jiē, sweep the streets." Chinese linguists refer to this phenomenon as 双音化 shuāngyīnhuà, binomization.

5.1.4   Differences between spoken and written forms

Written Chinese characters never have been primarily phonetic representations of the spoken word, so it should come as no surprise that some modes of expression in written Chinese will differ from modern spoken Chinese. One of the ways written Chinese differs from spoken forms is in its preference for brevity. For instance, in spoken Chinese the word most often used for "time" or "when" is "时候 shíhou." In written Chinese it will often be abbreviated into the single character/syllable "时 shí." The reason is very simple and practical: when listening, we cannot "see" which of the many "shí" the speaker has in mind, because there are more than twenty-five different characters pronounced "shí" in the second tone, at least four of which are very common: 时 shí, time; 十 shí, ten; 石 shí, stone; and 食 shí, food. The written form disambiguates the meaning for the reader, whereas the listener's key for disambiguation is the second syllable of "shíhou," which would be written "时候," as opposed to "石头 shítou," "食品 shípǐn," etc., in speech.

As stated above, the rules of Chinese grammar are fewer and less complex than those of most Western European languages, and are far fewer and far less complex than English grammar. When Chinese speakers utter a verb they need not worry, for instance, about distinguishing between past, present, and future forms of the verb:

(Yesterday) I went to his home (yesterday).
（我）昨天（我）去他家。
(Wǒ) zuótian (wǒ) qù tā jiā.
(I) yesterday (I) go his home.

(Today) I am going to his home (today).
（我）今天（我）去他家。
(Wǒ) jīntian (wǒ) qù tā jiā.
(I) today (I) go his home.

(Tomorrow) I shall go to his home (tomorrow).
（我）明天（我）去他家。
(Wǒ) míngtian (wǒ) qù tā jiā.
(I) tomorrow (I) go his home.

(Every day) I go to his home (every day).
（我）天天（我）去他家。
(Wǒ) tiāntiān (wǒ) qù tā jiā.
(I) every day (I) go his home.

The reason there is no need to change the verb form is simple enough: if the time of an action or state of affairs (past, present, or future) is significant enough to be mentioned, then it must be placed before the verb, hence removing the need to imbed a tense marker in the verb. The placement variable in the four sentences above is the subject, the first person pronoun, which may either precede or follow the time expression. In English, we may place a time expression at the very end of a sentence, because the verb's tense marker will have made it clear whether the action has or has not yet taken place. The time expression then serves to locate the point more specifically, as "yesterday," "last week," "tomorrow," "next year," or "when I was young." Nor is there any need to change verb forms when distinguishing between indicative and subjunctive moods:

If I were you…
要是我是你，。。。
yàoshi wǒ shi nǐ (literally, "if I am you")

Nor do we need to make any changes to nouns when we distinguish between singular and plural:
One mouse, two mice, many mice

一只老鼠， 两只老鼠， 许多老鼠
yìzhī lǎoshǔ, liǎngzhī lǎoshǔ, xǔduō lǎoshǔ
(one mouse, two mouse, many mouse)

This is because having said "two" or "many," we know beyond all doubt that we are referring to more than one mouse, so there simply is no need to distinguish between singular and plural forms of a noun. Sometimes this may frustrate or surprise non-native speakers of Chinese, when they hear the announcement:

客人来了！
Kèren lái le!
guest arrive

and have no idea whether it means "the guest has arrived," "a guest has arrived," "the guests have arrived," or "some guests have arrived." To the Chinese speaker, the reasoning is very simple and obvious: if one person is expected to arrive, the utterance means: "The guest has arrived." If more than one is expected, it means: "The guests have arrived." If no one is expected to arrive, the proper utterance would be:

来客了！
Lái kè le!
come guest (s)

Non-agency and non-anticipation of "guest arrival" outweighs the need to distinguish between singular and plural. We see a similar inversion of normal word order in expressions like "下雨了！ xiàyǔ le!, It's raining!" or "出太阳了 chū tàiyang le, The sun's come out," where something happens without agency and without volition on the part of the speaker.

5.2 Word order and syntax

Word order is paramount in Chinese speech. "Subject–Verb–Object" is the normal word order, with additional information, such as time of action, location of action, manner of action, extent of action, result of action, inserted into this core. As with English, the only difference between "Mom scolds the horse, 妈妈骂马 māma mà mǎ" and "The horse scolds Mom, 马骂妈妈 mǎ mà māma" is word order.

Time of action may be placed either immediately before the subject to focus attention on the time, or more often between the subject and the verb:

妈妈昨天骂马。
Māma zuótian mà mǎ.
Mom scolded the horse yesterday.

or

昨天妈妈骂马。
Zuótian māma mà mǎ.
Yesterday Mom scolded the horse.

The location of action is expressed after the subject and before the verb:

妈妈在院子里骂马。
Māma zai yuànzili mà mǎ.
Mom scolds the horse in the courtyard.

If the time and place are both stated in the same sentence, the time expression precedes the location:

妈妈昨天在院子里骂马。
Māma zuótian zai yuànzili mà mǎ.
Mom scolded the horse in the yard yesterday.

The manner of an action is expressed immediately before the verb:

妈妈昨天好好儿地骂马。
Māma zuótian hǎohāorde mà mǎ.
Mom gave the horse a good scolding yesterday.

The extent and/or result of an action, since they cannot be known until after the action has taken place, always follow the verb:

妈妈骂马骂得很利害.
Māma mà mǎ màde hěn lìhai.
Mom scolded the horse severely.

If an action takes place without the volition or anticipation of the speaker (without "agency"), the noun and verb are expressed in reversed order, often, but not always, referring to the weather (the "le" particle indicates a change of status):

下雨了。
Xiàyǔ le.
It's raining.

出事了。
Chūshì le.
There's been an accident.

下课了。
Xiàkè le.
Class is dismissed.

吃饭了!
Chīfàn le!
Dinner is served!

收工了.
Shōugōng le.
It's time to quit work.

散会了。
Sànhuì le.
The meeting is adjourned.

5.3 Topic-comment sentences

Chinese has been called a "topic-prominent language," meaning that the topic is what is being talked about, and the comment is what is said about the topic. On the surface, this may sound not too different from the basic division of an English sentence into a "subject–predicate" structure, but in fact it is not the same at all, as illustrated in the following typical sentence:

老张身体好。
Lǎo Zhāng shēntǐ hǎo.
Zhāng is in good health.

In this sentence, "Lǎo Zhāng" is the topic, "shēntǐ hǎo" is the comment. The comment itself consists of a subject, "shēntǐ" and a predicate "hǎo." The first reaction of an English speaker might be to express this type of sentence using a "topic marker" before "Zhāng," like "As for," "Concerning" or "Speaking of" but the natural English stylistic equivalent is simply "Zhang is in good health."
The topic may even be preceded by a contextualizing statement, such as:

去年老张身体好。
Qùnián Lǎo Zhāng shēntǐ hǎo.
Last year Zhang was in good health.

The time expression "qùnián, last year" could also be placed after the topic and before the subject:

老张去年身体好。
Lǎo Zhāng qùnián shēntǐ hǎo.
Zhang was in good health last year.

The "feeling" of the above sentence in English would be "As for Zhāng, last year he was in good health" but the most natural way of expressing it would be "Zhang was in good health last year."

An illustrative list of sample topic – comment sentences follows:

她年纪小.
Tā niánji xiǎo.
She is young.

那个饭店房间干净吗?
Nàge fàndiàn fángjiān gānjing ma?
Are the rooms in that hotel clean?

他们谁都不来参加座谈。
Tāmen shéi dōu bùlái cānjiā zuòtán.
None of them will come to participate in the discussion.

他朋友脾气很暴躁。
Tā péngyou píqi hěn bàozào.
His friend has a fiery temper.

那年夏天蒙特利尔天气非常不正常。

Nànián xiàtian Měngtèli'ěr tiānqi fēicháng búzhèngcháng.

The weather was very unusual in Montreal that summer.

房租纽约最贵。

Fángzū Niǔyuē zuì guì.

Apartment rental is most expensive in New York.

这个汉字结构很简单。

Zhège hànzì jiégòu hěn jiǎndān.

The structure of this Chinese character is quite simple.

他那个人笨手笨脚的。

Tā nàge rén bènshǒubènjiǎo de.

He is a very clumsy person.

5.4 Pronouns

5.4.1 Personal pronouns

There is no difference in form between singular nouns and plural nouns in Chinese, with the occasional exception that some may put a "men, 们" after nouns which indicate people, for example: 老师们 lǎoshīmen, the teachers; 学生们 xuéshengmen, the students. In pronouns, 代词 dàicí, however, there is a difference between singular and plural forms:

Number	Singular			Plural		
Person	1st	2nd	3rd	1st	2nd	3rd
Pronoun Possessive	我 wǒ 我的 wǒ de	你 nǐ 你的 nǐ de	他，她，它 tā 他的，她的，它的 tā de	我们 wǒmen 我们的 wǒmen de	你们 nǐmen 你们的 nǐmen de	他们，她们，它们 tāmen 他们的，她们的，它们的 tāmen de
English pronoun	I, me	you, you	he, him; she, her; it, it	we, us	you, you	they, them
English possessive	my, mine	your, yours	his, her, its; his, hers, its	our, ours	your, yours	their, theirs

The word "您 nín" is a polite form for "你 nǐ" or "你们 nǐmen." The plural form "您们 nínmen" is generally not used in the spoken form, but may appear in the written form.

The word "咱们 zánmen" also means "we, us" and is used more by northerners to include the listeners, so it is also known as "the inclusive 'we'."

The word "俩 liǎ" means "two of (persons)" and is always combined with two people's names or the plural form of personal pronouns. For example:

张三和李四俩
Zhāng Sān hé Lǐ Sì liǎ
Zhang San and Li Si: the two of them.

我们俩
wǒmen liǎ
we two

她们俩
tāmen liǎ
they two

5.4.2   Demonstrative pronouns

这 zhè/zhèi	this
这些 zhèxie/zhèixie	these
那 nà/nèi	that
那些 nàxie/nèixie	those
这样 zhèyang/zhèiyang	like this, this way
那样 nàyang/nèiyang	like that, that way
这么 zhème	so, like this
这么些 zhème xiē	so much, so many
那么 nàme, like that	in that way
那么些 nàme xiē	so much, so many

5.4.3   Interrogative pronouns

谁 shéi/shuí	who, whom
谁的 shéide/shuíde	whose
哪儿 / 哪里 nǎr/nǎli	where
哪 nǎ/něi	which, what
哪些 nǎxiē/něixiē	which ones
什么 shénme	what
什么时候 shénme shíhou	when
为什么 wèishenme	why
几 jǐ	how many (usually under ten)
多少 duōshao	how many, how much (usually over ten)
怎么 zěnme	how, how come
怎么样 zěnmeyàng	how

5.5 Location

The following are used to indicate location, relative location and position:

上边 shāngbianr/上面 shàngmian/上头 shàngtou	above, up there, on top
下边 xiàbianr/下面 xiàmian/下头 xiàtou	under, below, down there
前边 qiánbianr/前面 qiánmian/前头 qiántou	front, in front
后边 hòubianr/后面 hòumian/后头 hòutou	behind, in the back
左边 zuǒbianr	to the left, on the left side
右边 yòubianr	to the right, on the right side
这边 zhèbianr/这边 zhèibianr/这儿 zhèr/这里 zhèli/这里 zhèili	here, over here
那边 nàbianr/那边 nèibianr/那儿 nàr/那里 nàli/那里 nèili	there, over there
里边 lǐbianr/里面 lǐmian/里头 lǐtou	inside
外边 wàibianr/外面 wàimian/外头 wàitou	outside
旁边 pángbiānr	beside, by the side of, next to
中间 zhōngjiān/中间 zhōngjiànr	in the middle, in the center, in between
对面 duìmiànr	opposite, facing, across
斜对面 xiéduìmiànr	diagonally opposite to, kitty-cornered from
底下 dǐxia	underneath, under
东边 dōngbianr/东面 dōngmian	east, to the east of
南边 nánbianr/南面 nánmian	south, to the south of
西边 xībianr/西面 xīmian	west, to the west of
北边 běibianr/北面 běimian	north, to the north of

For example:

这所房子的上边是卧室和卫生间，下边是客厅、饭厅和厨房。
Zhèisuǒ fángzide shàngbianr shi wòshi he wèishēngjiān, xiàbianr shi kètīng, fàntīng he chúfáng.
The upstairs part of this house has bedrooms and bathrooms, and the downstairs part has the living room, dining room, and the kitchen.

他们家的前边有湖，后边有山。
Tāmen jiāde qiánbianr yǒu hú, hòubianr yǒu shān.

There is a lake in front of their house and there is a mountain behind it.

玛丽坐在汤姆和白恩的中间。
Mǎlì zuòzai Tāngmǔ hé Bái'ēn de zhōngjiān.
Mary sits in between Tom and Brian.

我就住在她家对面。
Wǒ jiù zhùzai tājiā duìmiànr.
I live right across from her house.

5.6 Measure words

Measure words, 量词 liàngcí, also known as classifiers, are mandatory when specifying or counting nouns. There are between 150 and 200 measure words in Chinese. Measure words also appear in English but there are very few of them. In "a bar of soap" or "two cups of coffee," "bar" and "cups" are like measure words in Chinese. In addition to the words used for length, area, weight, volume, capacity, year, time, temperature, and currency, there are other specific measure words for specific nouns. The word "月 yuè, month" takes "个 gè" as its measure word. For example, "ten months" is "十个月 shíge yuè."

A formula for the use of measure words is as follows:

这 zhè/zhèi, 那 nà/nèi, 几 jǐ, or 数字 shùzi, numeral + 量词 liàngcí, measure word + 名词 míngcí, noun

These are the most commonly used measure words:

把 bǎ	things with handles, a handful	两把椅子，三把伞，一把米
包 bāo	bundles, packets, bales	一包棉花，一包糖
杯 bēi	cups, glasses	一杯茶，四杯牛奶
本 běn	volumes, books, magazines	这本小说，那本杂志
遍 biàn	once over, frequency	写两遍，再看一遍
册 cè	volumes, books	第一册容易，第二册难
场 cháng	occurrences, happenings	下了一场大雨，一场火
次 cì	number of times an action is taken	一次手术，看了五次，写十次
打 dá	dozen	一打鸡蛋
袋 dài	bags, sacks	一袋面粉，一袋金子
滴 dī	drops	一滴眼泪，一滴汗，一滴血

点 diǎn	points, items	一点建议，几点好处
顶 dǐng	hats, caps	八顶新帽子
栋 dòng	houses, buildings	一栋旧房子，一栋大楼房
段 duàn	paragraphs, sections	一段文章，一段时间，一段距离
堆 duī	heaps, piles	一堆石头，一大堆衣服
对 duì	pairs, couples	六对花瓶，一对新婚夫妇
顿 dùn	regular meals, reprimands	每天吃三顿饭，骂一顿，打一顿
朵 duǒ	flowers, clouds	一朵茉莉花，几朵白云
份 fèn	copies of newspaper, portions	九份中文报，一份礼物，两份快餐
封 fēng	letters	十几封信
幅 fú	paintings	一幅世界名画
个 gè	persons, most things	两个演员，一个问题，六个答案，八个节目，一个念头，做了一个梦
根 gēn	long and slender things	几根火柴，一根针，一根棍子
盒 hé(r)	small boxes	一盒饼干，一盒香，一盒糖果
回 huí	times, cycles, frequency	怎么一回事，每回都看见他，去过一回
家 jiā	families, businesses	那家人很忙，那家饭馆很干净
间 jiān	rooms	四间屋子，一间病房
件 jiàn	articles, items of clothing	三件行李，四件大衣
句 jù	sentences, utterances	两句诗，十句话
棵 kē	trees, cabbages	三棵树，五棵大白菜
口 kǒu	persons, mouthfuls	他家有三口人，喝了两口茶
块 kuài	lumps, pieces, dollars	一块肥皂，一块砖，一块布，一块钱

粒 lì	grain, rice, sand	一粒种子，一粒米，一粒沙子
辆 liàng	vehicles	一辆自行车，一辆新汽车，一辆卡车
门 mén	relatives, courses, a discipline	好几门亲戚，选三门课，这是一门学问
面 miàn	things with flat surface	一面镜子，一面鼓，一面国旗
排 pái	rows of persons or things	一排学生，两排果树，三排楼房
盘 pán	coils, plates	一盘蚊香，一盘围棋，这盘菜很好吃
匹 pī	horses, camels, bolts of cloth	一匹白马，一匹骆驼，一匹红绸子
篇 piān	writings	一篇论文，一篇稿子，一篇日记
片 piàn	slices, pieces, vast expanse	一片面包，一片安眠药，一片空地
瓶 píng	bottles, jars	一瓶可乐，一瓶咳嗽药，一瓶酒
群 qún	crowd, flock	一群人，一群鸭子，一群牛
岁 suì	years (age)	八岁，六十岁
扇 shàn	doors, windows	这扇门，那扇窗户
首 shǒu	poems, songs	那首歌很好听，这首诗太棒了
束 shù	flowers, bunches	一束鲜花
双 shuāng	pairs (two of same kind)	一双手，一双黑皮鞋
所 suǒ	houses or other structures	一所房子，一所有名的大学
趟 tàng	scheduled transportation, actions such as "go," "come" etc.	这是最后一趟车，请你去一趟吧
套 tào	sets, suits	买一套百科全书，一套家具，借一套西装
条 tiáo	things narrow and long	一条裤子，两条裙子，十几条鱼
头 tóu	heads, animals	几十头奶牛，一头羊

碗 wǎn	bowls		吃一碗饭，喝一碗汤
位 wèi	persons (polite)		一位教授，一位老师，两位老人
些 xiē	some		买一些东西，有一些问题，一些好处
样 yàng	kinds, sorts		几样菜，两样水果，三样点心
页 yè	pages		请看第六页，看了十页书
张 zhāng	sheets, things with flat surface		一张火车票，两张照片，十三张桌子
只 zhī	one of a pair, some animals		一只耳朵疼，两只青蛙跳下水，三只小鸟
枝 zhī	branches, rod-shaped things		几枝桃花，一枝毛笔，一枝蜡烛
种 zhǒng	kinds, species		一种动物，各种看法，那种颜色
桌 zhuō	tables of		一桌客人，一桌酒席
座 zuò	mountains, big buildings		那座山很高，邮局在这座大楼里

5.7 Ways of asking questions

There are seven sentence patterns that are used to ask questions. They are listed below:

(1) Add 吗 ma, to the end of a statement:

> 妈妈骂马吗？
> Māma mà mǎ ma?
> Does Mom scold the horse?

> 妈妈没骂马吗？
> Māma méi mà mǎ ma?
> Didn't Mom scold the horse?

(2) Use an interrogative pronoun:

> 该谁骂马呢？
> Gāi shéi mà mǎ ne?
> Whose turn is it to scold the horse?

> 你以为她是谁？
> Nǐ yǐwéi tā shi shéi?
> Who did you think she was?

你能吃多少饺子？
Nǐ néng chī duōshao jiǎozi?
How many dumplings can you eat?

(3)   Ask the listener to choose between affirmative and negative forms:

妈妈骂不骂马？
Māma màbumà mǎ?
Does/Will Mom scold the horse?

她想不想看这本小说？
Tā xiǎngbùxiǎng kàn zhèběn xiǎoshuō?
Would she like to read this novel?

李老师来了没有？
Lǐ lǎoshī láile méiyou?
Has Professor Li arrived yet?

他们有没有孩子？
Tāmen yǒuméiyou háizi?
Do they have children?

(4)   Insert 是不是 shìbushi, into a statement:

妈妈是不是骂马？
Māma shìbushi mà mǎ?
Does Mom scold the horse or not?

他们两个是不是好起来了？
Tāmen liǎngge shìbushi hǎoqilai le?
The two of them have made up, have they?

他们两个好起来了，是不是？
Tāmen liǎngge hǎoqilai le, shìbushi?
The two of them have made up, haven't they?

是不是他们两个好起来了？
Shìbushi tāmen liǎngge hǎoqilai le?
Is it true that the two of them have made up?

(5)   Use 还是 háishi, to offer alternative choices:

妈妈骂马，还是打马？
Māma mà mǎ, háishi dǎ mǎ?
Will Mom scold the horse or beat it?

你去还是我去？
Nǐ qù háishi wǒ qù?
Shall you go, or shall I ?

你今天去还是明天去？
Nǐ jīntian qù háishi míngtian qù?
Will you go today or tomorrow?

你去纽约还是（去）旧金山？
Nǐ qù Niǔyuē háishi (qù) Jiùjīnshān?
Are you going to New York or to San Francisco?

你去滑冰还是（去）滑雪？
Nǐ qù huábīng háishi (qù) huáxuě?
Will you go ice skating or (will you go) skiing?

你去一个星期还是两个星期？
Nǐ qù yíge xīngqī háishi liǎngge xīngqī?
Are you going for one week or for two weeks?

(6) Use 多 duō, to ask about degree or quantity:

妈妈骂的马有多大？
Māma màde mǎ yǒu duōdà?
How big was the horse Mom scolded?

那一大包书有多重？
Nà yídàbāo shū yǒu duōzhòng?
How heavy is that big package of books?

您多大年纪？
Nín duōdà niánji?
How old are you?

她要去多久？
Tā yào qù duōjiǔ?
How long will she be away?

(7) Add 呢 ne, to a word or to a short phrase to ask where it is:

马呢？
Mǎ ne?
Where's the horse?

张老师呢？
Zhāng lǎoshī ne?
Where is Professor Zhang?

我的手套呢？
Wǒde shǒutàor ne?
Where are my gloves?

"呢 ne" may also be added at the end of other interrogative sentences when the speaker wishes to reveal curiosity and/or doubt, or to soften the tone:

你以为她是谁呢？
Nǐ yǐwéi tā shi shéi ne?
Who did you think she was?

你去还是我去呢？
Nǐ qù háishi wǒ qù ne?
Shall **you** go, or shall **I**?

她要去多久呢？

Tā yào qù duō jiǔ ne?

How long will she be away?

5.8 Auxiliary verbs/optative verbs

Verbs that help other verbs to express necessity, possibility and willingness are called auxiliary verbs or optative verbs, 能愿动词 néngyuàn dòngcí. We are familiar with auxiliary verbs in English: the "can" in "I can do it"; the "able" in "I am able to go"; the "may" in "You may go"; the "should" in "I should go." They appear in Chinese in the following forms:

5.8.1 Capability: 能 néng, 能够 nénggòu, 会 huì

"Néng, can" may indicate a general ability to do something, as in:

他明天不能跟我们去。

Tā míngtian bùnéng gēn wǒmen qù.

He can't go with us tomorrow.

我能够请三个人跟我去。

Wǒ nénggou qǐng sānge rén gēn wǒ qù.

I can invite three people to go with me.

"Huì" may mean "can" in the sense of "mastered the skill of," as in:

我不会游泳。

Wǒ búhuì yóuyǒng.

I can't swim (I don't know how to swim).

我不会抽烟。

Wǒ búhuì chōuyān.

I don't know how to smoke. (a polite way of saying "I don't smoke" without making the other person feel guilty for offering you a cigarette)

5.8.2 Possibility: 能 néng, 可能 kěnéng, 能够 nénggòu, 会 huì

"Néng, can, may" may also indicate possibility under certain conditions, as in:

他的车能坐五个人。

Tāde chē néng zuò wǔge rén.

His car can seat five people.

我们可能迟到。

Wǒmen kěnéng chídào.

We may possibly arrive late.

"Huì, may, might" may also indicate likelihood of someone doing something, as in:

这么晚，她不会来。
Zhème wǎn, tā búhuì lái.
It's so late. She won't come.

门票那么贵，他不会买。
Ménpiào nàme guì, tā búhuì mǎi.
The admission tickets are so expensive, he wouldn't buy them.

5.8.3 Permission: 可以 kěyǐ, 能 néng, 许 xǔ

"Néng" may also mean "can" in the sense of "be permitted to," as in:

教室里能抽烟吗？
Jiàoshìli néng chōuyān ma?
Can one smoke in the classroom?

教室里可以抽烟吗？
Jiàoshìli kěyǐ chōuyān ma?
May one smoke in the classroom?

教室里许抽烟吗？
Jiàoshìli xǔ chōuyān ma?
Is smoking allowed in the classroom?

5.8.4 Perceived obligation or likelihood: 应该 yīnggāi, 应当 yīngdāng, 该 gāi, 要 yào:

The feeling that something ought to be done, or that something is likely to happen, is usually expressed by the auxiliary verbs yīnggāi, yīngdāng, or the abbreviated form "gāi." For example:

十点了，我应该回家了。
Shí diǎn le, wǒ yīnggāi huíjiā le.
It's ten o'clock. I should go home now.

你不应当得罪她。
Nǐ bùyīngdāng dézuì tā.
You shouldn't offend her.

已经不早了，我该走了。
Yǐjīng bùzǎo le, wǒ gāi zǒu le
It's getting late. I should be leaving now.

下雪了，你开车要小心点儿。
Xià xuě le, nǐ kāichē yào xiǎoxīndiǎnr.
It's snowing. You should drive carefully.

5.8.5 Imperative obligation: 必须 bìxū, 必得 bìděi, 得 děi:

The requirement (as opposed to the feeling) that something must (as opposed to "ought to") be done is expressed using the auxiliary verb "bìxū, bìděi," or commonly "děi" before the verb, as in the following examples:

你后天必须出席开会。
Nǐ hòutiān bìxū chūxí kāihuì.
You really must attend the meeting the day after tomorrow.

我们必得参加毕业典礼。
Wǒmen bìděi cānjiā bìyèdiǎnlǐ.
We have to attend the graduation ceremony.

我有重要的约会，所以得早点儿下课。
Wǒ yǒu zhòngyàode yuēhuì, suǒyǐ děi zǎodiǎnr xiàkè.
I have an important appointment, so I have to leave class a bit
    early.

5.9 Negation

Negation in Chinese may be as simple and direct, or as roundabout and subtle, as the occasion requires. The simplest, most straightforward way to negate a verb is to attach the prefix "不 bù" to it.

你去吗?
Nǐ qù ma?
Are you going?

我不去。
Wǒ bú qù.
No, I'm not going.

If a sentence contains a string of verbs, or a principle verb preceded by a string of modifiers, then the "bù" is usually placed at the beginning of the string:

她不喝酒。
Tā bù hējiǔ.
She doesn't drink wine.

她不喜欢喝酒。
Tā bù xǐhuān hējiǔ.
She doesn't like to drink wine.

她不喜欢一个人在家里喝酒。
Tā bù xǐhuān yígeren zai jiāli hējiǔ.
She doesn't like to drink wine by herself at home.

"不 bù" can be used to negate any and all verbs except "有 yǒu, to have," which must be negated by "没 méi":

你有电脑吗?

Nǐ yǒu diànnǎo ma?

Do you have a computer?

我没有电脑。

Wǒ méiyou diànnǎo.

No, I don't have a computer.

The negative adverb "不 bù" is used to negate actions and intentions to act in the present and in the future, but for completed actions it is only used to negate the intention to act, not the action itself:

我今天不去。

Wǒ jīntian bú qù.

I'm not going today.

我明天不去。

Wǒ míngtian bú qù.

I'm not going tomorrow.

昨天我决定不去。

Zuótian wǒ juédìng bú qù.

Yesterday I decided I wouldn't go.

To negate a completed action, we place "没 méi" before the verb:

我昨天没去。

Wǒ zuótian méi qù.

I didn't go yesterday.

To negate sentences with auxiliary verbs, place "不 bù" before the auxiliary verbs.

5.10   Particles

Just as Chinese nouns and pronouns have no declension, so the verbs have no inflexion. Since Chinese verbs have no inflexion, the role of placing an action in the past, present, or future is performed by stating a time-when expression before the verb:

昨天我进城。

Zuótian wǒ jìnchéng.

I went downtown yesterday.

今天我进城。

Jīntian wǒ jìnchéng.

I'm going downtown today.

明天我进城。

Míngtian wǒ jìnchéng.

I will go downtown tomorrow.

It can also be achieved by adding a "perfective aspect" particle like "le" or "guò" to indicate that a specific action was or has been completed, or that something has been done before.

我进城了。
Wǒ jìnchéng le.
I went downtown.

我进过城。
Wǒ jìnguo chéng.
I've gone downtown before.

Mastery of particles, 助词 zhùcí, such as these is an extremely important part of using Chinese properly and effectively. Particles are added to a word, a phrase, or a sentence to indicate various supplementary meanings, grammatical relations, or mood. In this section we will examine the use and function of three different kinds of particles in Mandarin: structural particles, aspectual particles, and modal particles.

5.10.1 Structural particles: the three de

Structural particles are added to words or phrases to indicate grammatical relations. There are only three of them, and they are all pronounced "de" (neutral tone): 的，地，and 得.

The particle "的":

The particle "的" is used most commonly as a "possessive marker," as in the following sample sentences:

那是妈妈的马。
Nà shi māmade mǎ.
That's Mom's horse.

你的汉语真棒！
Nǐde Hànyǔ zhēn bàng!
Your Chinese is terrific!

It is also used at the end of an adjectival phrase, indicating that what precedes is a modifier, and what follows is being modified, as in:

蓝颜色的夹克
lán yánsède jiákè
a blue-colored jacket

相当便宜的汉堡包
xiāngdāng piányide hànbǎobāo
rather cheap hamburger

Note that a single-syllable adjective with no adverbial modifier such as 很 hěn or 真 zhēn or 非常 fēicháng preceding it, as in "好孩

子 hǎo háizi, good child," "红车 hóng chē, red car," or "小杯子 xiǎo bēizi, small cup" does not take a "的 de."

"的 de" is also used as a "subordinate clause marker," indicating that the preceding clause modifies what follows, often using the pattern "Subject + verb de + noun," the noun which/that the subject verbs, as in the following samples:

我看的杂志很有意思。
Wǒ kànde zázhì hěn yǒuyìsi.
The magazine which/that I am reading is very interesting.

这是妈妈昨天买的马。
Zhè shi māma zuótiān mǎide mǎ.
This is the horse which/that Mom bought yesterday.

The particle "的" is also frequently used in elliptical sentences in which the modified word is omitted because it is clearly understood by speaker and listener, as in the following examples:

红颜色的毛衣是你的，蓝的是我的。
Hóng yánsède máoyī shi nǐde, lánde shi wǒde.
The red sweater is yours, and the blue one is mine.

大的是你的，小的是我的。
Dàde shi nǐde, xiǎode shi wǒde.
The big one is yours, and the small one is mine.

The particle "地 de":

The second "地 de" (also pronounced "dì" when used as a noun meaning "place" or "land") is an adverbial modifier particle that always precedes the verb it modifies, as in the following examples:

他们高高兴兴地工作。
Tāmen gāogāoxìngxìngde gōngzuò.
They are happily going about their work.

她们很快地写完了第二本小说。
Tāmen hěn kuàide xiěwánle dì'èrběn xiǎoshuō.
They quickly finished writing their second novel.

Note: "地 de" is often not used following disyllabic adverbs such as "一起 yìqǐ," "一齐 yìqí," "一共 yígòng," "相当 xiāngdāng" and "非常 fēicháng," unless used for emphasis.

The particle "得 de":

The third "得 de" (also pronounced "dé" meaning "to get" or "to achieve," and "děi" meaning "must" or "have to" as a verb) is a verb complement particle. It always follows the verb and precedes complementary information which comments on the manner, extent, degree, or quality of the action.

To illustrate:

他说得太快，我听不懂。
Tā shuōde tài kuài, wǒ tīngbudǒng.
He talks too fast. I can't understand him.

她唱得非常好听。
Tā chàngde fēicháng hǎotīng.
She sings extremely well.

To negate the above two examples, we insert "不" after the "得," and not before the verb:

他说得不快，我听得懂。
Tā shuōde búkuài, wǒ tīngdedǒng.
He doesn't talk fast. I can understand him.

她唱得不好听。
Tā chàngde bùhǎotīng.
She doesn't sing well.

If the verb complement "得 de" particle is used with a "verb + object" structure, such as "说汉语 shuō Hànyǔ, speak Chinese," "写字 xiězì, write," "走路 zǒulù, walk," or "用筷子 yòng kuàizi, use chopsticks," the verb is usually repeated after stating the object, to form the pattern "Subject + verb + object + verb de + adjective," as in the following sample sentences:

他看书看得太多。
Tā kànshū kànde tài duō.
He reads too much.

妈妈骂马骂得很利害。
Māma mà mǎ màde hěn lìhai.
Mom scolded the horse severely.

老太太走路走得真慢。
Lǎotàitai zǒulù zǒude zhēn màn.
The old lady walks very slowly.

To negate the three sentences above, we simply replace "太 tài," "很 hěn," and "真 zhēn" with "不 bù" or "没那么 méi nàme Adjective, not that Adjective," or add "不 bù" before "太 tài" or "很 hěn." If the verb's complement is a clause rather than a simple adjective, the meaning becomes "to verb so…that …" as in these samples:

我累得都站不起来了。
Wǒ lèide dōu zhànbuqǐlai le.
I'm so tired that I can't stand up.

她笑得嘴都合不拢了。
Tā xiàode zuǐ dōu hébulǒng le.
She laughed so hard she couldn't close her mouth.

The "得 de" particle is also used as a "potential complement" (来得了 láideliǎo, be able to come; 吃得了 chīdeliǎo, be able to eat up; 来不了 láibuliǎo, unable to come; 吃不了 chībuliǎo, unable to eat up," etc.), as introduced in the "Complements" section above.

5.10.2   Aspect particles: le, ne, zhe, guo

When we speak of the "aspects" of an action, we are referring to five different stages, namely: "about to happen," "in progress," "in a continuing state," "in a completed state" and "a state of having been done before." They are used for actions that take place in past, present, or future.

About to happen "了 le":

The typical "about to happen" sentence structure is "Subject + 要 yào + verb + 了 le, The subject is about to verb," as in the following illustrative examples:

飞机要起飞了。
Fēijī yào qǐfēi le.
The airplane is about to take off.

秋天要来了。
Qiūtian yào lái le.
Autumn is about to arrive.

妈妈又要骂马了。
Māma yòu yào mà mǎ le.
Mom is about to scold the horse again.

To emphasize that the action will take place very soon, we may add an adverbial intensifier before the "要 yào," as follows:

客人就要来了。
Kèren jiù yào lái le.
The guests will be arriving very soon.

我快要饿死了。
Wǒ kuài yào èsǐ le.
I'm just about to die of starvation.

Note the similarity between the "about to happen 了 le" above, and the "change of status 了 le" below:

外边下雨了。
Wàibianr xiàyǔ le.
It's raining outside (it wasn't before).

天亮了。
Tiān liàng le.
It's getting bright outside (it was dark before).

Completed state "了 le":

The aspect particle "了 le" is used immediately after the verb in a simple "Subject + Verb" sentence to indicate that the action is, was, has been, or will have been completed:

他走了。
Tā zǒu le.
He left./He has left.

While it may refer to an action that has already taken place, it must not be seen as a "past tense marker," because it may just as well refer to present perfect or future perfect events. When a single syllable verb takes a single syllable object, the "le" follows the object at the end of the sentence:

他们吃饭了。
Tāmen chīfàn le.
They ate./They have eaten.

他打我了!
Tā dǎ wǒ le!
He hit me!/He has hit me!

Note that the verbal aspect particle "le" indicating completion and the sentence modal particle "le" indicating that a new situation has come about, may be used in the same sentence:

他们吃了饭了。
Tāmen chīle fàn le.
They have eaten.

他打了我了!
Tā dǎle wǒ le!
He hit me!

When the verb takes an object that is quantified, "le" follows the verb and precedes the object:

她喝了三杯水。
Tā hēle sānbēi shuǐ.
She drank/has drunk three glasses of water.

张教授写了两本书。
Zhāng jiàoshòu xiěle liǎngběn shū.
Professor Zhang wrote/has written two books.

When the verb takes a complement, "le" usually follows the complement:

张老师走进来了。
Zhāng lǎoshī zǒujinlai le.
Teacher Zhang walked in.

他们最近搬走了。
Tāmen zuìjìn bānzǒu le.
They moved away recently.

Following are more sample sentences:

谁来了？
Shéi lái le?
Who came?/Who has arrived?

她买书了。
Tā mǎi shū le.
She bought (the) book(s).

她买了书了。
Tā mǎile shū le.
She has bought (the) book(s).

她买了三本书。
Tā mǎile sānběn shū.
She bought/has bought three books.

她买到了那三本书。
Tā mǎidàole nà sānběn shū.
She was/has been able to buy those three books.

她买了书才去吃午饭。
Tā mǎile shū cái qù chī wǔfàn.
She went/will go to have lunch only after she had/has bought the
  book(s).

咱们等她来了再说吧。
Zánmen děng tā láile zài shuō ba.
Let's discuss it after she gets here.

我吃了十个饺子。
Wǒ chīle shíge jiǎozi.
I ate/have eaten ten dumplings.

我学了三年汉语。
Wǒ xuéle sānnián Hànyǔ.
I studied/have studied Chinese for three years.

我学汉语学了三年。
Wǒ xué Hànyǔ xuéle sānnián.
I studied/have studied Chinese for three years.

The "double le," Subject + verb 了 + quantified object + 了,
indicates "done so far, but not yet finished":

我已经吃了十个饺子了。
Wǒ yǐjing chīle shíge jiǎozi le.
I've already eaten ten dumplings (so far, and not yet finished eating
  them).

我学了三年汉语了。

Wǒ xuéle sānnián Hànyǔ le.

I've been studying Chinese for three years now (not finished yet).

我学汉语学了三年了。

Wǒ xué Hànyǔ xuéle sānnián le.

I've been studying Chinese for three years now (not finished yet).

In progress "呢 ne":

The typical "in progress" sentence structure is "Subject + 正在 zhèngzai/正 zhèng/在 zài + verb (+ 呢 ne)," as in the following examples:

她正在吃饭呢。

Tā zhèngzai chīfàn ne.

She was/is/will be eating.

她正在吃饭。

Tā zhèngzai chīfàn.

She was/is/will be eating.

她正吃饭（呢）。

Tā zhèng chīfàn (ne).

She was/is/will be eating.

她在吃饭（呢）。

Tā zai chīfàn (ne).

She was/is/will be eating.

她吃饭呢。

Tā chīfàn ne.

She was/is/will be eating.

The "in progress" aspect is negated by using "没 méi" instead of, or in front of "正在 zhèngzai," "正 zhèng," or "在 zài," and without "呢 ne," as in:

她在吃饭吗？

Tā zai chīfàn ma?

Was/Is/ she eating?

(1) 她没吃饭，她在打电话呢。

　　　Tā méi chīfàn, tā zai dǎ diànhuà ne.

　　　She was/is not eating. She was/is making a telephone call.

(2) 她没在吃饭，她在打电话呢。

　　　Tā méi zai chīfàn, tā zai dǎ diànhuà ne.

　　　She was/is not eating. She was/is making a telephone call.

Continuous or on-going state "着 zhe":

When we want to indicate the continuation of an action, or the on-going result of a completed action, we use the particle "着 zhe" immediately following the verb. Typical examples would be:

他高高兴兴地走着。
Tā gāogāoxìngxìngde zǒuzhe.
He was/is walking happily.

她忙着给丈夫打电话。
Tā mángzhe gěi zhàngfu dǎ diànhuà.
She was/is busy phoning her husband.

他现在还活着吗？
Tā xiànzài hái huózhe ma?
Is he still alive?

墙上挂着一张画儿。
Qiángshang guàzhe yìzhāng huàr.
A picture was/is hanging on the wall.

他的嘴可不会闲着。
Tāde zuǐ kě búhuì xiánzhe.
He cannot stop talking.

他们两个人说着说着吵起来了。
Tāmen liǎngge rén shuōzhe shuōzhe chǎoqilai le.
As those two were talking, they started to argue.

我不喜欢站着吃饭。
Wǒ bù xǐhuan zhànzhe chīfàn.
I don't like to eat standing up.

弟弟拍着巴掌笑。
Dìdi pāizhe bāzhang xiào.
Little brother laughed/laughs, clapping his hands.

The progressive and continuous aspects are often used together in the same sentence:

她正在图书馆看着报呢。
Tā zhèngzai túshūguǎn kànzhe bào ne.
She was/is reading a newspaper in the library.

他吃着饭看电视呢。
Tā chīzhe fàn kàn diànshì ne.
He was/is watching television while eating.

着 and 呢 are often used together as an adjectival suffix meaning "extremely adjective," as in:

大街上热闹着呢。
Dàjiēshang rènaozhe ne.
It's really bustling out on the street.

小王那个家伙厉害着呢。
Xiǎo Wáng nàge jiāhuo lìhaizhe ne.
That fellow Wang is really formidable.

Having been done before "过 guò":

The "experiential aspect" of an action or event, meaning "to have had the experience of verbing before" is expressed by adding "过 guò" immediately after the verb. Note that there are two different kinds of "experience": (1) to have done something ever before in one's life; and (2) to have done something which one does regularly (i.e., this year, this month, this week, today, etc.).

The following sentences illustrate both usages:

(1) 你坐过飞机吗？
     Nǐ zuòguo fēijī ma?
     Have you ever flown in an airplane?

     你去过桂林没有？
     Nǐ qùguo Guìlín méiyou?
     Have you ever been to Guilin?

     我没买过新车。
     Wǒ méimǎiguo xīn chē.
     I've never bought a new car before.

     你吃过四川菜没有？
     Nǐ chīguo Sìchuān cài méiyou?
     Have you ever eaten Sichuanese cuisine?

(2) 吃饭了吗？吃过了，谢谢。
     Chīfàn le ma? … Chīguo le, xièxie.
     Have you eaten yet? … Yes I have, thanks.

     你今年放过几天假？
     Nǐ jīnnián fàngguo jǐtiān jià?
     How many days of vacation have you taken this year?

     邮递员今天已经来过了。
     Yóudìyuán jīntian yǐjing láiguo le.
     The letter carrier has already come today.

5.10.3 Modal particles: a, ba, de, le, ma, ne

Modal particles are used at the end of sentences to verbalize emotions and moods that accompany an utterance. A few of the most commonly used are introduced below:

啊 a:

The modal particle "啊 a" is used to soften the tone of a sentence, leaving the meaning of the sentence unchanged. It may be used at the end of an interjection to express feelings of admiration, regret, contempt or worry, as in the following examples:

钱都用光了，怎么办啊！
Qián dōu yòngguāng le, zěnmebàn a!
The money's all spent. What'll we do now!

那个小孩子真聪明啊。
Nàge xiǎoháizi zhēn cōngming a.
That kid is really smart.

可惜啊！她来了那么一小会儿就走了。
Kěxī a! Tā láile nàme yìxiǎohuǐr jiù zǒu le.
Such a pity! She left after staying for such a short while.

他真是令人讨厌啊！
Tā zhēnshi lìngréntǎoyàn a!
He's truly disgusting!

It is also used to show agreement, affirmation, warning, or exhortation, as in the following:

是啊！我完全同意你的看法。
Shì a! Wǒ wánquán tóngyì nǐde kànfa.
Yes! I totally agree with your viewpoint.

你一定要来啊！
Nǐ yídìng yào lái a!
You really must come, you know!

行啊！我们按着你的想法做。
Xíng a! Wǒmen ànzhe nǐde xiǎngfǎ zuò.
Okay! We'll do it according to your idea.

It is often used at the end of interrogative sentences that use question words:

你到哪儿去啊？
Nǐ dào nǎr qù a?
Where are you going?

王经理最近怎么样啊？
Wáng jīnglǐ zuìjìn zěnmeyàng a?
How is Manager Wang doing these days?

And it is often used between items in a series, when pausing to think, rather like "uh…." in English, and often following a greeting:

狗啊，猫啊，都是宠物。
Gǒu a, māo a, dōu shi chǒngwù.
Dogs, cats, they're all pets.

老张啊，那个人很复杂。
Lǎo Zhāng a, nàge rén hěn fùzá.
Zhang, uh… is a very complex person.

再见啊，小黄！
Zàijiàn a, Xiǎo Huáng!
Goodbye, Huang!

吧 *ba:*

The modal particle "吧 ba" is used at the end of a statement to give the feeling of a suggestion or a request, to show expectation of agreement, or to indicate that the speaker thinks this might be the case, but is not certain:

我们不如一起去吧！
Wǒmen bùrú yìqǐ qù ba!
We might as well go together!

你帮我一个忙吧。
Nǐ bāng wǒ yíge máng ba.
How about giving me a hand?

那你的看法跟我的一样吧？
Nà nǐde kànfa gēn wǒde yíyàng ba?
Well then, you and I share the same view, don't we?

他们大概不会想吃凤爪吧？
Tāmen dàgài búhuì xiǎngchī fèngzhǎo ba?
They probably wouldn't want to eat phoenix claws (chicken feet), would they?

的 *de:*

As a modal particle at the end of a sentence, "的 de" conveys a sense of affirmation and certainty:

哪儿有这种道理的！
Nǎr yǒu zhèzhǒng dàolǐ de!
How unreasonable!

Used in the "是 shì...的 de" pattern, "de" conveys emphasis on the time, place, cause, manner, purpose, or agent of an action, most often a completed action. In a positive statement, the "shì" of the "shì...de" pattern may be omitted, but in the negative form "búshì," "shì" may not be omitted:

爷爷是哪年生的？
Yéye shì nǎnián shēng de?
What year was Grandpa born?

我（是）在多伦多大学学的汉语。
Wǒ (shi) zài Duōlúnduō Dàxué xuéde Hànyǔ.
I studied Chinese at the University of Toronto.

胖子不是一口吃的。
Pàngzi búshi yìkǒu chī de.
Fat people don't get that way from a single bite.

了 *le:*

The modal particle "了 le" at the end of a sentence often shows the emergence of a new situation, a change in understanding, opinion, ideas, etc.

For example:

天黑了。
Tiān hēi le.
It's become dark outside.

他们现在是博士了。
Tāmen xiànzài shi bóshì le.
They have now become Ph.D.s.

啊，我明白了，他不是你的舅舅。
À, wǒ míngbai le, tā búshi nǐde jiùjiu.
Oh, now I understand – he's not your uncle.

我有事，不能跟你去了。
Wǒ yǒu shì, bùnéng gēn nǐ qù le.
Something's come up, so now I can't go with you.

走了，走了，不能再等了。
Zǒu le, zǒu le, bù néng zài děng le.
Let's go! Let's go! We can't wait any longer.

吗 *ma:*

The interrogative modal particle "吗 ma" is added at the end of any declarative sentence to turn the sentence into a question. Note that "吗 ma" can never be added to a sentence that has already been made into a question using "question words," like "谁 shéi?" "什么 shénme?" "几 jǐ?" "多少 duōshǎo?" or after using the "Verb-bù-Verb" question form. We may say:

这是你的书吗？
Zhè shi nǐde shū ma?
Is this your book?

明天是星期三吗？
Míngtian shi xīngqīsān ma?
Is tomorrow Wednesday?

呢 *ne:*

The modal particle "呢 ne" is used at the end of a sentence to show "shades of feeling," such as softening the tone of an interrogative sentence (except interrogative sentences ending in "吗 ma"), toning down a rhetorical question, or softening an exclamation. Following the utterance of a simple noun phrase or a pronoun, it means "what about...?" or "where is...?" For example:

你怎么没有去呢？
Nǐ zěnme méiyou qù ne?
How come you didn't go?

她是谁呢？
Tā shi shéi ne?
Who might she have been/be?

我怎么会不知道呢？
Wǒ zěnme huì bùzhīdao ne?
How could I not have known/not know that?

诶？你太太呢？
Éi? Nǐ tàitai ne?
Oh! Where is your wife?

我想吃口东西，你呢？
Wǒ xiǎng chī kǒu dōngxi, nǐ ne?
I'd like to get a bite to eat, how about you?

你看，她的脸红着呢！
Nǐ kàn, tāde liǎn hóngzhe ne!
Look at her: her face is red!

怎么办呢？
Zěnme bàn ne?
What's to be done?

5.10.4 Other frequently used modal particles

呗 "bei"	to add the feeling that something is very obvious or easy to resolve.
嘛 "ma"	to add the feeling of obviousness or the tone of impatience.
啦 "la"	a fusion of the "change of status" 了 le + 啊 a.
嘞 "lei"	like 啦 la, but more informal, colloquial, or light-hearted.
咯 "lo"	a fusion of 了 le ＋噢 o, like the change of status "了 le," but more emphatic.
喽 "lou"	a fusion of 了 le and 呕 ou, colloquially intensifying the "了 le."
哪 "na"	same as 啊 a, but used following syllables ending with "-n" or "-ng."
哇 "wa"	same as 啊 a, but used following syllables ending with "-u," "-ao," or "-ou."
呀 "ya"	same as 啊 a, but used following syllables ending with "-a,""-e," "-i," "o," or "ü."
哟 "yo"	expresses an exclamatory or imperative sense.

5.11 Object inversion: "把 **bǎ**" sentences

The "把 bǎ" sentence is one of the most useful and characteristic structures in the Chinese language, because it "disposes" of specific things, or "settles" specific matters, giving the topic and the speaker a sense of completion and closure. An English language near-equivalent grammatical pattern might be: "The Subject takes the object and verbs it." Another way of explaining the use of the "bǎ" construction in structural terms is to say that it brings the object in front of an inseparable verb compound, such as "Verb + 过来 guòlai" or "Verb + 上去 shàngqu." The basic grammatical pattern is "Subject + bǎ + object + verb + complement." It is most important to remember that the "bǎ-inverted" object cannot be acted on by a single-syllable verb alone, but requires more syllables. The options are: reduplicate the single-syllable verb; add a complementary particle or phrase after the verb; or add the perfective aspect particle "了 le."

Specific circumstances wherein the "把 bǎ" construction is preferred include:

1. Giving a brief command:

   把它吃掉！
   Bǎ tā chīdiao!
   Eat it all up!

2. When the verb takes on a directional complement, "把 bǎ" is used to bring the object before the verb:

   请你把书拿过来。
   Qǐng nǐ bǎ shū náguolai.
   Please bring the book over here.

3. When we want to emphasize or exaggerate the way a person feels, or the way a person reacts to something, we may use "把 bǎ" with an adjective followed by a resultative complement:

   把她乐死了！
   Bǎ tā lèsile!
   She was thrilled to death!

   We may take the normal "S-V-O" sentence "妈妈骂马 māma mà mǎ, Mom scolds the horse" and turn it into a "把 bǎ" sentence, but we may not say: "māma bǎ mǎ mà," because "mà" alone does not imply disposition of a specific object.

   We may, however, say:

   妈妈把马骂了一顿。
   Māma bǎ mǎ màle yídùn.
   Mom gave the horse a good scolding.

妈妈把马骂得很利害。
Māma bǎ mǎ màde hěn lìhai.
Mom gave the horse a severe scolding.

妈妈把马骂来骂去。
Māma bǎ mǎ màlái màqù.
Mom scolded that horse over and over.

他把钱都花光了。
Tā bǎ qián dōu huāguāng le.
He spent all the money.

把门关上！
Bǎ mén guānshang!
Close the door!

差一点儿把她吓死了。
Chàyidiǎnr bǎ tā xiàsǐ le.
It almost scared her to death.

5.12　Commands and suggestions

The simplest and most common way to make a command is to utter
a verb with an abrupt tone of voice:

来！
Lái!
Come here!

去！
Qù!
Go!

吃！
Chī!
Eat!

Often the command may require the addition of a direct object,
an indirect object, a resultative complement, or a directional
complement, as in the following examples:

放手！
Fàng shǒu!
Let go!

给我！
Gěi wǒ!
Give it to me!

放开！
Fàngkāi!
Let go!

放下！
Fàngxia!
Put it down!

过来！
Guòlai!
Come over here!

出去！
Chūqu!
Get out!

A suggestion, as opposed to a direct command, can be made most simply by softening the tone of voice and adding a "吧 ba" at the end of the sentence:

来吧。
Lái ba.
Come.

去吧。
Qù ba.
Go.

吃吧。
Chī ba.
Go ahead and eat.

放手吧。
Fàng shǒu ba.
You can let go.

给我吧。
Gěi wǒ ba.
You can give it to me.

放开吧。
Fàngkāi ba.
You can let go.

放下吧。
Fàngxia ba.
You can put it down.

过来吧。
Guòlai ba.
Come on over.

出去吧。
Chūqu ba.
You can go out.

The sample phrases above may also be prefaced with a "请 qǐng, please" or with "应该 yīnggāi, should" or "不如 bùrú, might as well" to further soften the tone.

To give a negative command or suggestion, the normal and simplest way is to add a "别 bié, don't" before the command or suggestion:

别去!
Bié qù!
Don't go!

别站着吃饭。
Bié zhànzhe chīfàn.
Don't eat standing up.

别客气。
Bié kèqi.
You're welcome./You needn't be so polite.

别想跟他借钱。
Bié xiǎng gēn tā jièqián.
Don't even think about borrowing money from him.

别管她。
Bié guǎn tā.
Don't pay any attention to her.

5.13 Comparisons

5.13.1 Comparison of equality

The following two patterns are the basic ways of comparing similar things:

(1) A 和/跟 hé/gēn B 一样 yíyàng Adjective, A is as Adjective as B.

妈妈和马一样高.
Māma hé mǎ yíyàng gāo.
Mom is as tall as the horse.

中文和英文一样容易说。
Zhōngwén hé Yīngwén yíyàng róngyì shuō.
Chinese is as easy to speak as English.

马跟妈妈一样高。
Mǎ gēn māma yíyàng gāo.
The horse is as tall as Mom.

化学跟物理一样难学。
Huàxué gēn wùlǐ yíyàng nánxué.
Chemistry is as hard to learn as physics.

(2)   A 有 yǒu B 那么 nàme adjective, A is just as adjective as B.

妈妈有马那么高。
Māma yǒu mǎ nàme gāo.
Mom is just as tall as the horse.

这家的衣服有那家的那么便宜。
Zhèjiāde yīfu yǒu nàjiāde nàme piányi.
Clothes in this store are just as inexpensive as the clothes in that
    store.
Note: We cannot say: 妈妈有马那么很高, Māma yǒu mǎ nàme
hěn gāo. To convey both ideas, i.e., that Mom is very tall, and that
she is as tall as the horse, we would have to say:

妈妈很高，她有马那么高。
Māma hěn gāo, tā yǒu mǎ nàme gāo.
Mom is tall. She is as tall as the horse.

5.13.2   Negating comparison of equality

The two core patterns for negating comparisons of equality are:
"A and B are not equally adjective," and "A is not so adjective as B."
Variations are as follows:

(1)   A 和/跟 hé/gēn B 不一样 bùyíyàng adjective, A and B are not
equally adjective.

小张和小赵不一样聪明。
Xiǎo Zhāng hé Xiǎo Zhào bùyíyàng cōngming.
Zhang and Zhao are not equally intelligent.

中国跟加拿大不一样大。
Zhōngguo gēn Jiānádà bùyíyàng dà.
China and Canada are not the same size.

(2)   A 没有 méiyou B 那么 nàme adjective, A is not so adjective as B.

中国的总面积没有加拿大的那么大。
Zhōngguode zǒngmiànjī méiyǒu Jiānádàde nàme dà.
The total area of China is not so large as that of Canada.

5.13.3   Comparison of inequality

Comparison of inequality is not the same as negating comparison
of equality. When we compare inequality, we state which of two
subjects is more "adjective" than the other, as in the following
patterns:

(1)   A 比 bǐ B adjective, A is more adjective than B.

小张比小赵聪明。
Xiǎo Zhāng bǐ Xiǎo Zhào cōngming.
Zhang is more intelligent than Zhao.

(2) A 比 bǐ B 还 hái adjective, A is even more adjective than B.

加拿大的总面积比中国的还大。
Jiānádàde zǒngmiànjī bǐ Zhōngguode hái dà.
The total area of Canada is even larger than that of China.

5.13.4 Negating comparison of inequality

To say that one of two subjects is not more "adjective" than the other, we use the following pattern:

A 不比 bùbǐ B adjective, A is not more adjective than B.

小张不比小赵聪明。
Xiǎo Zhāng bùbǐ Xiǎo Zhào cōngming.
Zhang is not more intelligent than Zhao.

加拿大的总面积不比俄国的大。
Jiānádàde zǒngmiànjī bùbǐ Éguode dà.
The total area of Canada is not greater than that of Russia.

纽约的物价不比伦敦的贵。
Niǔyuēde wùjià bùbǐ Lúndūnde guì.
Prices in New York are not higher than those in London.

5.13.5 Degrees of inequality by comparison

When we want to say "A is more adjective than B" by a specified amount or degree, we may use one of the following sentence patterns:

(1) A 比 bǐ B adjective + number + measure word, A is X-measure word more adjective than B.

马比妈妈高一英尺。
Mǎ bǐ māma gāo yìyīngchǐ.
The horse is one foot taller than Mom.

妈妈比马矮一英尺。
Māma bǐ mǎ ǎi yìyīngchǐ.
mom is one foot shorter than the horse.

(2) A 比 bǐ B adjective 得多 deduō, A is much more adjective than B.

马比妈妈高得多。
Mǎ bǐ māma gāode duō.
The horse is a lot taller than Mom.

(3) A 比 bǐ B adjective 多了 duō le, A is much more adjective than B.

马比妈妈高多了。
Mǎ bǐ māma gāo duō le.
The horse is much taller than Mom.

(4) A Verb + object + verb 得 de 比 bǐ B adjective, A verb + object
     more adjective-ly than B.

> 妈妈骂马骂得比我多。
> Māma mà mǎ màde bǐ wǒ duō.
> Mom scolds the horse more often than I do.

> 他说汉语说得比我好。
> Tā shuō Hànyǔ shuōde bǐ wǒ hǎo.
> He speaks Chinese better than I do.

> 张三开车开得比李四快。
> Zhāng Sān kāichē kāide bǐ Lǐ Sì kuài.
> Zhang San drives faster than Li Si.

> 李四开车开得比张三慢。
> Lǐ Sì kāichē kāide bǐ Zhāng Sān màn.
> Li Si drives more slowly than Zhang San.

5.14 Complements

A complement, 补语 bǔyǔ, is a word or phrase that follows the main
verb of a sentence in order to enhance its meaning.

The following are different kinds of complements.

5.14.1 Complement of degree

For an ordinary declarative statement that someone "verbs" well or
poorly, quickly, slowly, sloppily, earnestly, etc., we use this simple
pattern:

(1) Subject + verb 得 de + adjective, The subject verbs adjective-ly.
     Used as a particle following a verb and preceding a resultative
     complement, a complement of degree, 程度补语 chéngdù bǔyǔ,
     "得 de" lets us know that what follows will tell us the extent or
     degree of the verbing, as in the following examples:

> 她跑得很快。
> Tā pǎode hěn kuài.
> She runs fast.

> 他走得很慢。
> Tā zǒude hěn màn.
> He walks slowly.

> 我写得不好。
> Wǒ xiěde bùhǎo.
> I write poorly.

> 她来得真早。
> Tā láide zhēn zǎo.
> She came really early.

你睡得很晚吗？

Nǐ shuìde hěn wǎn ma?

Do you go to bed very late?

他们玩儿得很高兴吧？

Tāmen wánrde hěn gāoxing ba?

Did they *have a good time together?

*The verb "玩 wánr" presents an interesting challenge for translation. If the subject is a young child, it usually means "to play," but for teenagers and adults it means "to spend a pleasant time together," and comes close to the current expression "to hang out."

(2) Subject + verb + object + verb 得 de adjective, The subject verbs + object adjective-ly.

For "Verb + Object" phrases, and for compound verbs that behave grammatically like a "Verb + Object" phrase, we use the following pattern:

她跑步跑得很快。

Tā pǎobù pǎode hěn kuài.

She jogs fast.

他走路走得很慢。

Tā zǒulù zǒude hěn màn.

He walks slowly.

我写汉字写得不好。

Wǒ xiě Hànzì xiěde bùhǎo.

I write Chinese characters poorly.

她听音乐听得很认真。

Tā tīng yīnyuè tīngde hěn rènzhēn.

She listens to music very seriously.

你睡觉睡得够不够？

Nǐ shuìjiào shuìde gòubugòu?

Do you get enough sleep?

他们打羽毛球打得很好玩儿吧？

Tāmen dǎ yǔmáoqiú dǎde hěn hǎowánr ba?

They had a very good time playing badminton, didn't they?

Asking a question using "complement of degree" pattern:

Subject + verb (or verb + object + verb) 得 怎么样 de zěnmeyàng?

As in the following example questions:

他跑得怎么样？

Tā pǎode zěnmeyàng?

How well does he run?

他跑步跑得怎么样?
Tā pǎobù pǎode zěnmeyàng?
How is he at jogging?

他跑步跑得多不多?
Tā pǎobù pǎode duōbuduo?
Does he jog a lot?

他跑步跑得快不快?
Tā pǎobù pǎode kuàibukuai?
Does he jog fast?

她唱得怎么样?
Tā chàngde zěnmeyàng?
How is she at singing?

她唱歌唱得怎么样?
Tā chànggēr chàngde zěnmeyàng?
How is she at singing?

她唱歌唱得好不好听?
Tā chànggēr chàngde hǎobuhaotīng?
Does she sing beautifully?

5.14.2 Directional complement

Simple Directional Complement:

The simple directional complement, 趋向补语 qūxiàng bǔyǔ, is added to a verb to indicate whether an action is moving towards the speaker or away from the speaker. For example, Verb + lai 来 = to verb in the direction of the speaker, as in the following examples:

拿来
nálai
bring (something) here (where the speaker is).

带来
dàilai
bring (something) along (to where the speaker is).

跑来
pǎolai
come running (in the direction of the speaker).

送来
sònglai
deliver (or send in the direction of the speaker).

飞来
fēilai
fly here (come flying in the direction of the speaker).

If we want to indicate that the action is moving away from the speaker, we use Verb + qu 去, as in the following examples:

拿去
náqu
take (something) over there (away from the speaker).

带去
dàiqu
take (something) along (away from the speaker).

跑去
pǎoqu
run (over there, away from the speaker).

送去
sòngqu
deliver (or send, away from the speaker).

飞去
fēiqu
fly there (away from the speaker).

Compound Directional Complements:

The compound directional complement, when added to a verb, adds more precise information in addition to whether the action is happening in the direction of the speaker or away from the speaker. For example: in an upward or downward direction; an inside or outside direction; returning to a point of origination; or crossing over. Using the same verbs as we used for the simple directional complement, we may add the further refinements of compound directionality:

拿上来 / 去
náshanglai/qu
bring/take up here/there

拿下来 / 去
náxialai/qu
bring/take down here/there

拿回来 / 去
náhuilai/qu
bring/take back here/there

拿过来 / 去
náguolai/qu
bring/take over here/there

跑上来 / 去
pǎoshanglai/qu
run up here/there

跑下来 / 去
pǎoxialai/qu
run down here/there

跑回来 / 去
pǎohuilai/qu
run back here/there

跑过来 / 去
pǎoguolai/qu
run over here/there

扔上来 / 去
rēngshanglai/qu
toss up here/there

扔下来 / 去
rēngxialai/qu
toss down here/there

Sample sentences using directional complements:

前门没开，我们怎么进去呢?
Qiánmén méikāi, wǒmen zěnme jìnqu ne?
The front door isn't open, so how are we to go in?

别忘了把我的书拿回来!
Bié wàngle bǎ wǒde shū náhuilai!
Don't forget to bring back my book!

他刚出去了，一会儿就回来，您请进来等他吧!
Tā gāng chūqule, yìhuǐr jiù huílai, nín qǐng jìnlai děng tā ba.
He has just stepped out, and will be back in a little while. Please
   come in and wait for him.

妈妈一开门，小鸟就飞出去了。
Māma yì kāimén, xiǎoniǎo jiu fēichuqu le.
As soon as Mom opened the door, the little bird flew out.

外边正下雨，我不想出去了。
Wàibian zhèng xiàyǔ, wǒ bùxiǎng chūqu le.
It's raining outside. I don't want to go out now.

Verb + place + directional complement:

请你上楼来。
Qǐng nǐ shànglóulai.
Please come upstairs (towards the speaker).

她下山去了。
Tā xiàshānqu le.
She has gone down the mountain (away from the speaker).

他们为什么还没回宿舍去呢？

Tāmen wèishénme háiméi huísùshèqu ne?

Why haven't they gone back to the dormitory yet?

听说你要到北京去。

Tīngshuō nǐ yào dào Běijīng qu.

I hear that you will go to Beijing.

5.14.3 Complement of time

Complement of time, 时间补语 shíjiān bǔyǔ, is an expression that tells about the duration of an action. The basic sentence pattern for such an expression is:

Subject + verb + duration. Some examples:

你每天晚上睡几个钟头？

Nǐ měitiān wǎnshang shuì jǐge zhōngtóu?

How many hours do you sleep every night?

你来了多久了？

Nǐ láile duōjiǔ le?

How long have you been here?

我在加拿大十年了。

Wǒ zai Jiānádà shínián le.

I've been in Canada for ten years.

她在这儿工作了三年。

Tā zai zhèr gōngzuòle sānnián.

She worked here for three years.

她在这儿工作了三年了。

Tā zai zhèr gōngzuòle sānnián le.

She has been working here for three years now.

If the action is a Verb + Object compound, the duration is expressed in either of two ways:

(1) Subject + verb + object + verb + duration:

你平常每天晚上睡觉睡几个钟头？

Nǐ píngcháng měitiān wǎnshang shuìjiào shuì jǐge zhōngtóu?

How many hours do you usually sleep every night?

我学汉语学了两年。

Wǒ xué Hànyǔ xuéle liǎngnián.

I studied Chinese for two years. (I'm no longer studying)

我学汉语学了两年了。

Wǒ xué Hànyǔ xuéle liǎngnián le.

I've been studying Chinese for two years now. (I'm still studying)

(2) Subject + verb + duration + de + object:

我们学了两年的汉语。

Wǒmen xuéle liǎngniánde Hànyǔ.

We studied Chinese for two years. (I'm no longer studying)

我们学了两年的汉语了。

Wǒmen xuéle liǎngniánde Hànyǔ le.

We've been studying Chinese for two years now. (I'm still studying)

5.14.4 Complement of quantity

Complement of quantity, 数量补语 shùliàng bǔyǔ, may be expressed using the same pattern as we use for duration of an act, but quantifying the number of objects acted upon by the verb, or the number of times the act has been performed or repeated, as below:

我买了三双皮鞋。

Wǒ mǎile sānshuāng píxié.

I bought three pairs of shoes.

他每天喝一大瓶酒。

Tā měitiān hē yídàpíng jiǔ.

He drinks a whole bottle of wine every day.

你有几条牛仔裤?

Nǐ yǒu jǐtiáo niúzǎikù?

How many pairs of jeans do you have?

我爬过二十次长城。

Wǒ páguo èrshicì Chángchéng.

I've climbed the Great Wall twenty times.

我爬长城爬了二十次。

Wǒ pá Chángchéng pále èrshicì.

I climbed the Great Wall twenty times.

你要等他请了三次才答应。

Nǐ yào děng tā qǐngle sāncì cái dāying.

You must wait until he has asked you three times before you agree.

5.14.5 Resultative complement

The resultative complement, 结果补语 jiéguǒ bǔyǔ, added to an action gives information about the resulting success of the action, clarity of the action, firmness of the action, etc. Examples are:

看 *kàn, to look* + 见 *jiàn, to perceive* = 看见 *kànjian, to see*

昨天我看见张老师了。

Zuótian wǒ kànjian Zhāng Lǎoshī le.

I saw Professor Zhang yesterday.

听 *tīng, to listen* + 见 *jiàn, to perceive* = 听见 *tīngjian, to hear*

我听了半天，也没听见。
Wǒ tīngle bàntiān, yě méitīngjian.
I listened for a long time, but I didn't hear it.

听 *tīng, to listen* + 懂 *dǒng, to understand* = 听懂 *tīngdǒng, to understand (what is/was heard).*

他的口音很重，我没听懂多少。
Tāde kǒuyīn hěn zhòng, wǒ méitīngdǒng duōshǎo.
He has a thick accent; I didn't understand very much.

写 *xiě, to write* + 好 *hǎo, well* = 写好 *xiěhǎo, to finish writing*

她还没写好昨天的作业。
Tā hái méixiěhǎo zuótiande zuòyè.
She still hasn't finished writing yesterday's homework.

学 *xué, to study* + 会 *huì, to know how* = 学会 *xuéhuì, to master something*

这个语法这么简单，你怎么还没学会呢？
Zhèige yǔfǎ zhème jiǎndān, nǐ zěnme hái méixuéhuì ne?
This grammar is so simple. Why haven't you mastered it yet?

做 *zuò, to do* + 完 *wán, to finish* = 做完 *zuòwán, to finish doing something*

你做完了体操没有？
Nǐ zuòwánle tǐcāo méiyou?
Have you finished your calisthenics?

今天的体操已经做完了。
Jīntiande tǐcāo yǐjing zuòwán le.
I've already finished doing today's calisthenics.

5.14.6 Potential complement

The potential complement, 可能补语 kěnéng bǔyǔ, is added to an action to indicate the possibility or impossibility of achieving the desired result or successfully completing the act. It is expressed by inserting the particle "得 de" or "不 bù" between the verb and its resultative or directional complement, as in Verb + de/bu + complement. Verb + de + complement = can succeed in the complementing, and Verb + bu + complement = cannot succeed in the complementing.
Examples are:

那本书我找了很久，怎么找都找不到。
Nàběn shū wǒ zhǎole hěnjiǔ, zěnme zhǎo dōu zhǎobudào.
I searched for that book a long time, but no matter how hard I
    searched, I couldn't find it.

你继续找吧，一定找得到。
Nǐ jìxù zhǎo ba, yídìng zhǎodedào.
Keep on searching; you can find it for sure.

他们听不懂广东话。
Tāmen tīngbudǒng Guǎngdōnghuà.
They don't understand Cantonese.

你的普通话，我听得懂。
Nǐde pǔtōnghuà, wǒ tīngdedǒng.
I can understand your Mandarin.

我吃不了那么多饺子！
Wǒ chībuliǎo nàme duō jiǎozi!
I can't eat that many dumplings!

我吃得了，你怎么吃不了呢？
Wǒ chīdeliǎo, nǐ zěnme chībuliǎo ne?
If I can eat them up, why can't you?

走错了路回得来，说错了话回不来。
Zǒucuòle lù huídelái, shuōcuòle huà huíbulái.
Having taken the wrong road, you can come back, but having said
the wrong thing, you can't take it back.

5.14.7 List of commonly used verbs with potential complements

Complement	Examples	Meaning
懂 dǒng	听懂；看懂	understand (listening or reading)
见 jiàn	听见；看见	hear; see (listen + perceive; look + perceive)
好 hǎo	写好；看好	finish writing, finish reading
完 wán	做完；吃完	finish doing, finish eating
来 lái	拿来；带来	bring; bring along
去 qù	进去；走去	go in; go on foot
到 dào	办到；送到	succeed in doing; succeed in sending
住 zhù	拿住；站住	hold firmly; stand still
了 liǎo	拿得了；做不了	able to hold; unable to do

Complement	Examples	Meaning
上 shàng	举上；搬上	raise up; carry up
下 xià:	坐下；放下	sit down; put down
会 huì:	学会	to master (through study)
起 qǐ	买得起；看不起	able to afford to buy; unable to look up to
动 dòng	走动；拿动	able to walk about; able to lift
清楚 qīngchu	看清楚；听清楚	see clearly; hear distinctly

5.15 Expressing whoever, whatever, wherever, however, and whenever

Structures like "whoever," "whatever," "wherever," "however" and "whenever" usually are expressed by adding "都 dōu, all" or "也 yě, also" after who, what, where, how, or when, as in the following examples:

谁都/也可以。
Shéi dōu/yě kěyǐ.
Anyone will be fine./Whoever will be fine.

什么都/也不要。
Shénme dōu/yě buyào.
(Subject) doesn't want anything at all./(Subject) wants nothing whatever.

哪儿都/也行。
Nǎr dōu/yě xíng.
Anywhere will do./ Wherever will do.

怎么做都/也好。
Zěnme zuò dōu/yě hǎo.
It's fine no matter how you do it./It's fine however you do it.

什么时候都/也 行。
Shénme shíhou dōu/yě xíng.
Any time is fine./It's fine whenever.

5.16   Expressing surprise

As with English speakers, Chinese speakers may express surprise upon seeing or hearing something out of the ordinary simply by raising their voice and widening their eyes while uttering a question word:

什么？！
Shénme?!
What?!

谁？！
Shéi?!
Who?!

多少？！
Duōshǎo?!
How much?!

Or they may utter typical expressions of surprise, such as:

哎呀！
Āiyā!
Oh! (sometimes "Oops!")

哎哟！
Āiyō!
Oh!! (more serious than "āiyā!")

我的天啊！
Wǒde tiān a!
Oh, my gosh!

真没想到！
Zhēn méixiǎngdào!
What a surprise!

5.17   Connecting words

Connecting words/conjunctions/conjunctives/correlatives are used to connect elements in sentences which have either more than one clause, or more than one predicate or comment related to the same subject or topic. These connecting words may occur independently, such as: 可是 kěshi, but; 但是 dànshi, but; 不过 búguò, however; 否则 fǒuzé, otherwise; 要不然 yàoburán, otherwise; 所以 suǒyǐ, so; 因此 yīncǐ, therefore.

They may also occur in correlated pairs, such as: 因为…所以…yīnwei…suǒyǐ…, because… (therefore)… 虽然…但是… suīrán…dànshi…, although… (yet)… 不但…而且… búdàn…érqiě, not only…(but also).

The following are illustrative examples of both types:

我劝了她，可是她不听。
Wǒ quànle tā, kěshi tā bùtīng.
I pleaded with her, but she wouldn't listen.

他很想参加，但是老板不准。
Tā hěn xiǎng cānjiā, dànshi lǎobǎn bùzhǔn.
He really wants to participate, but his boss won't let him.

我觉得已经太晚了，不过可以替你打听。
Wǒ juéde yǐjīng tàiwǎnle, búguò kěyǐ tì nǐ dǎtīng.
I think it's already too late, but I can enquire for you.

你最好写报告吧，否则可能有人找麻烦。
Nǐ zuìhǎo xiě bàogào ba, fǒuzé kěnéng yǒurén zhǎo máfan.
You'd better write up a report. Otherwise someone could make trouble.

她一定会去，要不然校长会生气。
Tā yídìng huì qù, yàoburán xiàozhǎng huì shēngqì.
She is certain to go. Otherwise the principal would get angry.

今天下大雨，所以野餐取消了。
Jīntiān xià dàyǔ, suǒyǐ yěcān qǔxiāo le.
It's raining heavily today, so the picnic is cancelled.

因为那个饭馆不收信用卡，所以我们去别的地方吃饭了。
Yīnwei nàge fànguǎnr bùshōu xìnyòngkǎ, suǒyǐ wǒmen qù biéde dìfang chīfàn le.
That restaurant doesn't accept credit cards, so we went someplace else to eat.

虽然他信佛教，但是他偶尔会吃肉。
Suīran tā xìn fójiào, dànshi tā ǒu'ěr huì chī ròu.
Although he is a Buddhist, he will occasionally eat meat.

她不但是我老师，而且是我最好的朋友。
Tā búdàn shi wǒ lǎoshī, érqiě shi wǒ zuìhǎode péngyou.
She is not only my teacher, but my best friend as well.

Note that although normally English will omit either the "because" or the "therefore," and omit either the "although" or the "yet" in such constructions, they may both be used in Chinese without sounding redundant.

Other connecting words are:

如果… 就… rúguǒ… jiù,… if… then

如果你能去，我就不必去了。
Rúguo nǐ néng qù, wǒ jiu búbì qù le.
If you can go, I won't have to go.

要是… 就… yàoshi… jiù…, if… ,then…

要是下雨，我就不去游泳。
Yàoshi xiàyǔ, wǒ jiu búqu yóuyǒng.
If it rains, I won't go swimming.

假如… 就… jiǎrú… jiù… if… ,then…

假如便宜一点儿，我就买两件。
Jiǎrú piányi yìdiǎnr, wǒ jiu mǎi liǎngjiàn.
If it's a little cheaper, I'll buy two.

一… 就… yī… jiù…, once… then…

天一黑，我就得回家。
Tiān yì hēi, wǒ jiùděi huíjiā.
As soon as it gets dark, I must go home.

既然… 就… jìrán… jiù…, since… then…

既然你不爱喝酒，我们就去咖啡店喝咖啡吧。
Jìrán nǐ bú'ài hējiǔ, wǒmen jiu qù kāfēidiàn hē kāfēi ba.
Since you don't like to drink alcohol, let's go to a coffee house for
    some coffee.

只要…，就… zhǐyào… jiù… if only…, then…

只要不下雨，我就跟你去游泳。
Zhǐyào búxiàyǔ, wǒ jiu gēn nǐ qù yóuyǒng.
As long as it's not raining, I'll go swimming with you.

只有…，才… zhǐyǒu… cái… only if… only then…

只有不下雨，我才跟你去游泳。
Zhǐyǒu búxiàyǔ, wǒ cái gēn nǐ qù yóuyǒng.
I'll go swimming with you, but only if it's not raining.

除非…，才…，chúfēi…, cái…, unless…; only then…

除非不下雨，我才跟你去游泳。
Chúfēi búxiàyǔ, wǒ cái gēn nǐ qù yóuyǒng.
I'll go swimming with you, unless it is raining.

除了… 以外,… chúle … yǐwài, …, except for… …

除了小张以外，人家都来了。
Chúle Xiǎo Zhāng yǐwài, rénjia dōu láile.
Except for Zhang, everybody else came.

不管…，也… bùguǎn… yě…, no matter…, still…

不管他要多少钱，我也要买。
Bùguǎn tā yào duōshao qián, wǒ yěyao mǎi.
No matter how much money he wants for it, I'm still going to
    buy it.

无论..., 都... wúlùn... dōu..., regardless... still...

无论她赢还是不赢，我都很佩服她。
Wúlùn tā yíng háishi bùyíng, wǒ dōu hěn pèifu tā.
Regardless of whether she wins or not, I still have great respect for her.

与其..., 不如... yǔqí... bùrú... rather than... better to...

与其得罪人，不如改变话题吧。
Yǔqí dézui rén, bùrú gǎibiàn huàtí ba.
Rather than offend someone, it would be better to change the subject.

一边... 一边... yìbiānr... yìbiānr..., (doing two things at the same time)

我们一边走，一边聊天。
Wǒmen yìbianr zǒu, yìbianr liáotiānr.
We chatted as we walked.

一面... 一面... yímiàn... yímiàn..., (doing two things at the same time)

我们一面讨论价钱，一面看画册。
Wǒmen yímiàn tǎolùn jiàqian, yímiàn kàn huàcè.
We perused the album of paintings as we discussed the price.

又... 又... yòu..., yòu..., both... and...

她又是我的老师，又是我的朋友。
Tā yòushi wǒde lǎoshi, yòushi wǒde péngyou.
She is both my teacher and my friend.

越... 越... yuè... yuè... the more... the more...

我越认识他，越觉得他不是一般的画家。
Wǒ yuè rènshi tā, yuè juéde tā búshi yìbānde huàjiā.
The more I know him, the more I feel he is not an ordinary artist.

或者... 或者... huòzhe... huòzhe..., either... or...

或者你去，或者我去，都可以。
Huòzhe nǐ qù, huòzhe wǒ qù, dōu kěyi.
Either you go or I'll go; either way is fine.

5.18   Emphasis using the "shì...de" pattern

The most common way of emphasizing agency, time, place, means/ manner, or purpose, i.e., who or what, when, where, how or why, etc. of an event in Mandarin is by using the "是...的 shì...de" pattern. There are three things about this pattern that are important: (1) the element that appears in between "shì" and "de" is emphasized;

(2) it is usually used for events that have already taken place; (3) "shì" is sometimes omitted. For example:

他昨天在城里买了一辆新车。
Tā zuótian zai chénglǐ mǎile yíliàng xīnchē.
He bought a new car downtown yesterday. (No emphasis)

新车是他买的。
Xīnchē shi tā mǎi de.
He is the one who bought the new car. (Emphasizing who)

他是昨天买的新车。
Tā shi zuótian mǎide xīnchē.
It was yesterday that he bought the new car. (Emphasizing when)

他昨天是在城里买的新车。
Tā zuótian shi zài chénglǐ mǎide xīnchē.
It was downtown that he bought the new car yesterday.
    (Emphasizing where)

他昨天在城里是跟他朋友一起买的新车。
Tā zuótian zài chénglǐ shi gēn tā péngyou yìqǐ mǎide xīnchē.
It was with his friend that he bought the new car downtown
    yesterday. (Emphasizing with whom)

他昨天在城里是用信用卡买的新车。
Tā zuótian zai chénglǐ shi yòng xìnyòngkǎ mǎide xīn chē.
It was with his credit card that he bought the new car downtown
    yesterday. (Emphasizing the means)

他是为了上班买的新车。
Tā shi wèile shàngbān mǎide xīnchē.
It was for going to work that he bought the new car. (Emphasizing
    the purpose)

Other common examples of emphasis using the "shì...de" pattern are:

这些菜都是她买的。
Zhèxiē cài dōu shi tā mǎi de.
She bought all these groceries. (who)

你什么时候来的？
Nǐ shénme shíhou lái de?
When did you come? (when)

他们昨天从北京来的。
Tāmen zuótian cóng Běijīng lái de.
They came from Beijing yesterday. (where)

我来买外套的。
Wǒ lái mǎi wàitào de.
I've come to buy a jacket. (purpose)

我坐火车来的。
Wǒ zuò huǒchē lái de.
I came by train. (means)

我跟同学们一起去的长城。
Wǒ gēn tóngxuémen yìqǐ qù de Chángchéng.
I went to the Great Wall with my fellow schoolmates. (with whom)

Note: The negative form of the "是...的 shì...de" pattern is: "不是...的 búshì...de" and in this pattern "是 shì" cannot be omitted.

5.19 Interjections

Interjections, 叹词 tàncí, express emotions and feelings. Examples are:

啊 ā	Expressing elation
啊 á	Expressing doubt or questioning
啊 ǎ	Expressing puzzled surprise
啊 à	Expressing agreement/approval
哎 āi	Hey!
唉 āi	Gosh!, My! (mild exclamation, sigh)
唉 ài	Expressing sympathy or disappointment
嗳 ài	No! (expressing disapproval)
欸/诶 ē/ēi	Hey! (to attract attention)
欸/诶 é/éi	Ah!, Oh!
欸/诶 ě/ěi	Huh?, What's this?
欸/诶 è/èi	Hey!
哈 hā	Aha! (expressing satisfaction)
咳 hāi	Hey!
嗨 hāi	Hey!
嗐 hài	Expressing pain, sorrow or regret
咳 hai	Expressing sorrow, surprise
呵 hē	Ah!, Oh!
嗬 hē	Ah!, Oh!
吓 hè	"Tut-tut," "Tsk-tsk"
嘿 hēi	Hey!
哼 hng	Humph!
嗯 ń or ńg	What? Huh?
嗯 ň or ňg	I wonder! I'm suspicious!
嗯 ǹ or ǹg	Okay; understood; agreed
哦 ó	Expressing half believing, half doubting
哦 ò	Expressing a newly gained understanding
呸 pēi	Bah! Pooh! Expressing disgust and disdain
喂 wèi	Hey!; "Hello?" when answering the telephone
吁 xū	Wow! Expressing surprise or amazement

吁 yū	Whoa! Calling on a horse to stop
噫 yī	Expressing regret or surprise
咦 yí	Eh? Expressing surprise or disapproval
唷 yō	Oh! I forgot!
啧 zé	tsk-tsk: the sound of tongue-clicking, "Shame on you!"
嗨哟 hāiyō	"Heave-ho"
哎呀 āiyā	Expressing wonder, admiration, or shock
哎哟 āiyō	(also ēiyō) Expressing surprise or pain, more serious than "āiyā"
哎唷 ēiyō	Same as "āiyō" above
喔唷 wōyō	Oh!, Ouch!

5.20 Passive voice

5.20.1 Structural passive

Passive voice, 被动式 bèidòngshì, is expressed by using the passive indicator 被 bèi, by/让 ràng, let or 叫 jiào, let. The last two are most often used orally. The passive voice is not commonly used in Chinese, but it is more often used for stress, or sometimes used to express more unfortunate events.

The sentence structure is as follows:

Object (receiver) + bèi/ràng/jiào + subject (doer)* + verb + other elements.

*The doer can be omitted (this does not apply to when ràng or jiào is used) or 人 rén may be used if it is not clear who the doer is.

新闻报道：很多人的房子被大水淹了。
Xīnwén bàodào: hěnduō rénde fángzi bèi dàshuǐ yānle.
According to news reports, many people's houses were flooded by the high waters.

报纸被丢进垃圾桶了。
Bàozhǐ bèi diūjìn lājītǒng le.
The newspaper was thrown into the garbage can.

她买的那件很贵的衣服被人偷走了。
Tā mǎide nàjian hěn guìde yīfu bèi rén tōuzǒule.
That expensive dress she bought was stolen by someone.

If an adverb or an auxiliary verb or a negative is used, the order is as follows:

Object + adverb/auxiliary verb/negative + bèi + subject + verb + other elements*.

*If the verb is more than one syllable, there is no need for other elements.

270

这幅很有名的画一定会被他们拍卖掉。

Zhèifú hěn yǒumíngde huàr yídìng huì bèi tāmen pāimàidiao.

This very famous painting will definitely be auctioned off by
them.

他的朋友很可能被选出来当主席。

Tāde péngyou hěn kěnéng bèi xuǎnchūlai dāng zhǔxí.

It is very possible that his friend will be elected as the chairperson.

要是不被送去英国学习，他们真的会非常失望。

Yàoshi bú bèi sòngqu Yīngguó xuéxí, tāmen zhēnde huì fēicháng
shīwàng.

They will really be disappointed if they are not sent to England to
study.

她的歌唱得那么好，绝对会被很多人欣赏。

Tāde gēr chàngde nàme hǎo, juéduì huì bèi hěnduō rén xīnshǎng.

She sings so well. She will definitely be appreciated by many
people.

5.20.2 Notional passive

When the subject of a sentence does not do the action and is the
receiver of the action, and when the doer of the action is either
unknown or unnecessary to express, the passive indicator 被 bèi/让
ràng/叫 jiào, is not used. This is known as the notional passive and
the sentence structure is usually as follows:

Object (receiver) + verb + other elements.

汽车已经修好了。

Qìchē yǐjīng xiūhǎole.

The car is already repaired.

信昨天就寄出去了。

Xìn zuótian jiu jìchuqule.

The letter was already mailed yesterday.

我订的书今天早上送来了。

Wǒ dìngde shū jīntian zǎoshang sòngláile.

The book I ordered was delivered this morning.

5.21 Reduplications

5.21.1 Reduplication of verbs

Functions of reduplicated verbs:

(1) to show that the action is short and quick.
(2) to indicate an attempt or trial.
(3) to show that the action is casual.

What verbs can be reduplicated:

(1)   action and behavioral verbs
(2)   verbs with a positive feeling

How to reduplicate the verbs:

1.   when monosyllabic verbs are reduplicated: AA

请你先看看。
Qǐng nǐ xiān kànkan.
Please have a look first.

您尝尝好吃不好吃。
Nín chángchang hǎochī bu hǎochī.
Try it and see whether it tastes good.

我们工作了一整天了，晚上应该听听音乐了。
Wǒmen gōngzuòle yìzhěngtiān le. Wǎnshang yīnggāi tīngting
    yīnyuè le.
We have been working hard the whole day. We should listen to
    some music this evening.

2.   for disyllabic verbs which are Verb–Object combinations: AAB

有时侯游游泳对身体非常好。
Yǒushíhou yǒuyouyǒng duì shēntǐ fēicháng hǎo.
It is very good for one's health to have a swim sometimes.

今天天气很好，我们想去海边散散步。
Jīntian tiānqi hěnhǎo, wǒmen xiǎng qù hǎibianr sànsanbù.
The weather is so nice today, we would like to go to the beach for
    a stroll.

我们应该不时开开会，大家可以表达一下意见。
Wǒmen yīnggāi bùshí kāikāihuì, dàjiā kěyi biǎodáyíxià yìjian.
We should have meetings from time to time so that everyone has a
    chance to express his/her opinion.

Note: "一 yī" can be inserted between the reduplicated verb (A 一
yī A) to mean the same thing and to have the same function.

请你先看一看。
Qǐng nǐ xiān kànyikan.
Please have a look first.

他很想去散一散步。
Tā hěn xiǎng qù sànyisànbù.
He wants very much to go for a walk.

Note: "了 le" can be inserted between the reduplicated verb (A 了
le A) to emphasize the completion of the verb.

她尝了尝不好吃。
Tā chánglechang bù hǎochī.
She tried it and it did not taste good.

昨天他们虽然很累，可是还游了游泳。
Zuótian tāmen suīrán hěn lèi, kěshi hái yóuleyouyǒng.
Although they were very tired yesterday, they still had a swim.

3.   when disyllabic verbs are reduplicated: ABAB
Note: the reduplicated part of the verb is pronounced in the neutral tone.

这件事我们还是考虑考虑再做决定吧。
Zhèjian shì wǒmen háishi kǎolükaolü zài zuò juédìng ba.
Perhaps we should think this over before we make a decision.

今天虽然天气不太好，他们还是应该出去运动运动。
Jīntian suīrán tiānqi bútàihǎo, tāmen háishi yīnggāi chūqu
    yùndongyundong.
Although the weather is not very good today, they still should go
    out to have a bit of exercise.

你忙了这么久，实在应该放两个星期的假休息休息。
Nǐ mángle zhème jiǔ, shízài yīnggāi fàng liǎnggexīngqīde jià
    xiūxixiuxi.
You have been busy for such a long time. You really should take a
    two-week vacation to relax a bit.

What verbs cannot be reduplicated:

(1)   verbs expressing feelings and emotions:

爱 ài, love; 喜欢 xǐhuan, like; 怕 pà, fear; 嫉妒 jìdu, jealous; 希望
xīwang, hope.

(2)   verbs expressing change or development:

开始 kāishǐ, begin; 结束 jiéshù, finish; 发展 fāzhǎn, develop; 变
化 biànhuà, change.

(3)   verbs expressing existence, judgement, possession:
是 shì, to be; 在 zài, to be at; 有 yǒu, to have; 象 xiàng, to
    resemble; 好像 hǎoxiàng, to be like.

(4)   verbs showing directions:
上 shàng, go up; 下 xià, go down; 出 chū, exit; 进 jìn, enter.

5.21.2   Reduplication of nouns

Some nouns can be reduplicated to mean "each and every + noun":

他们家人人都有收入。
Tāmen jiā rénrén dōu yǒu shōurù.
Each and every one in their family has an income.

本市不是家家都有孩子。
Běnshì búshi jiājiā dōu yǒu háizi.
Not every family in this city has children.

我多么希望天天都是晴天！
Wǒ duōme xīwang tiāntiān dōushi qíngtiān!
How I wish every day was a sunny day!

祝你事事顺利！
Zhù nǐ shìshì shùnlì!
I hope everything goes smoothly for you!

岁岁平安！
Suìsuì píng'ān!
May you have peace year after year!

她年年都有新发明。
Tā niánnián dōu yǒu xīn fāmíng.
She has a new invention each and every year.

他们世世代代都有人做教授。
Tāmen shìshìdàidài dōu yǒurén zuò jiàoshòu.
There have been professors in their family in each and every
    generation.

新年的时候家家户户都喜气洋洋的。
Xīnniánde shíhou jiājiāhùhù dōu xǐqì yángyángde.
Each and every household is brimming with happiness during the
    New Year.

5.21.3 Reduplication of adjectives

***The reduplicated adjectives give a more vivid and lively
description.***

(1) Reduplicated adjective + 的 de = adjective
(2) Reduplicated adjective + 地 de = adverb
(3) Not all adjectives can be reduplicated.

1. Monosyllabic adjectives are reduplicated as: AA
    The duplicated syllable may be pronounced in the first tone and
    followed by the "r" ending.
    The following are some adjectives that are commonly reduplicated:
    快快儿 kuàikuāir, fast; 慢慢儿 mànmānr, slow; 远远儿 yuǎnyuānr,
    far away; 好好儿 hǎohāor, fine, well; 高高儿 gāogāor, tall; 矮矮儿
    ǎi'āir, short; 胖胖儿 pàngpāngr, chubby; 瘦瘦儿 shòushōur, skinny;
    长长儿 chángchāngr, long; 短短儿 duǎnduānr, short; 大大儿 dàdār,
    large, big; 小小儿 xiǎoxiāor, small.

    湖里清清儿的水真象一面镜子。
    Húli qīngqīngrde shuǐ zhēn xiàng yímiàn jìngzi.
    The wonderfully clear water in the lake is just like a mirror.

274

她黑黑儿的头发使人觉得她很年轻。

Tā hēihēirde tóufa shǐ rén juéde tā hěn niánqīng.

Her dark black hair makes one think she is very young.

他慢慢儿地走来走去，不知道在想什么。

Tā mànmānrde zǒulái zǒuqù, bùzhīdao zai xiǎng shénme.

He walks back and forth slowly and I do not know what's on his mind.

小王紧紧地抱住她不放。

Xiǎo Wáng jǐnjīnrde bàozhu tā bú fàng.

Wang held her tightly and would not let go of her.

2. Disyllabic adjectives are reduplicated as: AABB

These are some commonly reduplicated adjectives: 仔仔细细 zǐzǐxìxì, careful, attentive; 清清楚楚 qīngqīngchūchū, clear; 漂漂亮亮 piàopiàoliàngliàng, beautiful; 高高兴兴 gāogāoxìngxìng, happy; 舒舒服服 shūshūfūfū, comfortable; 辛辛苦苦 xīnxīnkǔkǔ, working hard; 干干净净 gāngānjìngjìng, clean; 整整齐齐 zhěngzhěngqīqī, tidy; 客客气气 kèkèqīqī, polite; 认认真真 rènrènzhēnzhēn, serious, careful.

冬天的时候她总是把孩子穿得暖暖和和的才让他们去上学。

Dōngtiande shíhou tā zǒngshi bǎ háizi chuānde nuǎnnuanhuōhuōde cái ràng tāmen qù shàngxué.

She always dresses the children warmly before letting them go to school in winter.

开学了，孩子们都高高兴兴地去上学了。

Kāixué le, háizimen dōu gāogāoxìngxìngde qù shàngxué le.

School started and the children all went to school happily.

5.21.4 Reduplication of measure words

Measure words can be reduplicated for emphasis to mean "each and every + measure word":

她说的普通话句句都很清楚。

Tā shuōde pǔtōnghuà jùjù dōu hěn qīngchu.

Every sentence she spoke/speaks in Mandarin was/is very clear.

这家服装公司的衣服件件都很好看。

Zhèijiā fúzhuāng gōngsīde yīfu jiànjiàn dōu hěn hǎokàn.

Each and every item of clothing in this garment company is beautiful.

那个咖啡店的咖啡杯杯都好喝。

Nèige kāfēidiànde kāfēi bēibēi dōu hǎohē.

Every cup of coffee in that coffee house tastes delicious.

他们卖的水果种种都很新鲜。

Tāmen màide shuǐguo zhǒngzhǒng dōu hěn xīnxian.

Each and every kind of fruit they sell is very fresh.

那家汽车行卖的汽车辆辆都是高贵的汽车。
Nàjiā qìchēháng màide qìchē liàngliàng dōushi gāoguìde qìchē.
Every car sold in that dealership is a high-class car.

我们觉得他画的画张张都值得收集。
Wǒmen juéde tā huàde huàr zhāngzhāng dōu zhíde shōují.
We think every one of his paintings is worth collecting.

5.22 Prepositions

The following are the more commonly used prepostions:

按 àn: based on, on the basis of, according to

按小时工作收费的叫小时工。
Àn xiǎoshí gōngzuò shōufèide jiào xiǎoshígōng.
Those whose wages are paid according to hours worked are called
    "hourly workers."

按照 ànzhào (cannot be followed by monosyllabic words): according to

按照她的意思我们最好先学习汉语。
Ànzhào tāde yìsi wǒmen zuìhǎo xiān xuéxí Hànyǔ.
According to her opinion, we had better study Chinese first.

朝 cháo/往 wàng/向 xiàng: toward, towards

你朝 / 往 / 向东走一百米就到了。
Nǐ cháo/wàng/xiàng dōng zǒu yìbǎi mǐ jiù dào le.
Walk 100 meters east and you will be there.

趁 chèn: take advantage of

你还是趁天气好的时候去旅游吧。
Nǐ háishi chèn tiānqi hǎo deshíhou qù lǚyóu ba.
Why don't you go traveling while the weather is good.

除了chúle/除了chúle... 以外 yǐwài: except for, besides

除了游泳（以外），你还做别的运动吗？
Chúle yóuyǒng (yǐwài), nǐ hái zuò biéde yùndong ma?
Do you do other exercises besides swimming?

从 cóng: from

那个人到底是从哪儿来的呢？
Nàge rén dàodǐ shì cóng nǎr lái de ne?
Where did that person really come from?

从 cóng... 起 qǐ: starting from

从下星期一起，他们就要上班了。
Cóng xià xīngqīyī qǐ, tāmen jiùyao shàngbān le.
They have to start going to work next Monday.

从 cóng... 到 dào: from...to, from...till

坐飞机从这儿到伦敦要多久？
Zuò fēijī cóng zhèr dào Lúndūn yào duōjiǔ?
How long does it take to fly from here to London?

他们的会从早上一直开到晚上。
Tāmende huì cóng zǎoshang yìzhí kāidao wǎnshang.
Their meeting lasted all the way from morning till night.

对 duì: to, towards

他这样对你说话是不可以的。
Tā zhèyang duì nǐ shuōhuà shi bùkěyide.
He should not talk to you like this.

给 gěi: for, to

要是有机会的时候，请你告诉他给我打电话，好吗？
Yàoshi yǒu jīhui deshíhou, qǐng nǐ gàosu tā gěi wǒ dǎdiànhuà,
  hǎo ma?
If there is an opportunity, please tell him to phone me, won't you?

他什么时候才把书还给你呢？
Tā shénme shíhou cái bǎ shū huán gěi nǐ ne?
When will he ever return your book to you?

跟 gēn/和 hé (the written form is often "与 yǔ"): with, from

你别担心，我不会跟你去华盛顿的。
Nǐ bié dānxīn, wǒ búhuì gēn nǐ qù Huáshèngdùn de.
Don't worry. I won't go to Washington D.C. with you.

他们想跟你们借一万块钱买房子。怎么办呢？
Tāmen xiǎng gēn nǐmen jiè yíwànkuàiqián mǎi fángzi. Zěnmebàn
  ne?
They want to borrow ten thousand dollars from you to buy a
  house. What are you going to do?

关于 guānyu: about, concerning, with regard to

今天的校报上有一篇关于她得奖的消息。
Jīntiande xiàobàoshang yǒu yìpiān guānyu tā déjiǎngde xiāoxi.
There is an item concerning her getting a prize in the university
  newspaper today.

经 jīng: through, as a result of

经他们的介绍，我才认识她。
Jīng tāmende jièshao, wǒ cái rènshi tā.
I only got to know her through their introduction.

据 jù: based on, according to

据他说，他认识的教授都已经退休了。

Jù tā shuō, tā rènshide jiàoshòu dōu yǐjīng tuìxiū le.

According to him, all the professors he knew have already retired.

离 lí (the written form can be: 距 jù): from, to

现在离上课的时间还有十五分钟。

Xiànzài lí shàngkède shíjiān hái yǒu shíwǔ fēnzhōng.

There is still fifteen minutes to class time.

她的办公室离家不远，可以走路去。

Tāde bàngōngshì lí jiā bù yuǎn, kěyi zǒulù qù.

Her office is not far from her home and she can walk to work.

为 wèi/替 tì: for, on account of

她已经是大人了，你别再为她头疼了。

Tā yǐjīng shi dàren le, nǐ bié zài wèi tā tóuténg le.

She is already an adult. You should not worry yourself over her
    any more.

为了 wèile: in order to, for the purpose of

为了得到奖学金，她不分昼夜地努力学习。

Wèile dédao jiǎngxuéjīn, tā bùfēnzhòuyède nǔlì xuéxí.

In order to get the scholarship, she studies hard day and night.

向 xiàng: from, towards

他是个好学生，我们都应该向他学习。

Tā shi ge hǎo xuésheng, wǒmen dōu yīnggāi xiàng tā xuéxí.

He is a good student. We all should learn from him.

依 yī: according to, in light of

依她的经验，我们都应该每天早起早睡。

Yī tāde jīngyan, wǒmen dōu yīnggāi měitian zǎo qǐ zǎo shuì.

In light of her experience, we all should get up early and go to
    bed early every day.

以 yǐ: with, use, to

他们特别以你的成绩为骄傲。

Tāmen tèbié yǐ nǐde chéngjī wéi jiāo'ào.

They are especially proud of your achievements.

这座大山以北是一条大河。

Zhèzuò dàshān yǐběi shi yìtiáo dàhé.

To the north of this big mountain is a big river.

由 yóu: by, for

下个月的座谈会应该由你主持。

Xiàge yuède zuòtánhuì yīnggāi yóu nǐ zhǔchí.

Next month's seminar should be chaired by you.

这种事当然是由大学校长负责。

Zhèzhǒng shì dāngrán shi yóu dàxué xiàozhǎng fùzé.

Matters like this should naturally be the responsibility of the
university president.

由于 yóuyú: due to, owing to

他们这次重要的发现是由于他们仔细的观察。

Tāmen zhècì zhòngyàode fāxiàn shi yóuyú tāmen zǐxìde guānchá.

Their important discovery this time is due to their careful
observation.

在 zài: at, on, in

她是不是在南京出生的？

Tā shìbushi zài Nánjīng chūshēng de?

Was she born in Nanjing?

他们在八月八日那天就结婚了。

Tāmen zài bāyue bāri nàtian jiù jiéhūn le.

They got married on August 8th.

在 zài...看来 kànlái: in someone's...view, from...someone's point
of view

在他们看来，学拉丁文是很有用的。

Zài tāmen kànlái, xué Lādīngwén shi hěn yǒuyòngde.

From their point of view, learning Latin is very useful.

自从 zìcóng: since

自从上了大学他开始对汉语感兴趣。

Zìcóng shàngle dàxué tā kāishǐ duì Hànyǔ gǎn xìngqu.

He began to be interested in Chinese since he entered university.

For the uses of 把 bǎ, 被 bèi, 叫 jiào, 给 gěi, 让 ràng and 比 bǐ, see
the following:

把 bǎ	see "bǎ sentences," p.248
被 bèi, 叫 jiào, 让 ràng	see "passive voice," p.270
比 bǐ	see "comparisons," p.251

5.23 Subjunctive mood

Subjunctive mood, 假设式 jiǎshèshì, in Chinese is expressed by using
certain connecting words, the context of the sentences, or the tone
of voice if spoken.

1. 要是 yàoshi A, 就 jiù B, when/if A...then B

    要是她能来就好了！

    Yàoshi tā néng lái jiù hǎo le!

    It would have been nice if she could have come!

要是今天天气有昨天那么好，一定有很多人来参加野餐。

Yàoshi jīntian tiānqi yǒu zuótian nàme hǎo, yídìng yǒu hěnduō rén lái cānjiā yěcān.

If the weather today were as nice as it was yesterday, many people would have come to the picnic.

2. (要是 yàoshi) A 的话 dehua, 就 jiù B..., if A...then B

(要是)她是个百万富翁的话，她就能买那所房子。

(Yàoshi) tā shi ge bǎiwànfùwēng dehua, tā jiu néng mǎi nàsuǒ fángzi.

If she were a millionaire, she could have bought that house.

3. 只要 zhǐyào A, 就 jiù B, if only A...then B

只要他们肯出钱，他们就会像你们一样现在在夏威夷度假了。

Zhǐyào tāmen kěn chūqián, tāmen jiu hui xiàng nǐmen yíyàng xiànzài zài Xiàwēiyí dùjià le.

If only they were willing to spend the money, they would have been enjoying a vacation in Hawaii like you are now.

4. 要不是 yàobúshi A, 就 jiù B..., if not A, then B

要不是她告诉我，我到现在还不会知道他们已经去了美国了。

Yàobúshi tā gàosu wǒ, wǒ dào xiànzài hái búhuì zhīdao tāmen yǐjīng qùle Měiguó le.

If she had not told me, I would not have known that they have already gone to the United States.

5. Instead of 要是 yàoshi, which can also be omitted, any one of the following can be used: 如果 rúguǒ, 假如 jiǎrú, 假使 jiǎshǐ, 假若 jiǎruò, or 倘若 tǎngruò.

5.24 Sentences without subjects

Sentences without subjects occur in the following situations:

1. Expressing weather conditions:

出太阳了。
Chū tàiyang le.
The sun has come out.

晴天了。
Qíngtiān le.
It has cleared up.

下雨了。
Xiàyǔ le.
It's raining.

下雪了。
Xiàxuě le.

It's snowing.

下雹子了。
Xiàbáozi le.
It's hailing.

下雾了。
Xiàwù le.
It's foggy.

刮风了。
Guāfēng le.
It's windy.

打雷了。
Dǎléi le.
It's thundering.

闪电了.
Shǎndiàn le.
It's lightning.

2. Expressing time and season:

十一点了。
Shíyīdiǎn le.
It's eleven o'clock.

半夜了。
Bànyè le.
It's midnight.

天黑了。
Tiān hēi le.
It's dark now.

十二月了。
Shí'èryuè le.
It's December now.

冬天了。
Dōngtian le.
It's winter now.

圣诞节了。
Shèngdànjié le.
It's Christmas now.

3. Expressing a factual condition:

出汗了。
Chūhàn le.
(Subject +) is sweating/broke into a sweat.

流泪了。

Liúlèi le.
(Subject +) is shedding tears/started to shed tears.

吃饭了。
Chīfàn le.
Dinner's ready.

上课了。
Shàngkè le.
Class is going to start./Class has started.

下班了。
Xiàbān le.
Time to quit work.

来客了。
Lái kè le.
Guests have showed up./We have guests.

着火了!
Zháohuǒ le!
Fire!/A fire has started.

4.   Expressing a command:

该起床了。
Gāi qǐchuáng le.
Time to get up.

小心汽车!
Xiǎoxīn qìchē!
Be careful of cars!

欢迎参观。
Huānyíng cānguān.
Welcome (for a visit by sightseers and other visitors).

请别吸烟。
Qǐng bié xīyān.
Please do not smoke.

努力学习。
Nǔlì xuéxí.
Study hard!

6 Body language

Body language is a behavioral complement to spoken language and is an important part of communication. It is communication beyond words, a silent language that adds cues to vocal language and is particularly important for face-to-face interaction.

Much of the body language of Chinese speakers is the same as, or similar to, that of English speakers, but there is some which is different or even significantly different. On the other hand, not all the Chinese body language described here is shared by all Chinese.

Here are some examples of typical Chinese body language:

Appearance: Chinese usually stand and sit with a slight modest bend. A person with very straight body and lifted head is considered to be too proud. Long hair and beards are generally worn only by old men or artists. It is rare to see married men and women wearing wedding rings. Most people will dress according to the occasion, but they will seem more casual to the Western eye. Normally people do not wear clothing that stands out too much in design or color. It is not considered modest for older women to wear bright colors.

Applause: to praise, encourage, or welcome.

Cough: to catch people's attention or announce one's presence.

Covering the mouth: This is sometimes done by women and children when they feel embarrassed or shy.

Distance: Personal space is limited, so when conversing standing up, the distance between speakers will be closer than normal for North Americans; standing too close or too far can lead to misunderstandings. When a subordinate is talking to a superior or when a male is talking to a female, the distance between them is slightly greater than normal.

Eye contact: When talking, it is polite to establish eye contact but to avoid direct eye gaze from time to time. A constant gaze is impolite. However, an older person or a superior can look at a younger person or a subordinate for a much longer time. Looking left or right when talking is also considered impolite. No eye contact indicates that one does not value the person spoken to, or the listener is not paying much attention to the topic of conversation. If a person looks at someone from the corner of his/her eye, it means he/she looks down on or harbors suspicions about that person. Women often lower their gaze to show modesty, obedience, and respect. When a child is scolded, he/she is supposed to bow his/her head with eyes downcast to show shame.

Facial expression: Most well-brought-up Chinese are supposed to keep their personal feelings inside rather than exhibiting them openly or publicly. Sometimes if one has no facial expression it means this person does not want to express opinions or does not agree with the opinion expressed by someone else.

Gestures:

Finger snapping: feeling bored; having fun or keeping a beat.

Hand and arm extended, palm downward and waving towards oneself: beckoning, "Come here."

Handing business cards, gifts or other objects to someone with two hands: very polite gesture.

Index finger pointing to chest or nose: "I," "me."

Nodding: agreement; an expression of greeting.

Palm facing outward, waving hand left and right in front of face: no, wrong, mistaken, won't do.

Palm facing outward, move hand from left to right and from right to left: goodbye.

Pointing: it is more polite to use an open hand, fingers together, palm upward.

Pointing index finger to the temple and drawing a circle: think, think please, use your brain.

Pointing finger to temple or forehead: this person is stupid or crazy.

Putting index finger by cheek and repeatedly scraping from back to front: shame, shame!

Scratching the head: hesitating, not knowing what to do.

Shaking the head: no, disagree.

Stamping feet: angry.

Tapping the table with one or three fingertips beside the teacup after someone has poured tea: "Thank you!"

Wrinkling the brow: feeling bothered, unable to understand, disagreement, feeling impatient, feeling sad or contemplative.

Greeting: handshake, nod, or slight bow. Most Chinese handshakes are not firm, with no tight grip, but they do it seriously. It is sometimes accompanied with a nod or smile or a slight bow. Shaking hands without standing up is considered impolite.

Posture: Good and proper posture is considered important. Some say that one should "stand like a pine, sleep like a bow, walk like the wind and sit like a temple bell" (立如松 lì rú sōng, 睡如弓 shuì rú gōng, 行如风 xíng rú fēng, 坐如钟 zuò rú zhōng). Putting one's feet on a desk, or sitting on a desk while teaching or talking is considered very rude.

Sighing: feeling sad, regretful, or tired.

Silence: "Silence is golden": it is respected, tolerated, and customary. Silence is used for contemplation. During a conversation, if there is silence, Chinese do not rush to fill in the void. Silence is sometimes a "no" and is considered much less rude than a direct spoken answer of "no."

Smile: A smile may show any of the following: friendliness, happiness, willingness, agreement, appreciation, request, understanding, apology, refusal, disagreement, regret, embarrassment.

Thumbs up: This gesture says: "It's great!" or "That's excellent!"

Timing: Appointments and functions usually take place in a punctual manner. For a dinner party, it is a general practice that guests leave shortly after the meal. During a conversation, people take turns speaking. Interruption is considered very impolite.

Touch: There is generally no kissing or hugging in public, especially between people not closely related or in love. However, adults do not hesitate to touch children to show care and affection. People will also touch older people in order to help or guide them. Although different sexes may hesitate to hold arms or hands, people of the same sex may hold hands to show friendliness, especially younger and older people.

China is a large country and many of the habits and customs will differ from the north to the south, and even from place to place within the same region. As a result, some body language may differ in meaning, or the same meaning may be expressed through different body language.

Bibliography

Bao, Zhiming. *The Structure of Tone*. New York: Oxford University Press, 1999.

毕继万。中外文化比较 （上册，下册）。北京：北京语言学院三系，
1986。

毕继万译，莱杰·布罗斯纳安著。中国与英语国家非语言交际对比。
(translated from the manuscript, *Chinese and English Gestures: Contrastive
Nonverbal Communication*, written by Leger Brosnahan) 北京：北京语言学
院出版社，1991。

毕继万。跨文化非语言交际。北京：外语教学与研究出版社，1999。

Chao, Yuen Ren. *A Grammar of Spoken Chinese*. Berkeley: University of
California Press, 1968.

Chen, Matthew Y. *Tone Sandhi: Patterns across Chinese Dialects*. Cambridge:
Cambridge University Press, 2000.

Chen, Ping. *Modern Chinese: History and Sociolinguistics*. Cambridge: Cambridge
University Press, 1999.

陈松岑。礼貌语言初探。北京：商务印书馆，1989。

Cheung, Hung-nin Samuel, in collaboration with Sze-yun Liu and Li-lin Shih.
A Practical Chinese Grammar. Hong Kong: The Chinese University Press,
1994.

Chinnery, John D. 秦乃瑞 and Cui Mingqiu 崔鸣秋. *Corresponding English
and Chinese Proverbs and Phrases* 英汉俚谚合壁. Beijing: New World Press,
1984.

Chu, Chauncey Cheng-Hsi. *A Reference Grammar of Mandarin Chinese for English
Speakers*. New York and Berne: Peter Lang Publishing, 1983.

A Discourse Grammar of Mandarin Chinese. New York and Berne: Peter Lang
Publishing, 1998.

Chu, Vicky, and Don Starr. *Dictionary of Basic Chinese Grammar*. Honolulu:
University of Hawaii Press, 2002.

Clark, Herbert H. *Using Language*. Cambridge: Cambridge University Press,
1996.

戴雪梅，张若莹。实用汉语语法三百点 *Speaking Chinese: 300 Grammatical
Points*. Beijing: 新世界出版社 New World Press, 1999.

DeFrancis, John. *The Chinese Language: Fact and Fantasy*. Honolulu: University of
Hawaii Press, 1984.

杜学增。中英（英语国家）文化习俗比较。北京：外语教学与研究出版
社，1999。

Ernst, Thomas. Conditions on Chinese A-not-A Questions. *Journal of East Asian
Linguistics* 3: 241–264, 1994.

Negation in Mandarin Chinese. *Natural Language and Linguistic Theory* 13: 665–707, 1995.

房玉清。 实用汉语语法。 北京：北京语言学院出版社，1993。

Fast, Julius. *Body Language*. New York. Pocket Books, Simon & Schuster Inc., 2002.

郭玉玲， 钱肃文编。锡勇勤译。实用汉语常用成语 1000 例 *Speaking Chinese: 1000 Practical Chinese Idioms*. Beijing: New World Press 新世界出版社，2002。

Guo, Zhenhua 郭振华. *A Concise Chinese Grammar* 简明汉语语法。 Beijing: Sinolingua, 2000.

Hall, Edward T. *The Hidden Dimension*. Garden City, N.Y.: Anchor Press, 1969.
The Silent Language. Garden City, N.Y.: Anchor Press, 1973.
Beyond Culture. Garden City, N.Y.: Anchor Press, 1977.

Halliday, M. A. K. Comparison and Translation. In Halliday, M. A. K., Angus McIntosh and Peter Strevens, *The Linguistic Sciences and Language Teaching*. London: Longman, 1964.

Han, Dezhi. *Fifty Patterns of Modern Chinese*. Hong Kong: The Chinese University Press, 1993.

Han, Yang. A Pragmatic Analysis of the BA Particle in Mandarin Chinese. *Journal of Chinese Linguistics* 23: 2, 99–127, 1995.

胡文仲。 跨文化非语言交际。 北京：外语教学与研究出版，1999。

Jin, Shaozhi (compiled). *An Introduction to Modern Chinese Vocabulary* 现代汉语词汇概论。 Beijing: Sinolingua, 1988.

Joos, Martin. *The Five Clocks*. Bloomington: Indiana University Press, 1962.

冷玉龙， 韦一心等。中华字海。 *Sea of Chinese Characters*. 北京：中华书局， 1994。

Li, Charles N., and Sandra A. Thompson. *Mandarin Chinese: A Functional Reference Grammar*. Berkeley: University of California Press, 1989.

Li, Dejin and Meizhen Cheng 李德津，程美珍. *A Practical Chinese Grammar for Foreigners* 外国人实用汉语语法. Beijing: Sinolingua 外语教学与研究出版社，1988。

Li, Eden Sum-hung. *Systemic Functional Grammar of Chinese: A Text-Based Analysis*. London: Continuum International Publishing Group, 2007.

李峻。态势语言论略。北京：中国文联出版社，2000。

李行健，曹聪孙，云景魁主编。周自厚，王铁昆，杜淑芬， 尹淑英，冯瑞生，王小龙编。新词新语词典。北京：语文出版社，1993。

Li, Ying-che. *An Investigation of Case in Chinese Grammar*. South Orange, N.J.: Seton Hall University Press, 1971.

林大津。跨文化交际研究：与英美人交往指南。福州：福建人民出版社，1996。

Lin, Helen T. *Essential Grammar for Modern Chinese*. Boston: Cheng & Tsui Company, 1981.

Lu, Fubo. *Practical Chinese Grammar for Foreign Learners*. Beijing: Beijing Language and Culture University Press, 2005.

吕叔湘主编。李临定，刘坚，范继淹，史有为，范方莲，孟琮，马树钧，李珠，陈建民，詹开第，郑怀德，陶宝祥编写。 现代汉语八百词。Beijing: The Commercial Press 商务印书馆，1996。

Marney, John. *A Handbook of Modern Chinese Grammar*. San Francisco: Chinese Materials Center, 1977.

Norman, Jerry. *Chinese*. Cambridge: Cambridge University Press, 1988.

曲阜师范大学本书编写组编著。现代汉语常用虚词词典。浙江教育出版社，1992。

Quirk, R.S. Greenbaum, G. Leech and J. Svartvic. *A Comprehensive Grammar of the English Language*. London: Longman, 1985.

Ross, Claudia, and Jing-Heng Sheng Ma. *Modern Mandarin Chinese Grammar: A Practical Guide*. London and New York: Routledge, 2006.

Tao, Hongyin. *Units in Mandarin Conversation: Prosody, Discourse and Grammar*, Studies in Discourse and Grammar, Vol. V. Amsterdam: John Benjamins, 1996.

Taylor, Insup and Martin M. Taylor. *Writing and Literacy in Chinese, Korean and Japanese*. Amsterdam; Philadelphia: John Benjamins, 1995.

Tian, Shou-be. *A Guide to Proper Usage of Spoken Chinese* (Simplified Chinese Edition) 漢語口語指引。 Hong Kong: The Chinese University, 2005.

US State Department, Bureau of East Asian and Pacific Affairs, Background Note: China www.state.gov/r/pa/ei/bgn/18902.htm, April, 2006.

Wang, James J. *Outrageous Chinese: A Guide to Chinese Street Language*. San Francisco: China Books & Periodicals, Inc., 1994.

王泉根。中国人名文化。北京：团结出版社，2000。

吴叔平编著。汉语动词380例 *380 Most Commonly Used Chinese Verbs*. 北京：华语教学出版社 Sinolingua, 2000。

徐宗才，应俊玲编著 张清常审定。俗语词典。北京：商务印书馆，1998。

姚汉铭主编。新词新语词典。西安：未来出版社，2000。

尹斌庸编著，韩晖翻译。谚语 *100 Pearls of Chinese Wisdom*. 北京：华语教学出版社，1999。

Yip, Po-Ching and Don Rimmington. *Chinese: An Essential Grammar*. London and New York: Routledge, 1997.

于根元主编。周洪波，刘一玲，张朝炳，宋孝才，程国富，凌云 编。现代汉语新词词典。北京：北京语言出版社，1994。

张拱贵主编。王聚元，王福良，崔如萍编写。汉语委婉语词典。北京：北京语言文化大学出版社，1996。

Zhao, Yongxin. *Essentials of Chinese Grammar for Foreigners*. Beijing: Beijing Foreign Languages Institute, 1994.

Zheng, Yide, etc. 郑懿德等。 *Difficult Points in Chinese Grammar* 汉语语法难点释疑。Beijing: Sinolingua, 1996.

周苓仲，何泽人编译。典故 *The Stories Behind 100 Chinese Idioms*. 北京：华语教学出版社 Sinolingua, 1999。

Zhou, Yimin and James J. Wang. *Mutant Mandarin: A Guide to New Chinese Slang* 时髦汉语。San Francisco: China Books & Periodicals, Inc., 1995.

Zuckermann, Ghil'ad. Language Contact and Globalisation: The camouflaged influence of English on the world's languages – with special attention to Israeli (sic) and Mandarin. *Cambridge Review of International Affairs*, 16: 2, 287–307, 2003.

Index